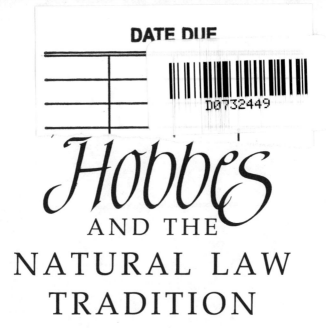

Hobbes
AND THE
NATURAL LAW
TRADITION

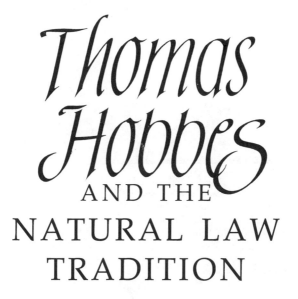

Thomas Hobbes
AND THE
NATURAL LAW
TRADITION

NORBERTO BOBBIO

Translated by
Daniela Gobetti

THE UNIVERSITY OF CHICAGO PRESS
CHICAGO & LONDON

The University of Chicago Press, Chicago 60637
The University of Chicago Press, Ltd., London
© 1993 by The University of Chicago
All rights reserved. Published 1993
Printed in the United States of America

02 01 00 99 98 97 96 95   5 4 3 2

ISBN (paper): 0-226-06248-1

Originally published as *Thomas Hobbes,* © 1989 Giulio Einaudi editore s.p.a.,
Turin.

Library of Congress Cataloging-in-Publication Data

Bobbio, Norberto, 1909–
    [Thomas Hobbes. English]
    Thomas Hobbes and the natural law tradition / Norberto Bobbio ;
translated by Daniela Gobetti.
        p.   cm.
    Includes index.
    ISBN 0-226-06247-3 (cloth). — ISBN 0-226-06248-1 (pbk.)

    1. Hobbes, Thomas, 1588–1679—Contributions in political science.
    2. Hobbes, Thomas, 1588–1679—Contributions in natural law.
    I. Title.
    JC153.H66B6313   1993
    320′.01—dc20   92-17978
                                                         CIP

⊗ The paper used in this publication meets the minimum requirements of
the American National Standard for Information Sciences—Permanence of
Paper for Printed Library Materials, ANSI Z39.48-1984.

Contents

Preface   vii

Author's Note   xv

One   The Conceptual Model of
Natural Law Theory   1

1. Elements of the Model 1 / 2. Variations on the Theme 3 / 3. The
Alternative Model 5 / 4. Elements of the Alternative
Model 8 / 5. The Conceptual Model of Natural Law Theory and
Bourgeois Society 10 / 6. The Family and the State of
Nature 13 / 7. The Family in the Conceptual Model of Natural Law
Theory 15 / 8. The Bourgeois Family 18 / 9. A Proof "to the
Contrary" 20 / 10. The End of the Model 23

Two   Hobbes's Political Theory   26

1. Works 26 / 2. The Leading Idea 29 / 3. The
Method 32 / 4. Artificial Man 35 / 5. The State of
Nature 38 / 6. The War of All against All 41 / 7. The Dictates of
Right Reason 44 / 8. The Covenant of Union 46 / 9. Sovereignty Is
Irrevocable 49 / 10. Sovereignty Is Absolute 53 / 11. Civil
Laws 56 / 12. Sovereignty Is Indivisible 60 / 13. Church and
State 63 / 14. Hobbes and His Critics 66 / 15. Hobbes
Interpreted 69

Contents

Three Introduction to *De Cive* 74

Appendix: Introduction to *A Dialogue between a Philosopher and a Student of the Common Law of England* 107

Four Natural Law and Civil Law in the Political Philosophy of Hobbes 114

Five Hobbes and Natural Law Theory 149

Six Hobbes and Partial Societies 172

Seven By Way of Conclusion 197

Appendix 201

Considerations upon the Reputation, Loyalty, Manners and Religion of Thomas Hobbes of Malmesbury 201 / A Brief History of Hobbesian Historiography 205 / Three Books on Hobbes 212

Index 221

Preface

When Luigi Firpo conceived of the series "Political Classics" for Utet, he asked me to take charge of Hobbes's work. *Leviathan* had already been translated. I therefore decided to edit the translation and prepare the critical apparatus of *De Cive*, which had been only partially translated.[1] In the first two years after the liberation of Italy,[2] I was at the University of Padua, where I taught two courses on the history of natural law theory in modern times.[3] In those courses, I devoted one section to Hobbes's political philosophy. My first writing on Hobbes had been the review of Carl Schmitt's book, *Der Leviathan in der Staatslehre des Thomas Hobbes*, which had appeared in *Rivista di Filosofia* in 1939. This book brought into stark relief Hobbes's mechanistic view of the state. Reading it suggested to me the contrast between the state as machine and the state as person. This contrast was the theme of my address

1. T. Hobbes, *Il cittadino*, translation and preface by P. D'Abbiero (Lanciano: Carabba, 1935). It includes the first two parts of the work, and excludes the third on religion.

2. From the German occupation of Italy after the armistice, between September 1943 and April 1945. —Trans.

3. Published as *Le origini del giusnaturalismo moderno e il suo sviluppo nel secolo XVII* (Padua: Litografia Tagliapietra, 1946); and *Il diritto naturale nel secolo XVIII* (Turin: Giappichelli, 1946).

at the beginning of the academic year at the University of Padua in 1946, which I entitled "La persona e lo stato."[4]

Dr. Clelia Guglielminetti translated *De Cive*, which appeared in 1948. I revised this translation and provided an introduction, which is now the third chapter of this book. In 1959 a second edition was published, followed by the first Italian translation of *A Dialogue between a Philosopher and a Student of the Common Law of England*, in a book entitled Thomas Hobbes, *Opere politiche*, vol. 1, (the first and only volume to appear).

Since then I have repeatedly come back to this great and unparalleled builder of the first theory of the modern state. Hobbes captivated me from my first reading of him. With each subsequent sounding I gained an increased awareness of the complexity of his thought, which today impatient critics often mistake for incongruity and which they attribute to an unwitting lack of clarity. The last piece in this collection is the fruit of this uninterrupted work of ever deeper analysis. In it I explored the theme, neglected at the time, of "Hobbes and partial[5] societies," which appeared in *Filosofia* in 1982.

The first and the last piece of this collection were written, respectively, in 1948 and 1982. In between these two, the volume includes an appendix with minor essays, two articles on Hobbes and natural law, which appeared in 1954 and 1962, and the broader essay on Hobbes's political philosophy, written for the volume of the *Storia delle idee politiche, economiche e sociali*, edited by Luigi Firpo for Utet, which was published in 1980. A piece of a more general character, "Il modello giusnaturalistico" (1973), introduces this collection. I sketch in it two opposite approaches to the problem of the origin and foundation of political power. I call these two approaches, respectively, the Aristotelian and the natural law conceptual

4. Published in "Annuario dell'Università di Padova dell'a.a 1946–47" (Padua: Successori Penada Stampatori, 1948), pp. 15–26.

5. I have translated literally the Italian term *parziali*, for want of a better solution. By *"parziali"* Bobbio means associations—within or without the state—which lack the two defining features of a "complete" society (that is, by definition, the state): independence from any superior power and absoluteness, that is, the unquestioned supremacy of its legal order.—TRANS.

models. The latter is mainly the result of my reflections on Hobbes's works. In the last forty years Hobbes's reputation as a political writer and a philosopher has grown enormously. The bibliography on him grows larger every year.[6] When I began to study him, Hobbes occupied a much smaller place in the history of philosophical and political thought, at least in Italy. It may be by chance, but the author of *Leviathan* was the only one among the great political philosophers of the seventeenth and eighteenth centuries to whom my teacher Gioele Solari did not devote any specific study. In those years the charge weighed on him, wholly unfounded, of having been a precursor of the totalitarian state. One of the most important studies of his political thought, written by Carl Schmitt, cited above, came from an author who was politically suspect.[7] Leo Strauss's monograph, *The Political Philosophy of Hobbes*, appeared in 1936 but was, however, ignored in Italy. Hobbes had not been included in our curriculum of philosophical studies, since idealism, then the dominant philosophy, had set him aside. Croce did not even mention him, in his short—and even scanty— history of political philosophy.[8] In addition, it is well known that Hegel devoted few pages to Hobbes in his *History of Philosophy*. One finds in these pages that there is nothing properly philosophical in Hobbes's thought, and that his views are superficial and empirical. The main Italian work on Hobbes, written by Rodolfo Mondolfo, was published long ago, in 1903.[9] The most complete monograph on Hobbes, written by

6. See D. Felice, "Thomas Hobbes in Italia: Bibliografia (1880–1981)," *Rivista di Filosofia* 73 (1983): 440–70; A. L. Schino, "Tendenze della letteratura hobbesiana di lingua inglese degli ultimi venticinque anni," *Materiali per una storia della cultura giuridica* 17 (1987): 159–98; F. Viola, "Hobbes tra moderno e postmoderno: Cinquant'anni di studi hobbesiani," *Materiali per una storia della cultura giuridica* 19 (1989): 27–84. G. Sorgi has published a wide-ranging analysis of the debate on Hobbes in recent years, *Quale Hobbes? Dalla paura alla rappresentanza* (Milan: Angeli, 1989).
7. Carl Schmitt was a Nazi sympathizer.—TRANS.
8. B. Croce, "Sulla storia della filosofia politica: Noterelle," *La critica* 22 (1924): 193–208, then in *Elementi di politica* (Bari: Laterza, 1925), pp. 59–90.
9. R. Mondolfo, *Saggi per la storia della morale utilitaria. I. La morale di T. Hobbes* (Verona-Padua: F.lli Drucker, 1903).

Preface

Adolfo Levi, and published in 1929, did not devote any particular attention to his political thought.[10]
In the past forty years things have changed greatly. The fourth edition of my translation of De cive was published in 1988. A new translation, edited by Tito Magri, was published in 1979 by Editori Riuniti. The old translation of Leviathan by Mario Vinciguerra, which came out in the well-known series by Laterza, Classics of Modern Philosophy, promoted by Croce and Gentile, has been followed by two others. One is by Roberto Giammanco for Utet, in 1955; the other is by Gianni Micheli for Nuova Italia in 1976. In 1968 Nuova Italia also published the translation of Hobbes's first political work, Elements of Natural and Political Law, edited by the late Arrigo Pacchi.

Thus in Italy as well, Hobbes's political thought has become the subject of a growing number of up-to-date and accurate studies. In the year of his centenary (1988), Hobbes even appeared in the newspapers. A chorus of approving voices, including mine, arose from their pages.[11]

It is not for me to say what place my writings occupy in the immense literature that exists on Hobbes. His political works have been scoured in their most hidden corners. Differences between works, which are significant, but in my opinion marginal to the original nucleus of Hobbes's theory, have been emphasized. The more diverse and divergent interpretations have been argued. For despite the apparent and seductive clarity of Hobbes's works, which emerges at first reading, it has been repeatedly observed that his writings are not lacking in ambiguous and contradictory passages. These provide a difficult test even for sophisticated interpreters, who at times become exasperated, to the point of mistaking the inessential for

10. A. Levi, La filosofia di Tommaso Hobbes (Milan: Dante Alighieri, 1929).
11. N. Bobbio, "Hobbes della pace," La Stampa, 31 May 1988, reprinted in this volume with the title "By Way of Conclusion." Among other reviews, S. Veca, "Hobbes inventore dell'anarchia," Corriere della Sera, 5 April 1988, and the insert of Il Manifesto, 21 January 1988, which includes an interview I gave M. D'Eramo.

the essential, the variation upon a theme for the radical change of theme.[12]

In the study of the classics of philosophical thought, the analytical and historical methods stand in opposition to one another. The former aims at the conceptual reconstruction of a text, and at a comparison between texts by the same author. The latter aims at placing a text within the context of the debates of its times, in order to explain the origin and the effects of a work. As a matter of fact the two methods are not incompatible. They complement each other well. A dispute, such as the only which has recently taken place between the supporters of one side or the other is, in my opinion, otiose.[13] Having said this much, I warn the reader that the two essays about Hobbes and natural law theory are a consciously chosen exercise in the analytical method. Hobbes's writings are especially suited to this kind of inquiry, which is not usual in Italy, the fatherland of historicism. However, the other writings also aim at the analysis of concepts and at the reconstruction of Hobbes's system, rather than at the recreation of the so-called historical context. Between natural law theory and legal positivism, I put Hobbes on the side of the latter rather than the former. Between the two interpretive extremes, one considering Hobbes the precursor of the totalitarian state, the other reading him as the precursor of the liberal state, I accept neither. The central theme of Hobbes's political thought is the unity of the state; it is neither the citizen's liberty nor the total state.

12. In his book *Quale Hobbes* (cited in n.6), Sorgi concludes from an analysis of the incongruities, ambiguities, and contradictions remarked in recent years by the many and bellicose interpreters of Hobbes's work, that Hobbes is a thinker "with many souls" (pp. 147ff.).

13. I refer here to John A. Pocock's and Quentin Skinner's criticisms of the followers of the analytical method. See M. Viroli, "Revisionisti e ortodossi nella storia delle idee politiche," *Rivista di filosofia* 78 (1987): 121–36. I have dealt more extensively with this question in an essay, "Ragioni della filosofia politica," which is about to appear in the collection of works dedicated to the memory of L. Firpo.

I mistrust recent interpretations which have attempted to place particular stress on the religious dimension of Hobbes's political thought. The essential part of his political theory, despite variations from work to work, is the rational justification of the origin of the state and its mission in this world. This enterprise represents a decisive moment in the process of the secularization of politics; the state ceases to be *remedium peccati* [a remedy for sin], and becomes the strongest and most reliable disciplinary authority of the passions. One cannot dismiss the fact that the growth of interpretations has offered an important contribution to a better understanding of Hobbes's thought. But such variety has in the end prevented readers from understanding the core of his theory, and has obscured the fact that Hobbes is a thinker who pursues one idea all his life. If there is a work in which the leading theme is insistently, even obstinately expressed, that work is *Leviathan*, which completes Hobbes's trilogy of political writings. This leading idea is that human beings have only one way out of the natural anarchy that is a consequence of their nature; and they have only one way to establish peace, which is prescribed by the first law of nature. This way is the institution by artifice of a shared power, that is, the state.

The contemporaneity of a thinker is always a thorny issue. The person who declares a thinker "contemporary" founds his judgment on an interpretation of the author's thought, and of the social reality of his own time. The same work may or may not be contemporary, depending on the various possible interpretations of both the author's and the interpreter's own age. I have identified the nucleus of Hobbes's thought in the institution of a shared power to which human beings resort in order to leave the state of anarchy and establish a stable peace. If we accept this interpretation we become aware that today this is the problem of realizing an international order. Such international order is still grounded, despite the permanent union of states represented by the United Nations, on a system of unstable equilibrium. And it is grounded on the "balance of terror," as it was called (until yesterday?), on the "reciprocal fear" which, according to Hobbes, characterizes the state of nature, where peace is nothing more than a truce between two wars. There is a clear analogy between the *multitudo* [multitude] of individuals who must become a *populus* [people], and the *multitudo* of states which must become the *populus* of sovereign powers, in order to give life to a truly global *commonwealth*. It is far from certain whether this passage from the domestic to the international level is feasible. But there is no question that the only way to make this happen is a *pactum unionis* [covenant of union] among the members of the international community. These must obtain the authority to unite by consent, that is in Hobbesian terms, through an act of authorization by the members of each and every political community. The pursuit of perpetual peace is a long process, which may well remain incomplete. This process is surely not the fiat, the act of divine creation, to which Hobbes, on the famous first page of *Leviathan*, compares the pact through which the body politic is born. But this does not detract from the ideal validity of the "Hobbesian model" as the motivating force of this process.

The idea of collecting my principal studies on Hobbes is not mine, but rather belongs to Luigi Bonanate, Michelangelo Bovero, and Pier Paolo Portinaro. Its realization has been possible thanks to the fervent support of Guido Davico Bonino, of the Casa Editrice Einaudi. To each and everyone of them go my warm thanks.

Author's Note

The material in this volume was originally published as follows:

"Il modello giusnaturalistico," *Rivista internazionale di filosofia del diritto* 50 (1973): 603–22.

"La teoria politica di Hobbes." In *Storia delle idee politiche, economiche e sociali,* ed. L. Firpo. Vol. IV, *L'età moderna.* Turin: Utet, 1980. Book 1, pp. 270–317.

"Introduzione al *De Cive.*" In T. Hobbes, *Elementi filosofici sul cittadino,* ed. N. Bobbio. Turin: Utet, 1948. Pp. 9–40. The Appendix, "Introduzione al *Dialogo tra un filosofo e uno studioso del diritto comune d'Inghilterra,*" was originally published in the second edition, entitled T. Hobbes, *Opere politiche,* ed. N. Bobbio. Turin: Utet, 1959. Vol. I, pp. 36–41.

"Legge naturale e legge civile nella filosofia politica di Hobbes." In *Studi in memoria di Gioele Solari.* Turin: Edizioni Ramella, 1954. Pp. 61–101. Reprinted in N. Bobbio, *Da Hobbes a Marx.* Naples: Morano, 1965. Pp. 11–49.

"Hobbes e il giusnaturalismo." *Rivista critica di storia della filosofia* 17 (1962): 470–85. Reprinted in Bobbio, *Da Hobbes a Marx,* op cit. Pp. 51–74.

"Hobbes e le società parziali." *Filosofia* 33 (1982): 375–94.

"A guisa di conclusione." Published in *La Stampa*, 31 May 1988, with the title "Hobbes della pace," on the occasion of the four hundredth anniversary of Hobbes's birth.

In the Appendix:

"Le considerazioni sulla reputazione, sulla lealtà, sulle buone maniere e sulla religione." *Rivista di filosofia* 42 (1951): 399–423, introduction to the translation of Hobbes's work of the same title.

"Breve storia della storiografia hobbesiana" (hereafter cited as *Hobbes Studies*). In *Questioni di storiografia filosofica: Dalle origini all'Ottocento*, ed. V. Mathieu. Brescia: La Scuola, 1974. Pp. 324–28.

Review of C. Schmitt, *Der Leviathan in der Staatslehre des Thomas Hobbes. Revista di Filosofia* 30 (1939): 283–84.

Review of J. Bowle, *Hobbes and His Critics: A Study in Seventeenth-Century Constitutionalism. Rivista di filosofia* 44 (1953): 212–14.

Review of S. I. Mintz, *The Hunting of Leviathan. Rivista di filosofia* 54 (1963): 249.

Passages from Hobbes's works are cited from the following editions:

Leviathan, M. Oakeshott. Oxford: Basil Blackwell, 1946.

De Cive (*Philosophical Rudiments concerning Government and Society*), in T. Hobbes, *English Works* (hereafter cited as *EW*), ed. W. Molesworth. 11 vols. London: J. Bohn, 1845. Vol. II.

Considerations upon Reputation, upon Loyalty, upon Good Manners and upon Religion. In *EW*, vol. IV.

A Dialogue between a Philosopher and a Student of the Common Law of England. In *EW*, vol. VI.

Six Lessons to the Savilian Professors of the Mathematics. In *EW*, vol. VII.

The Elements of Law Natural & Politic, ed. F. Tönnies. Cambridge: Cambridge University Press, 1928.

De Corpore, De Homine, and passages from Hobbes's Latin writings, Thomae Hobbes, *Opera philosophica quae latine scripsit omnia* (cited as *OL*), Studio et labore G. Molesworth, 5 vols. Londini: Apud Joannem Bohn, 1839–45); Aalen: Scientia Verlag 2d reprint, 1966, vols. I and II.

One

The Conceptual Model
of Natural Law Theory

1. *Elements of the Model*

As has generally been done, we may speak with some degree
of approximation of the "conceptual model of natural law theory," which concerns the origin and foundation of the state, or
of political (that is, civil) society. From Hobbes (who is its fountainhead) to Hegel, all the major political philosophers of the
modern age employ this model without modifying its struc-
tural elements, although they do subsume under them a
remarkably wide range of substantive features. (I speak delib-
erately of "political philosophers," rather than of "political
writers" in the broad sense of the term. I wish here to refer to
writers on politics who aim at constructing a rational theory of
the state, deduced from, or somehow juxtaposed with, a general theory of man and society. These writers range from
Spinoza to Locke, from Pufendorf to Rousseau, from Kant to
the first Fichte, and to the myriad of minor Kantian thinkers
who come with the end of the school of natural law.)

As is well known, the conceptual model of natural law theory is built on the great dichotomy "state of nature—civil society." Its characteristic features can be listed as follows:

1. The state of nature, which is a non-political and anti-political condition, is the starting point for the analysis of the origin and foundation of the state.
2. The state of nature and civil society are opposed to one another, since civil society arises in antithesis to the state of nature, in order to correct or eliminate the shortcomings of the latter.
3. The constitutive elements of the state of nature are primarily and fundamentally individuals, who do not live in society but are sociable. (I say "primarily" and not "exclusively" because in the state of nature there may exist natural societies such as families.)
4. The constitutive elements of the state of nature (either individuals, or families for those who accept their existence) are free and equal. Therefore the state of nature is always depicted as a condition of freedom and equality. (There are, however, noticeable variations, depending upon the notational range attributed to the two terms.)
5. The passage from the state of nature to civil society does not occur by necessity, because of the nature of things; it rather takes place through one or more conventions. These are voluntary and deliberate acts, performed by individuals who are interested in leaving the state of nature. Consequently, civil society is conceived as an "artificial" being, or, as we should say today, as the product of "culture" rather than of "nature." (Hence there derives the ambiguity of the term "civil," which is an adjective related to both "civitas" and "civilitas.")
6. The principle of legitimation of political society is consent; this is not true of any other type of natural society. In particular, it is not true of domestic society, that is, of the family/household.

I do not use the term "model" by whim, or to make use of a fashionable word, but only because I wish to convey directly the idea that such a historical and social formation has never actually existed. In their historical evolution, the institutions typical of the modern state have gone from the feudal state to the *Ständestaat*, from the *Ständestaat* to absolute monarchy, from absolute to constitutional monarchy, and so forth. The image of a state that arises through the reciprocal consent of individuals who are originally free and equal is a pure construct of the intellect.

2. Variations on the Theme

In seventeenth- and eighteenth-century literature we can find many variations on this theme, of which the most important are

1. Those regarding the state of nature, which are articulated around the following classical themes:
   a. Whether the state of nature is a historical or merely fictional condition (a rational hypothesis, an ideal condition, and so forth).
   b. Whether it is a condition of peace or of war;
   c. Whether it is a condition of isolation (in the sense that each individual lives by himself, with no need for others), or a social condition (even if of a primordial society).
2. The variations regarding the form and content of the contract or contracts upon which civil society is founded. The classical discussions generated by this issue revolve around the following themes:
   a. Whether the social contract is a contract among individuals in favor of the community, or in favor of a third party.
   b. Whether the contract among individuals (the so-called *pactum societatis* [pact of union]) should be followed by a second contract between *populus* and *princeps* [prince] (the so-called *pactum subjectionis* [pact of subjection]).
   c. Whether, once stipulated, contracts may or may not be rescinded, and on what conditions. (This depends on whether the transfer of power from

isolated individuals to the people, or from the
people to the prince, is conceived as a permanent
alienation or as a temporary concession.)
d. Whether the object of the contract or contracts is
the partial or complete renunciation of natural
rights.
3. The variations regarding the nature of the political
power which ensues from the contract. That is,
whether that power is absolute or limited,
unconditioned or with conditions attached,
indivisible or divisible, irrevocable or revocable, and
so forth.

It is worthy of note that no one of these variations affects and
modifies the essential elements listed in the first paragraph
above. These elements are the starting point (the state of nature), the point of arrival (civil society), and the means by
which the passage from the one to the other takes place (the
social contract). The antithesis between prepolitical and political conditions, which I analyzed in the first paragraph, point b
is so strong as to characterize all analyses which accept it. Even
those who proceed from a social or peaceful state of nature are
forced by the logic of the conceptual model itself to do one of
two things. *Either* they consider the state of nature a peaceful,
but imperfect and insufficient condition, in which sociability is
weak, unsafe, and provisional, always on the brink of a crisis
or breakdown; *or* they divide the prepolitical condition into
two: the state of nature in the narrow sense of the term, and a
state of nature which has degenerated into a state of war,
which makes necessary the passage to civil society. This latter
solution is typical both of the Lockean and the Rousseauian
models. For Locke, the state of nature is not in itself a state of
war. But once the state of war has begun, it can be stopped only
by instituting political power. For Rousseau, there are no
longer two, but rather three moments in the development of
history. These are

a. the state of nature as a state of innocence and
primordial happiness;

b. "civil society," which reproduces some of the features of the Hobbesian state of nature;

c. the state born through the social contract.

Rousseau does not reproach Hobbes for having described the state of nature as a state of war, but instead for having located it at the beginning of human history, rather than at a subsequent moment. In doing so, Rousseau justifies his own triadic (and no longer diadic) conception of history. He can thus suggest that the state born in the third stage is a return to, or recovery of a primordial condition. But Rousseau does not give up one of the fundamental theses of the conceptual model, according to which political society is born as the antithesis (not the continuation) of the immediately preceding condition.

3. The Alternative Model

The elaboration of a model and the subsuming under it of a varied and multiform reality may appear to be an arbitrary and sterile operation. I believe that in this case the operation can be shown to be legitimate (and useful), for political philosophers, who came before natural law theorists, received and handed down from one to another a conceptual model which was entirely different from, and in most aspects nearly opposite to, the conceptual model of natural law theorists. This model may be called "Aristotelian," from the name of its author. In the first pages of the *Politics* Aristotle explains that the state, as the *polis* or city, starts from the family, and then grows through the intermediate phase of the village. His own words are

> The first form of association naturally instituted for the satisfaction of daily current needs is thus the family. . . . The first form of association—which is also the *first* to be formed from more households than one, and for the satisfaction of something more than daily recurrent needs—is the village. . . . When we come to the final and perfect association, formed from a number of villages, we have already reached the polis—an

association which may be said to have reached the
height of full self-sufficiency; or rather we may say that
while it *grows* for the sake of mere life, it *exists* for the
sake of a good life.[1]

It is surprising how lasting, permanent, stable, and vital this
way of conceiving the origin of the state has been over the centuries. To confirm this, I have chosen two fundamental works
of political theory, one from the Middle Ages, and the other
from the modern age (before Hobbes). In his *Defensor pacis*,
Marsilius begins by asserting that human beings have pro-
gressed from imperfect communities to increasingly perfect
ones. In establishing the stages of this evolution he follows the
Aristotelian approach: the "first and smallest combination of
human beings" is that of the man and the woman; the second
is the aggregation of dwellings called "village," or "hamlet," in
which "the first "community" arose; the third and last is the
stage in which "the things which are necessary for living and
for living well were brought to full development by men's reason and experience, and there was established the perfect
community, called the state."[2] Bodin begins his treatise *The Six
Bookes of a Commonweale* by offering the following definition of
the state: "A Commonweale is a lawfull government of many
families, and of that which unto them in common belongeth,
with a puissant soveraigntie."[3] In a subsequent passage, having to comment upon the part of that definition regarding "different families," he explains that the family "is the seminaire
and beginning of every Commonweale, as also a principal
member thereof."[4] Bodin is critical of some aspects of Aris-

1. Aristotle, *Politics*, trans. E. Barker, (London: Oxford University Press,
1958), (1252b), p. 4.

2. Marsilius of Padua, *Defensor Pacis* (Toronto: University of Toronto Press,
1967), I, III, 4–5, pp. 10–13.

3. A. facsimile reprint of Knolles's translation, 1606, (Cambridge: Harvard
University Press, 1962; New York: Arno Press Reprints, 1979), I, p. 1. [I quote
from Knolles's translation because it is the only complete translation into English of Bodin's *De la république*, and it is the version which was available to
Hobbes.—TRANS.]

4. Ibid., II, p. 8.

totle's theory, and does not emphasize the intermediate step of
the "village." Nonetheless, he insists that the state originates
from the family; so much so that he discusses the question of
how many families are necessary to form an association which
may be called "state."

At the beginning of the seventeenth century, right before the
appearance of Hobbes's great work, Johannes Althusius, the
author of the most complex political work of the time, still defines the city as an association of the second degree (or the
third, or the fourth, depending on the number of intermediate
steps). The city is a public association, which differs from the
various private associations, in that it is an aggregation of
lesser associations. The first of these in time is the family:
"A universal association is the gathering together of many
couples, families, and lesser societies inhabiting the same territory, and is turned into an association through certain laws.
This universal association is also called the state."⁵ If we observe the unfolding of Althusius's work, we cannot fail to
notice that its plan still conforms to the model of the great Aristotelian edifice. This is so even if Althusius's construction is
more complex and articulated than the Aristotelian one. (In
particular, he stresses colleges [*collegia*], that is, civil societies,
together with families, which are natural societies.) Althusius
begins his account by speaking of the domestic association,
that is, the family (chap. II). He then speaks of the neigh-
borhood [*consociatio propinquorum*] (chap. III), and of inferior
species of civil societies, the colleges (chap. IV). He finally
arrives, through successive steps and broader and broader
circles, at the city (differentiated into rural and urban); and
from cities through provinces at the kingdom (which corresponds more or less to our state), defined as the major universal association [*universalis maior consociatio*] (chap. X). What
characterizes Althusius's model is not so much the number
and kinds of degrees of associations, but rather the progress

5. *Politica methodice digesta of Johannes Althusius* (Cambridge: Harvard University Press, 1932), V, 8, p. 39 [The translation of passages from Althusius is
mine.—TRANS.]

from inferior associations to the state. The state is thus considered a great association, more precisely the greatest of associations, composed of smaller ones. There is no better way of expressing this idea than Althusius's own words: "Human society becomes differentiated into states by progressing from private to public societies according to fixed steps."[6]

4. Elements of the Alternative Model

The best way to emphasize the differences between the conceptual model of natural law theory and the Aristotelian one is to see how the elements typical of the former model (listed in section 1 above) appear in the latter.

1. The analysis does not begin with a generic state of nature in which human beings would find themselves before the state is instituted. The analysis begins with a specific, concrete, and historically determined kind of human society: the family is the original natural association.
2. The relation between this original society, the family, and the last and perfect one, the state, is not one of opposition, but rather of continuity, or development, or progress. In passing from the state of families to the civil state, human beings have gone through several intermediate steps. The state is the natural outcome and the point of arrival, rather than the antithesis of the previous associations.
3. The natural condition is not one of isolation. Individuals live in organized groups, as domestic associations are in fact. The state must therefore be portrayed as an aggregation of families, or a big family, and not as an aggregation of individuals.
4. Since individuals live in families from the time of their birth, the prepolitical condition is not one of freedom and equality. It is rather a condition in which the fundamental relationships existing in a

6. Ibid., V, Preface.

hierarchical society, such as the family is, are between superiors and inferiors. Such are the relationships between father (and mother) and child, or between master and servant.

5. The passage from the prepolitical to the political condition takes place, as noted, through a natural process of evolution from the lesser associations to the major association. This change thus does not occur thanks to a convention, that is, a voluntary and deliberate act. But it is the product of natural causes such as territorial expansion, population growth, security requirements, the need for procuring the means of subsistence, and so forth. As a consequence, the state is no less natural than the family.

6. The principle of legitimation of political society is not consent, but rather necessity (or *natura rerum*).

If we compare the six features of the two conceptual models, there emerge some of the great dichotomies which characterize the long road of political philosophy up to Hegel;

a. rationalistic or historical-sociological conceptions of the state;
b. the state as antithesis or complement of natural man;
c. atomistic and individualistic, or social and organicistic conceptions of the state;
d. idealized conception of the prepolitical condition, from which ensue the theories of natural rights; or realistic conception of human beings as living in society, and therefore always subjected to one another and unequal;
e. contractual or naturalistic conceptions of the foundation of the power of the state;
f. theory of legitimation of political power by consent or through the nature of things.

These are the great dichotomies which concern the fundamental issues of any theory of the state: the issues of (a) the origin, (b) nature, (c) structure, (d) end, (e) foundation, and

(f) legitimacy of political power which is superior to any other type of power exercised over human beings.

5. *The Conceptual Model of Natural Law Theory and Bourgeois Society*

In the historiography on natural law theory, it has so often been remarked as to become commonplace that the elaboration, transmission, and refinement of the conceptual model of natural law theory accompanies the rise and development of bourgeois society. This model, which is founded on the antithesis state of nature–civil society, would, wittingly or unwittingly, be the theoretical reflection of the historical process. The *ideological* meaning of the *theoretical* model appears to lie in its being a reflection of a historical situation. It goes without saying that this ideological interpretation has been a characteristic theme of Marxist historiography. (It was begun by Marx himself, whose famous *Jewish Question* is devoted to the critique and reinterpretation of the rights of man and citizen as an expression of class-stratification and conflict.) C. B. Macpherson is the author of a recent and highly debated (and debatable) version of this type of interpretation.[7] Macpherson sees in Hobbes's state of nature the first representation of market society instead of a description of the civil war, as has always been assumed. Hobbes would portray a specific kind of market society, which Macpherson labels "possessive," in order to distinguish it from simpler kinds of market societies. But in Hobbes's account, market society is still at the embryonic stage, if compared with the version we find reflected in Locke's theory. In the latter, the state of nature is a full-fledged market society, and the state is an association of property owners. In any case, independently of the varying interpretations, it cannot be denied that the state born of the French Revolution was informed by the fundamental principles of the school of natu-

7. C. B. Macpherson, *The Political Theory of Possessive Individualism* (Oxford: Clarendon Press, 1962). I have devoted a broader discussion to this interpretation in a collection of studies on Locke, now reprinted in *Da Hobbes a Marx* (Naples: Morano, 1965), pp. 108–16.

ral law. In the nineteenth century this type of state became the prototype of the bourgeois state, as the constitutional, liberal, parliamentary, and representative state.

According to the most widespread interpretations, the outstanding connections between the conceptual model of natural law theory and bourgeois society are the following:

1. Natural law theorists see the state of nature as the condition in which human beings experience the most elemental, simple, and immediate relations, that is, economic relations. Through these, human beings provide for their subsistence by fighting for the possession of the goods necessary to their survival. This is the discovery of the economic domain as distinct from the political domain; in other words, of the private sphere as distinct from the public. This separation reflects the rise of a society different from feudal society, which was characterized by the overlapping of economic and political power and the confusion between private and public.

2. The discovery that the economic and the political spheres are distinct and even, as remarked above, antithetical to one another, reflects the rise of a social class that is about to become emancipated from and economically hegemonic over the existing state. This discovery is articulated as the identification of a prepolitical and antipolitical society, which is regulated by natural laws. This society is the basis upon which political society is built. The latter is an artificial entity, created by the will of owners of resources who wish to see their property secured. (And to see secured all the rights that enable them to acquire and enjoy that property, such as liberty, equality, independence, and so forth.)

3. The state of nature which precedes political society is a condition in which the agents are individuals who enjoy full religious, moral, and economic autonomy. Considered abstractly, they are independent of one

another, but they come into contact or conflict with one another to gain possession of and to exchange goods. This portrait reflects an individualistic conception of human society and history, which is usually seen as a characteristic feature of the bourgeois ethics and worldview.

4. The ideals of liberty and equality which find their (imaginary) place of actualization in the state of nature, describe and point to a normative conception of life in society which is antithetical to the traditional one. According to the latter, human society is built upon a hierarchical and tendentially stable order. On the contrary, the ideals of liberty and equality characterize an egalitarian and libertarian conception of society, which has inspired bourgeois uprisings against the social, ideological, economic, and political bonds that pose obstacles to the emancipation of the bourgeoisie.

5. The notion that the state is founded on the consent of the individuals who will be its members represents the trend toward the political, and not only the social and economic emancipation of the new class. This class aims at gaining control of political power, which is the most important means of domination employed by any group of human beings seeking to obtain obedience from others. In other words, the contractual conception of the origin of the state reflects the idea that a class which is in the process of establishing its ideological and economic hegemony must also seize political power by creating the state in its own likeness.

6. The idea that the exercise of power is legitimate only if founded on consent, is proper to those who are struggling to conquer a power which they do not yet have. And yet, they are the first to hold the opposite thesis, once they have realized their aim.

6. The Family and the State of Nature

In my opinion, we can best show the validity of this ideological interpretation of the conceptual model of natural law theory by comparing it with the Aristotelian model. From this point of view, the comparison is not only an academic exercise, but also has a heuristic value, which to my knowledge, has not yet been adequately explored. In brief, the modern conceptual model substitutes the dichotomy state of nature–civil society for the dichotomy domestic society–political society. In both models, the political condition is the final stage of a finite process, which has been preceded by a prepolitical condition. But the difference lies in the fact that this prepolitical condition is represented by the domestic association in the classical model, and by the state of nature in the modern one. As Hobbes (but Locke and others too) devoted the first chapter of his political treatises to the state of nature, so Aristotle devoted the first chapter of the *Politics* to the family. The state of nature becomes such a faithful mirror of (private) economic relations, that it may appear as the idealized description of mercantile society. In the classical model, the description of domestic society which Aristotle offers in book one of the *Politics*, and which has been handed down to posterity over the centuries, includes not only the relationships between husband and wife, and parent and child, but also that between master and servant. The household is thus the fundamental nucleus of economic life in that type of society, a nucleus around which are organized all relations of production relating to it. (It must not be forgotten that "economy" in Greek means "management of the household," and that book one of Aristotle's *Politics* has been considered one of the major treatises on economics.) From the success of words we should not derive any more meaning than is allowed us as historians of concepts, rather than of words. And we should not forget that modern economic science began with the study of the exchange and circulation of goods, activities which Aristotle had called *chrematistic*. Nonetheless, the distinction between domestic society and political society plays the same role in the classical model as does the distinction between state of nature and civil society in the modern one. For both dichotomies distinguish between the initial moment of organized social life, in which human beings provide for their subsistence, and the later moment of political rule.

In the modern model, the family has thus been suppressed or set aside as the prepolitical society by definition, and it has been replaced by the state of nature. The latter progressively assumes the features of the society in which the network of elemental economic relations develops. (So much so that Hegel calls its "bourgeois" or "civil society.") We may consider the family and the state of nature from the point of view of the roles they play when we distinguish between the economic and the political phases of society taken as a whole. If we do so, we can interpret these phases as the reflections, at the theoretical level, of the great transformation from feudal to bourgeois society, and from the "management of the household" to market economy. In other words, this change is an indicator of the dissolution of the household as an economic enterprise and of the rise of capitalism; or of the passage from a primarily agricultural society (*gemeinschaftlich* in Tönnies's terminology, or traditional in the Weberian sense of the term), to a society characterized by a more complex economic structure (*gesellschaftlich* in Tönnies's sense, and rational in Weber's sense).

The latter type of society is characterized by the progressive separation of the management of the household from the management of the (economic) firm. The procreation and education of children remain functions typical of the family; whereas economic functions, ideally carried out among free and equal individuals, are entrusted to associations in which the criteria for the organization of power are legal and rational, rather than personal and traditional. It is thus legitimate to interpret this complex dynamic as follows. The natural society of free and equal individuals replaces the domestic association as the first moment of social life. This change provides a simple and synthetic, and yet significant version of all those phenomena which scholars usually take into account when characterizing the rise of bourgeois society. In similar fashion, the traditional family in which the head of household was at the same time husband, father, and master was considered for centuries the propelling motor of economic life, until the development of modern economic science in the eighteenth century. We may note that this image of the traditional household was reproduced unchanged for centuries, thus outliving the historic institution on which it had been based. (But this depends on the well-known inertia of abstract thought, which changes much more slowly than empirical reality.)

7. The Family in the Conceptual Model of Natural Law Theory

It is impossible in a few lines to give an account of the role of the family in the most famous works of natural law theorists. If we try to do so, we run the risk of engaging in a vague and futile exercise. We may observe, however, that in these works the analysis of the family, as both domestic and despotic society, usually follows the account of the state of nature. Natural law theorists introduce this theme in their political theories (which are always theories of society as a whole), because they aim at showing that domestic and political power do differ, and ought to be kept distinct. More precisely, power relations between both father and child and master and servant are different, and ought to be kept distinct from political power relations, that is, from the power relations between ruler and ruled. In political society the foundation of power is, or should be, the consent of the ruled;[8] whereas in domestic society the foundation of power is generation, and, in despotic society, force (as victory in a just war shows). To these three kinds of foundations of power correspond the three classical kinds of sources of obligations: *ex contractu, ex generatione, ex delicto.* Natural law theorists are inclined to prove, or rather to maintain with plausible arguments, that civil power differs (or should be kept distinct) from the power of the father over his children, and of the master over his servants, because the three types of power differ in the foundation of their legitimacy. One

8. I say "should be," for the political philosophy of natural law theorists has a deontological vocation: it rationalizes, not to say idealizes, the existing state of affairs.

can thus see why the family is not and can no longer be the first link in a chain of which the last link is the state. On the contrary, there is a qualitative leap, from the natural condition of human beings, to which belongs the formation of the family, both as domestic and as despotic society, to civil society.

This qualitative leap is what allows humankind to go from nature to civilization. It is true that Hobbes does not rule out the fact that, in a primitive society, the "small family" plays the role of the state.[9] Nor does he exclude from consideration that in the historical evolution of society from the small group to the state, there have been states, such as patrimonial monarchies, which have assumed the features of families "writ large."[10] And it is also true that Locke, whose main polemical target is Filmer's theory of the origin of the state from the family, concedes that *"Fathers of Families*, by an insensible change, became the *politick Monarchs* of them too," and that "they laid the Foundations of Hereditary, or Elective Kingdoms,"[11] and that originally the first governments were monarchical, for the father had been recognized as king.[12] But it is also apparent that in Hobbes and Locke, we must distinguish the description of what happened from their proposals for a new form of legitimation of political power. As has been correctly remarked with regard to Locke, we must distinguish the problem of the historical origin of government from the problem of its ethical foundation.[13] From the point of view of the foundation of a new principle of legitimacy, neither domestic nor despotic society offers a valid model for political society.

9. *Leviathan*, XVII, pp. 109–10.
10. *De Cive*, IX, 10, pp. 121–22; *Leviathan*, XX, p. 133. These aspects of Hobbes's thought have been subtly and precisely analyzed by S. Landucci in a very interesting book, *I filosofi e i selvaggi* (Bari: Laterza, 1972), pp. 114ff., especially notes 73 and 74.
11. J. Locke, *Two Treatises of Government*, ed. P. Laslett (New York: A Mentor Book, 1965), II, vi, 76, p. 361.
12. Ibid., II, viii, 107, pp. 382–83.
13. G. J. Schnochet, "The Family and the Origins of the State in Locke's Political Philosophy," in *John Locke: Problems and Perspectives* (Cambridge: Cambridge University Press, 1969), pp. 91ff. This theme has also been explored by J. Dunn, *The Political Thought of John Locke* (Cambridge: Cambridge University Press, 1969), in which Dunn explicitly refers to Schochet, p. 113, note 1.

This is one of the profound themes of the political philosophy of natural law theory: if consent, expressed through one or more conventions, must be the foundation of legitimacy of political power, it follows that political power rests on foundations different from those on which rest domestic and despotic power. And yet, no one of the writers taken in consideration here is willing to exclude that there also exist states which have different foundations: these are patrimonial monarchies and despotic states. In the former, power is modeled upon domestic power; in the latter, upon despotic power. But natural law theorists, who are also proponents of an ideal, incline to rule out the possibility that these states are, ideally, legitimate.

Three examples will suffice. Hobbes starkly distinguishes among the three kinds of power which one human being may have over another,[14] after describing the transition from the state of nature to civil society through the social contract; that is, after describing the formation of the state based upon a convention (which he calls state by institution). This type of state, which is founded on consent, clearly becomes an ideal model with regard to all other forms of domination. From the very first pages of the *Second Treatise of Government*, Locke makes explicit what his aim is, when saying that "the Power of a *Magistrate* over a Subject, may be distinguished from that of a *Father* over his Children, a *Master* over his Servant, a *Husband* over his Wife, and a *Lord* over his Slave." So that we need to show "the difference betwixt a Ruler of a Common-wealth, a Father of a Family, and Captain of a Galley."[15] Rousseau's *Social Contract* begins with a critique of the theories that give political power a foundation of legitimacy different from consent. He then comments upon domestic society, the right of the stronger, and finally, slavery. Although he calls domestic society "the first model of political societies,"[16] he remarks, as did Locke, that this society is precarious. And in his discussion of slavery, he contends that neither consent nor the right of war provide le-

14. *De Cive*, VIII, 1, pp. 114–25.
15. J. Locke, *Two Treatises*, II, i, 2, p. 308.
16. J.-J. Rousseau, *The Social Contract*, trans. M. Cranston (Harmondsworth: Penguin Books, 1984), I, 2, p. 50.

gitimate foundations. It is not by chance that, after refuting those doctrines which seek to found the legitimacy of political power on something other than freely expressed consent, Rousseau begins the following chapter with the heading: "That We Must Always Go Back To an Original Covenant."[17]

8. The Bourgeois Family

The family thus leaves the stage as the initial phase in the formation of the state, and ceases to be a small state *in potentia,*[18] to be replaced by a new sociological account. The state of nature is no longer populated by fathers and children, and masters and servants, tied to one another by organic links. But it is populated by economic man, free, equal, and independent, who has no ties other than the ones created by his own need to exchange the fruits of his labor. By losing its position as the initial phase of social life, the family also loses its economic function. And by losing the latter, it preserves as its sole functions the procreation and education of children (which will become the typical feature of the bourgeois family). As bourgeois society becomes more and more emancipated from existing political society, productive laborers will no longer be the members of domestic society, seen as an organic whole, but rather legally independent producers.

In Locke's theory we can already find a mature expression of the transformation of the family from economic enterprise to ethical and pedagogical institution. After discussing the state of nature and the state of war, Locke deals with the theme of the foundation of private property. This theme concerns the passage from the original possession in common of all things to the right of an individual to the exclusive appropriation of some of those things. This transition takes place in the state of nature, that is, before the institution of civil society. As is well known, Locke solves this traditional problem by rejecting the

17. Ibid., I, 5, p. 58.
18. To the image of the family as a small state corresponded the image of the state as a big family.

two classical solutions. The first of these holds that occupation assigns a legitimate title; the second derives the right of private property from a contract. According to Locke, private property, that is, the exclusive right which an individual claims to the enjoyment and disposal of a good, derives from the effort made by an isolated individual to appropriate it, and, if necessary, to transform it and increase its value through his own labor. It goes without saying that this theory of the foundation of private property is one of the most original and innovative of Locke's theses. Nothing comparable can be found in the other famous treatises of political philosophy that adopt the conceptual model of natural law theory. With his value theory of labor, his theory of original accumulation, and of the function of money, Locke is the first political writer to deal with themes which would later become the specific object of a new science, political economy.

In view of our concerns, Locke's theory of private property is important for three reasons. First, Locke makes it fully explicit that the prepolitical condition, or state of nature, or natural society, however one wishes to call it, coincides with the sphere of economic relations. This is the domain in which human beings establish and develop their relationships with nature in order to transform it to their own advantage through their own labor. Second, the protagonist of this prepolitical condition, which coincides with economic society, is the isolated individual. He is considered to have the personal capacity for appropriating things which have been held in common, and for transforming them to his own benefit and the benefit of society. Third, the fundamental institution of bourgeois economy, private property, comes into existence already complete and perfect in the state of nature, that is, before the rise of the state. (Unlike what we find in the theories of Hobbes and Rousseau.)

These remarks enable us to understand the new function played by the family in Locke's system. Locke (unlike Hobbes) deals with the family before discussing political society, but after treating the theme of private property. What meaning can we assign to this succession of themes? Since Locke analyzes the family before political society, he appears to consider it a natural society. But since he analyzes it after private property, and the related themes of labor, the appropriation of land and its increase in value, and money, he shows that the institution of the family has nothing to do with economic enterprise, which is essentially an individual activity. In his analysis of the family Locke insists on two points in particular;

a. The family is a "temporary" society, for it is destined to last only until children come of age. It therefore cannot be confused with political society, which is a "permament" society, and which accompanies the individual from the cradle to the grave.

b. The family has as its only function the feeding, upbringing, and education of children, and therefore cannot be confused with economic society, in which the agents are independent individuals (as can be found in the state of nature). (The functions typical of the family further differentiate it from political society. Since political society must perform much more important functions, much broader powers must be assigned to political rulers.) To conclude, the Lockean family well represents the end of the traditional conception which considered domestic and despotic society as the original nucleus of society. In so doing, the traditional view also assigned economic functions to the household, which are prepolitical activities by definition.

9. A Proof "to the Contrary"

There is a proof to the contrary that the conceptual model of natural law theory represents a break from the classical model; a break which assumes an ideological meaning in the analyses of the formation of the modern state. This proof to the contrary is provided by the fact that, once the conceptual model of natural law theory has become hegemonic, it is reactionary thinkers who retrieve the classical model.[19] It is they who emphasize the family as the origin of political society, thus denying that there ever existed a state of nature constituted of free and equal individuals. It is they who offer a close critique of the social contract, thereby asserting that the state is a product of nature. It is they who reject the antithesis of state of nature and civil society, insisting that the state is an outgrowth of domestic society.

I offer two typical examples of this polemical strategy, the first from the beginning, and the second from the end of the period when the conceptual model of natural law theory flourished. The former is developed by Robert Filmer, one of the last supporters of monarchichal restoration in England in the second half of the seventeenth century. And the latter is developed by Ludwig von Haller, one of the most famous ideologists of the Restoration following the French Revolution.

Filmer's polemical target is the theory of natural freedom of human beings. From it writers derived the right for human beings to choose the form of government which they prefer. (Filmer considers this contention blasphemous and without foundation.) For Filmer, monarchy is the only legitimate form of government, because the foundation of every power is the right of the father to govern his children. Kings were originally fathers of families, and, in the course of time, the descendants of those fathers or their delegates. While contractual theories hold an "ascending" conception of power, Filmer holds a rigidly descending one. According to Filmer, power is never transmitted from below, but only from above to below. The power of the father over his children is paradigmatic of every form of power of a human being over another. Therefore, for Filmer there is not a difference in kind, but only of degree between domestic and political society. He thus contends: "If we compare the natural duties of a father with those of a king, we find them to be all one, without any difference at all but only in the latitude or extent of them. As the father over one family, so

---

19. I here mean by "reactionaries" those writers who are hostile to the great economic and political upheavals that have the bourgeoisie as protagonist.

the king, as father over many families, extends his care to preserve, feed, clothe, instruct and defend the whole commonwealth."[20]

Haller proceeds along the same lines. Although he does not
know Filmer's work, he declares that its title seems to indicate
a fundamentally correct idea (albeit too narrow, as he warns
soon afterwards). In his major work, *Restoration of the Science of
Politics,* Haller reasserts over and over that one of his aims is to
show that "the human groups which we call States differ from
other associations not in nature, but only in degree."[21] Haller
pursues this project with a continuous attack on all versions of
contractual theory, described as a "chimera," and with the
thesis that the state is no less natural than the most natural
forms of social life. So much so that we cannot find any difference between natural societies and those which have falsely
been called "civil." "The ancients ignored, as still today the
whole world ignores (except for the philosophical schools), the
whole terminology which pretends to be scientific, and which
establishes an essential difference between the state of nature
and civil society."[22] States have not been created through an act
of human reason, but rather they have taken shape through a
natural process. Therefore, "the difference between states and
other social relations only consists in their independence, that
is, in the higher degree of their power and liberty."[23] One
could not state more clearly that the difference between prepolitical societies and the state is one of degree and not of substance. Societies are piled up one on top of the other in a finite
chain. It is thus inevitable that we reach a society on which all
others depend, but which does not depend on any other. This
ultimate society is the state. But a society can become a state,
and cease to be a state, without changing its nature.

20. R. Filmer, *Patriarcha,* in *Patriarcha and Other Writings,* ed. J. P. Sommerville
(Cambridge: Cambridge University Press, 1991), I, 10, p. 12.
21. K. L. von Haller, *Restauration de la science politique* (Lyon: Rusand, 1824–
30), II, p. 8. [Translation mine.—TRANS.]
22. Ibid., XVI, pp. 534–35.
23. Ibid., p. 541.

10. The End of the Model

I said in the first pages of this essay that the success of the conceptual model of natural law theory lasts until Hegel. But Hegel's attitude toward the natural law tradition is complex, for it is an attitude both of rejection and acceptance. It is undeniable that Hegel, on the one hand, does not miss a chance to criticize the basic features of the conceptual model of natural law theory: the state of nature, the social contract, the state as a voluntary association rather than an organism, and so forth. He contrasts the atomistic conception of the state typical of his predecessors with his conception of the state as an "ethical totality," as an organism, and as the organization of society as a whole through the constitution, which expresses the spirit of the nation. But it is also undeniable, on the other hand, that Hegel appropriates the same elements. At the right place and moment he inserts them in his account of the "objective Spirit," thus making them essential, if not exclusive features of his system. The state of nature is eliminated as the original condition of humankind, but reappears at the end of the deployment of the objective Spirit, in the relations among states. The phase of economic man, which constitutes the main element of the social atomism of natural law theorists, also makes its appearance in Hegel's system, in the section immediately preceding the state. In this section, which regards "civil society" (to be taken here to mean "bourgeois society"), Hegel, not by chance, calls "system of atomistic" the part devoted to the "system of needs." Hegel includes in the moment of "abstract right," with which the movement of the objective Spirit begins, most topics that previous writers had included in the analysis of the state of nature, or of natural law as opposed to positive law. (The latter only comes into being with the foundation of the state.)[24]

24. I have explored in greater detail the relationship between Hegel and natural theory in a long essay entitled "Hegel e il giusnaturalismo," *Rivista di filosofia* 58 (1966): 379–407. Later I returned to the same topic in the essay "Hegel e il diritto," in *Incidenza di Hegel*, ed. F. Tessitore (Naples: Morano, 1970), pp.

Hegel's seeming ambiguity toward the doctrine of natural law depends, as has often been remarked, on the complexity of his system. This system is difficult to understand in its multiple articulations, which describe a totality both extremely differentiated and extremely compact. I think that the contrast of the classical and modern conceptual models, outlined in the previous paragraphs, may help us to clarify the complexity of Hegel's system. It is a commonplace that the Hegelian system is so inclusive as to leave out nothing essential of the previous systems—at least, nothing which Hegel deemed essential. But even if it is a commonplace, it continues to amaze us because of its truth. This is confirmed every time we approach Hegel's system in order to make a further step in understanding the deeper layerings on which it rests. The contrast of the two models now becomes a means for deconstructing and reconstructing the complexity of Hegel's system, thus enabling us to reach a better understanding of it.

Until Hegel, the two conceptual models had been kept starkly distinct, as the example of Hegel's contemporary, Haller, which I have just discussed, shows. I mean to say that, until Hegel, the whole tradition of political philosophy proceeded on two parallel tracks: the Aristotelian track, based on the pair family-state; and the Hobbesian track, based on the pair state of nature–civil society. Hegel is the first (and the last) to merge the two models in his system. His system of practical philosophy is a synthesis because it tries to mediate between, or more precisely, not to drop the classical as well as the modern tradition of political philosophy. Hegel attempts to preserve both of them, and to insert them into an organic totality. He can perform this operation because he articulates his system in triads rather than pairs.

Let us consider the last moment of the objective Spirit, ethical life, with its tripartition into family, civil society, and state. After all that has been said in the previous pages, it is now ap-

217–49, and "La filosofia giuridica di Hegel nell'ultimo decennio," *Rivista critica di storia della filosofia* 27 (1972): 293–319. These and other works have been collected in the volume *Studi hegeliani* (Turin: Einaudi, 1981).

parent that this triad results from the combination of the two great dichotomies which precede it. The movement begins with the family, as in the classical conceptual model, and then continues with civil society. But the first moment of civil society, the system of needs, reproduces fundamental themes of the state of nature in its more mature expressions. Thinkers had increasingly seen the state of nature as the domain of economic man. This is the condition in which the new economic relations of bourgeois society develop, thus prompting analysts to elaborate a new science, economics, which is no longer taken to mean "management of the household." In the two previous conceptual models, which are both diadic, prepolitical society is *either* the family, as the first natural society, *or* the state of nature, as the sphere of exchange relations among individuals in competition with one another. But in the Hegelian model, which is triadic, before the state there are *both* the family *and* bourgeois society. In other words, Hegel recovers from the traditional theory the moment of the family as the original moment in the development of human society. But he does not eliminate, as reactionary writers do, the moment when the agents of social relations are individuals (or social classes), rather than fathers of families. This is the moment when individuals (or classes) are in conflict with one another, and, as has been remarked, it is seen to reflect the rise of mercantile bourgeois society. In Hegel, the passage from the family to the state occurs neither directly, nor gradually, but through an intermediate negative moment. This moment represents, on the one hand, the dissolution of the family, and, on the other, the necessary premise for the reconstitution of social life at a higher level, that is, the state. As in the classical conceptual model, the state is an ethical organism like the family (and unlike civil society). Nonetheless, as in the modern conceptual model, the state is the antithesis of the system of needs, in which conflicting relations among individuals and classes prevail. In the two previous models the state was seen either as the continuation or the antithesis of the former condition. In Hegel's model, the state is at the same time continuation (of the family) and antithesis (of civil society).

TWO

Hobbes's Political Theory

1. *Works*

As a philosopher, Thomas Hobbes (1588–1679) was long considered one of the minor disciples of Bacon, until Ferdinand Tönnies's reassessment of his role. Hobbes divided the entire subject matter of philosophy into three parts which he published in his books *De Corpore, De Homine, De Cive*. But he was mainly a political philosopher, as shown by the fact that he elaborated *De Cive* (1642), the part specifically devoted to politics, many years before the other two when England was on the threshold of civil war. A careful reading and comparison of these three parts clearly shows that *De Cive* is also the one which Hobbes formed fully, despite the decade or so which separates it from *De Corpore* (1655) and *De Homine* (1658). In addition, his first philosophical work, *Elements of Law Natural and Politic*, written before the outbreak of the Civil War, is, despite its title, a complete philosophical tract, a sort of trial run for Hobbes's system. There the broadest and most elaborate part by far is the one devoted to the theory of the state, so much so that commentators unanimously consider it to be the first draft of Hobbes's major work, *Leviathan*, which was published in 1651. Finally, if we take into account the various editions of Hobbes's works—both of the works cited here and of his minor writings on similar subjects—edited by Hobbes himself, we can realize how pervasive and continuous was his interest in political reflection throughout his life:

a. 1640, *Elements,* already cited;
b. 1642, the first private edition of *De Cive;*
c. 1647, the first published edition of *De Cive,* with notes added in response to objections;
d. 1650, *De Corpore Politico, or the Elements of Law, Moral and Politic,* separate publication of the part of the *Elements* devoted to the state;
e. 1651, *Leviathan* (in English);
f. 1666, *A Dialogue between a Philosopher and a Student of the Common Law of England;*
g. 1670, Latin edition of *Leviathan,* probably written in part before the English version, but published only in Hobbes's old age, substantively unchanged, except for a few corrections of mistakes in the exposition of religious doctrines.

To complete the picture, we should not forget to what extent Hobbes's historiographical work was also politically engaged. This begins with the translation of Thucydides in which, according to the critics' unanimous opinion, readers can observe Hobbes's beginnings as a political writer. Hobbes's last historiographical work is the narration of the events which provided the background and the stimulus to his reflections on politics: *Behemoth: The History of Causes of the Civil Wars of England.*

Among the works listed, the three which follow are essential to an understanding of Hobbes's political thought: *Elements,* the second edition of *De Cive,* and the English version of *Leviathan.* The last named is usually considered the most complete and reliable version of Hobbes's theory. And most recently, scholars are inclined to emphasize rather than to downplay differences among Hobbes's works, although more with regard to methodological than to substantive issues. Nonetheless, the central nucleus of Hobbes's theory is already fully presented and developed in *Elements,* and it remains unaltered in the subsequent works.

Unlike the majority of political writers, Hobbes never engaged in active politics, either as a party man or as an advisor to the prince. He was a political philosopher, in the fullest and most narrow sense of the term. In comparison with Machiavelli, he was merely an "erudite," as a British historian has described him. Hobbes spent most of his very long life in the shadow of the Cavendish family, Earls of Devonshire, first as tutor, then as secretary, and finally as an honored guest. In his younger years he made three trips for study to the continent (1610–13, 1629–30, 1634–37), which allowed him to make contact with the great philosophers and scientists of the time (he met both Descartes and Galileo.) At the end of 1640, before the beginning of the *Long Parliament* (November 1640), he went into exile in France. He was not being persecuted, but he was afraid of persecution, because in the same year he had written and circulated a work (the already cited *Elements*) in which he contended that monarchy is the best form of government (part II, chap. V). He spent eleven years in France, nearly always in Paris, where he frequented the scientific circle around Father Mersenne. In 1646 he was called to teach mathematics to the Prince of Wales (the future Charles II), who was also in exile in Paris. But he never established such close ties to the Court as to force him to accept the consequences of the Stuarts' defeat.

After Cromwell restored the peace, Hobbes returned to England, having just published his major work, *Leviathan* (1651). He was accused of writing *Leviathan* in order to obtain the favor of the winner—a charge which is, all things considered, unjust. Indeed, in the age of Cromwell, Hobbes could enjoy the ease of an independent scholar, and thus published all his major nonpolitical works: *De Corpore* in 1655; *The Questions concerning Liberty, Necessity and Chance*, in which he collected all his writings pertaining to the controversy with Bishop Bramhall, in 1656; and *De Homine*, in 1658. He willingly accepted the regime born of the revolution which he had abhorred. But he never compromised himself with the new lord to the point that his former pupil Charles II could not accept him with benevolence when the Restoration occurred in 1660.

He devoted his old age to his beloved studies, interrupted now and then by polemics, most often provoked by adversaries (such as the methematician John Wallis) in scientific and religious matters rather than by political enemies. He wrote *An Historical Narration concerning Heresy and the Punishment thereof* (1665–66), left unfinished, in order to defend *Leviathan* from charges of impiety and atheism. It was less pressing to defend it from political attacks, for, apart from its anticlericalism, *Leviathan* could well be interpreted and accepted as the justification and apology for the Restoration. This is how the young Locke interpreted and accepted it, when, as lecturer at Christ Church at Oxford, he wrote his first political tracts on the civil magistrate.

2. The Leading Idea

Although he never was a political activist, Hobbes did write about politics starting from the real and crucial problem of his time, the problem of the unity of the state. This unity was threatened, on the one hand, by religious controversies and the conflict between Church and state, and, on the other, by the conflict between Crown and Parliament and the dispute over the separation of powers. Two great antitheses dominate the political thought of all times: oppression-freedom, and anarchy-unity. Hobbes definitely belongs in the company of those whose political thought has been inspired by the latter antithesis; the ideal which he defends is not liberty against oppression, but unity against anarchy. Hobbes is obsessed by the idea of the dissolution of authority, the disorder that ensues from the freedom to disagree about what is just and what is unjust, and with the disintegration of the unity of power, doomed to become reality when human beings begin to contend that power must be limited. In one word, he is obsessed by the threat of anarchy, which he considers to be the return of humankind to the state of nature. The evil which Hobbes most fears is not oppression, which derives from the excess of power, but insecurity, which derives, on the contrary, from the lack of power. And Hobbes feels called upon to erect his philosophical system as the supreme and insuperable defense against insecurity. Insecurity, first of all, of one's life, which is the *primum bonum;* second, of material goods; and, last, of that small or great liberty which a human being may enjoy while living in society.

During the years of Hobbes's adulthood, the dissolution of the state in England reached the extreme phase of civil war. The theme of civil war acquires a starker relief as we go from the *Elements*, written before the upheavals, to *Leviathan*, written when the long and bloody struggle among the various factions had culminated in regicide. At first, civil war is a nightmare from which we must free ourselves; then it is a calamity which we must try to avert for the future. The theme of the factions which tear the state apart appears in both the *Elements* and *Leviathan*. (Together with the marvelous simile of Medea and her sisters who cut their father into pieces so that he can be born again.) But in *Leviathan*, this theme elicits the image of civil war twice; whereas in the *Elements*, Hobbes speaks generically of "rebellion." In *Leviathan* there are frequent references to civil war as the worst of all evils,[1] not only to civil war in general, but specifically to the one that has raged and still rages in England while the author writes: "Howsoever it may be perceived what manner of life there would be, where there were no common power to fear, by the manner of life, which men that have formerly lived under a peaceful government, use to degenerate into, in a civil war" (XIII, p. 83). In the first page of the *Introduction*, Hobbes offers the famous comparison between the human body and the body politic, and compares sedition to a sickness, civil war to death (p. 5). Civil war is an *idée fixe*. In discussing the "unguided" association of thoughts, in the part of the book which is devoted to psychology, before the part on politics, Hobbes reports the example of the person who "in a discourse of our present civil war" asks "what was the value of a Roman penny" (III, p. 14). In *De Homine*, in talking about presumption, that is, of the defect of those who believe themselves to be wiser than they are, Hobbes introduces judges who claim thay they can give laws

---

1. *Leviathan*, ed. M. Oakeshott (Oxford: Basil Blackwell, 1946), pp. 120, 136, 219. Hereafter the page numbers in parentheses following quotations from *Leviathan* refer to this edition.

to the state, rather than apply the laws issued by the sovereign. Hobbes thus comments: "This is the beginning of civil wars" (XIII, 6, p. 115).

In chapter I of *De Corpore*, Hobbes praises philosophy. The mechanical arts, which have contributed to the improvement of human life, were born from natural philosophy; the prudent man can derive the art of good government from civil philosophy. And what does it mean to govern well? It means to build the state on foundations so strong that its dissolution becomes impossible. That is, it means to avert the danger of civil war, from which, Hobbes remarks, "derive massacres, desolation, and scarcity" (I, 7, p. 7).[2] Immediately afterwords, in speaking of civil war again, Hobbes calls them "the greatest calamities." Hobbes keeps returning to the same point.[3] Just when Hobbes explains to us what he means by philosophy and what its aim and usefulness are, his attention is drawn once more by the problem of civil war: "The utility of moral and civil philosophy is to be judged not from the advantages which we derive from knowing it, but from the calamities which befall us by ignoring it. On the other hand, all calamities which can be avoided thanks to human industry arise from war, especially from civil war" (ibid.).

Hobbes is prompted to philosophize by worry over the danger of the dissolution of the state. He is convinced that the major cause of this evil is to be sought in the minds of human beings, in the false opinions they hold, or receive from evil teachers, concerning what is just and unjust, and concerning the rights of sovereigns and the duties of subjects. One of the recurrent themes in his three political works is the condemnation of seditious opinions, which he sees as the main cause of disorders. In arguing in favor of the right of the sovereign to condemn opinions contrary to the well-being of the state, Hobbes thus comments: "For the actions of men proceed from

2. Translation of passages from Hobbes's Latin works are mine; page references are to the Latin edition of the works quoted cited in the Author's Note—TRANS.

3. In Italian, "la lingua batte dove il dente duole"—the tongue touches where the tooth aches.—TRANS.

their opinions; and in the well-governing of opinions, consisteth the well-governing of men's actions, in order to their
peace, and concord" (*Leviathan*, XVIII, p. 116). In the passage
already quoted from *De Corpore*, the analysis of the link between philosophy and civil war continues as follows: "The
cause of civil wars is that we ignore the causes of peace and
war. Very few have learnt their duties, thanks to which peace is
reinforced and preserved, that is, the true rules of social life"
(I, 7, p. 7). In the "Preface to the Readers" of *De Cive*—one of
the most beautiful passages in Hobbes's works—he compares
the "hermaphrodite opinions" of the moral philosophers who
have preceded him, to Centaurs, "a fierce, and fighting, and
unquiet generation." For the former, like the latter, are "partly
right and comely, partly brutal and wild; the causes of all contentions and bloodshed" (p. xiii).

3. The Method

If the main cause of the evils which afflict civil society is philosophical in nature, the remedy can only come from philosophy. But what philosophy?

The problem of good philosophy, which must finally drive
out the old philosophy which has dominated minds and led
them astray for too long, is tightly connected to the problem of
method. After devoting himself for years to humanistic studies, Hobbes became convinced, through his contacts with
some of the major scientists of his time, whom he met during
his trips to the continent, that the only developed sciences
were the ones that had applied the rigorously deductive
method of geometry. These kinds of sciences alone had developed so much that they had radically transformed the conception of the universe. Should one not infer from this that the
reason for the backwardness of the moral sciences lay in a defect in their method? In an environment so enthusiastic about
the successes of the natural sciences had the time not come to
put the study of humankind and society onto the same path as
the one which the study of nature had followed so successfully? The major cause for the disturbance of social peace

was, as remarked, the variety of opinions. But differences of opinions essentially depended on the fact that moral philosophers had never tried, either out of ignorance or bias, to transform political science into a rigorous science. In geometry and the demonstrative sciences there was no room for otiose disputes about truth and falsehood. Geometry—we can read in one of the many passages which might be quoted in this regard—"is the only science that it hath pleased God to bestow on mankind," and, a little farther, "[Its] conclusions have thereby been made indisputable" (*Leviathan*, IV, p. 21; V, p. 27). And yet moral philosophy was the one most in need of a rigorous method. "For in matters wherein we speculate for the exercise of our wits, if any error escape us, it is without hurt; neither is there any loss, but of time only. But in those things which every man ought to meditate for the stearage of his life, it necessarily happens that not only from errors, but even from ignorance itself, there arise offences, contentions, nay, even slaughter itself" (*De Cive*, Preface, p. xi).

Hobbes believed he knew that one of the causes of the backwardness of the moral sciences was that their truths could hinder "man's ambition, profit or lust" (*Leviathan*, XI, p. 68). He had no doubt that, "if it had been contrary to any man's right of dominion, or to the interest of men that have dominion, *that the three angles of a triangle, should be equal to two angles of a square;* that doctrine should have been, if not disputed, yet by the burning of all books of geometry, suppressed, as far as he whom it concerned was able" (*Elements*, Epistle Dedicatory, p. xvii). From the very first lines of his first book Hobbes distinguishes two kinds of knowledge, mathematical and dogmatic. The former is "free from controversies and disputes," because it only deals with shapes and movement, and does not interfere with anyone's interest. Whereas "in the later there is nothing not disputable, because it compareth men, and meddleth with their right and profit" (*ibid.*). In the paragraph already quoted from *De Corpore*, Hobbes offers another variation on this theme, and contrasts the "scientific" writings of mathematicians to the "verbose" writings of moral philosophers, who are only concerned to "boast about their eloquence and genius" (I, 7, p. 8). In a passage from *Leviathan*, he compares moral and civil science to the telescope, which enables us to see things from afar; and he contrasts it with those lenses, multipliers of passions, which deform even things that are close to us (XVIII, p. 120).

In this struggle in favor of a rigorous political science, Hobbes aims at knocking down several targets at once. His most illustrious adversary is Aristotle, for whom ethics and politics were sciences of what is probable, not of what is certain. Those sciences were not domains reserved for logic, but for rhetoric. In the dedicatory epistle of the *Elements*, Hobbes may be alluding to this point of view in a passage in which he apologizes for his bad style, saying that he has consulted "more with logic than with rhetoric" (p. xvii). By opposing this ancient and revered Aristotelian doctrine, Hobbes establishes one of the most characteristic principles of modern natural law theory: the pursuit of a demonstrative ethics.

The next rank of adversary, more heavily populated, is composed of the scholastics, old and new. These swear *in verba magistri* [by the words of the master (Aristotle)]; they base their theories not on reason and experience, but on the authority of precedent, which they follow blindly, either by inertia, or in order to please the powerful. They are also the holders of a purely bookish knowledge. Hobbes criticizes those who waste their time "fluttering over their books; as birds that entering by the chimney, and finding themselves enclosed in a chamber, flutter at the false light of a glass window, for want of wit to consider which way they came in" (*Leviathan*, IV, p. 22). In another passage, he compares them to the person who "trusting to the false rules of a master of fence, ventures presumptuously upon an adversary, that either kills or disgraces him" (V, p. 30). Since their infected nests are the universities, Hobbes's antibookish and antischolastic polemics goes hand in hand with his critique of the universities. There is no place in them for the study of true philosophy and geometry. As long as "the authority of Aristotle is only current there, that study is not properly philosophy . . . but *Aristotelity*" (*Leviathan*, XLVI, p. 439).

In the times in which he writes, Hobbes faces a third group of enemies of reason, which is also the most dangerous and turbulent. These are the "inspired," that is, fanatics, enthusiasts, visionaries, and false prophets. They all speak not by reason but by faith, mistake their own ghosts for truths revealed by God, and are driven to utter their seditious opinions by the satanic pride of believing themselves to be the few saved among the multitude of the damned. In a passage from *De Cive*, Hobbes calls them "apostates from natural reason" (XII, 6, p. 156). In another passage from *Leviathan*, he considers inspiration as a true instance of madness (VIII, p. 47), and he portrays its victims as follows: "They presently admire themselves, as being in the special grace of God Almighty, who hath revealed the same to them supernaturally, by his Spirit" (VIII, p. 48).

4. Artificial Man

What method Hobbes followed in dealing with his subject matter, whether he ever actually had one, or whether he formulated several mutually conflicting methods while applying others, these are all highly disputed questions, which may not even be essential. In order to understand the deeper reasons for his attempt to found a rigorous science of ethics, it is important to remark that Hobbes's effort is based on a nominalistic theory of knowledge. Unlike those who argued in favor of the stark separation between mathematics and ethics, between demonstrative sciences of nature and nondemonstrative sciences of the human kind, Hobbes holds that the type of knowledge most similar to geometry is politics. As has been remarked several times,[4] Hobbes's argument is the same as the one which Vico employed to show that history is knowable.

In a passage from *De Homine*, Hobbes distinguishes sciences that are demonstrable a priori, that is, in a rigorous way, from those that are not demonstrable. Demonstrable sciences are

4. As an example, see A. Child, *Making and Knowing in Hobbes, Vico, and Dewey*, (Berkeley, University of California Press, 1953).

those concerning objects that are created by the human will. Therefore, geometry is demonstrable because "we ourselves create its shapes," whereas physics is not demonstrable, "because the causes of natural things are not in our power, but rather in God's power." Ethics and politics are demonstrable like geometry, "for we have created the principles thanks to which we know what is just and what is fair, and what is unjust and unfair, that is, the causes of justice, which are laws and compacts" (X, 5, pp. 93–94).[5]

I wish to leave aside the problem of the validity of this thesis, and to emphasize instead its fundamental importance for our understanding of Hobbes's thought and the evaluation of its historical role. One of the characteristic features of Renaissance thought, which profoundly marks the philosophy of Bacon, Hobbes's first master, is the transformation of the relationship between nature and artifice, in comparison with the conception of the ancients.[6] Artifice no longer imitates nature, but is equal to it. This change is a sign that things made by human beings, and human industry in general, are now seen in a new light and valued more highly. Nature is now conceived as a great machine; to penetrate the secret of nature means to reach a comprehension of the laws which regulate its mechanisms. But once this secret has been discovered, human beings can, by building other machines, recreate nature, perfect it, increase its power, and not merely imitate it. For Hobbes, the state is one of these machines produced by human beings in order to compensate for the shortcomings of nature, and to replace the deficient products of nature with a product of human ingenuity, that is, an *artificium*.

This conception of the state is part of a much wider plan, which consists of depriving a not always beneficent nature of a part of its ancient kingdom; and of considering products tradi-

5. Hobbes presents the same view, more or less with the same words, in the *Dedicatory Epistle* of *Six Lessons to the Professors of the Mathematics* (*EW*, VII, p. 183).
6. I here refer to P. Rossi's illuminating pages in his *I filosofi e le macchine, 1400–1700* (Milan: Feltrinelli, 1960), appendix 1, "Il rapporto tra natura-arte e la macchina del mondo," pp. 139–47.

tionally attributed to nature to be the result of human creativity and inventiveness. According to Hobbes, not only are figures and numbers, political bodies and life in society products of humankind: so too is language. We should add a third demonstrable science to geometry and politics: logic, if we consider logic nothing more than the set of tools which allows us to use language rigorously. Of this program, Hobbes developed most extensively and coherently the part regarding political science. Starting from the assumption that the state is an automaton, Hobbes divided the entire field of philosophy into two parts: natural philosophy and civil philosophy. The former is concerned with "what is the work of nature"; the latter, with what "is constitued by the human will through conventions and compact among men" and "is called state" (*De Corpore*, I, 9, p. 10). History too is divided into natural history, that is history "of such facts, or effects of nature, as have no dependence on man's *will;* such as are the histories of *metals, plants, animals, regions,* and the like. The other is *civil history;* which is the history of the voluntary actions of men in commonwealths" (*Leviathan*, IX, p. 53).

As early as the "Preface to the Reader" of *De Cive*, Hobbes compares the state to the archetypal machine, the clock: "For as in a watch, or some such small engine, the matter, figure, and motion of the wheels cannot well be known, except it be taken insunder and viewed in parts; so to make a more curious search into the rights of states and duties of subjects, it is necessary, I say, not to take them insunder, but yet that they be so considered as if they were dissolved" (p. xiv). The Introduction to *Leviathan*, which contains the manifesto of Hobbes's theory of the state, begins with these words: "Nature, the art whereby God hath made and governs the world, is by the *art* of man, as in many other things, so in this also imitated, that it can make an artificial animal" (p. 5). After saying that art can even imitate "that rational and perfect work of nature, which is man," Hobbes explains: "For by art is created that great Leviathan called a Commonwealth, or State, in Latin *civitas,* which is but an artificial man." Hobbes continues with the minute and painstakingly detailed comparison between the parts of the natural machine, man, and those of the artificial machine, the state. In the state, finally, Hobbes compares "the *pacts* and *covenants,* by which the parts of this body politic were at first made, set together, and united" to the fiat pronounced by God at the creation (p. 5).

Hobbes contrasts the state, *societas civilis,* as something built by human beings, and as an artifact, with the unsocial natural condition. As I shall explain more clearly in the following section, this idea is the foundation of Hobbes's political theory. It is sufficient to recollect here that besides comparing the state with the clock, Hobbes compares it with what is "built" by definition, that is, with a house, as the following passage illustrates: "Time, and industry, produce every day new knowledge. And as the art of well building is derived from principles of reason, observed by industrious men, . . . long after mankind began, . . . to build: so, long time after men have begun to constitute commonwealths, imperfect, and apt to relapse into disorder, there may be principles of reason found out, by industrious meditation, to make their constitution, excepting by external violence, everlasting" (XXX, p. 220).

Either as clock maker or architect, man, or more precisely humankind in its historical development, has built, by instituting the state, the most complicated, perhaps the most delicate, and surely the most useful mechanism. Only this mechanism allows human beings to survive in a natural environment which is not always friendly. If we accept that human beings are called to correct and not only to imitate nature, the highest and noblest expression of their capacity as *artifices* is the institution of the state.

5. The State of Nature

Hobbes's three main political works offer us descriptions of the state of nature which are substantively identical, ·except for a few variations, and which are meant to play the same functional role. Hobbes presents his arguments for justifying the creation of artificial man in chapter XIV, part I, of *Elements,* chapter I of *De Cive*, and chapter XIII of *Leviathan*. These arguments emerge from an analysis of the objective conditions in which human beings happen to find themselves in the state of nature (conditions which are independent of their wills) and on the basis of human passions (partially fueled by those objective conditions).

The principal objective condition is that human beings are, de facto, equal. Being equal by nature, they are capable of causing the greatest of evils to one another: death. To this is to be added the second objective condition: scarcity of goods, which is the reason why it may happen that several human beings desire the same thing. In the presence of relative scarcity, equality raises everyone's hope of attaining his end. The combination of equality and relative scarcity of goods generates a permanent state of reciprocal lack of trust, which induces all to prepare for war, and to make war if necessary, rather than to seek peace. Among the objective conditions, *Elements* and *De Cive* emphasize in particular the *ius in omnia*. This is the right to all things which nature gives to anyone living outside civil society. To have a right to all things means that, where civil laws have not yet introduced a criterion to distinguish between mine and thine, every human being has the right to appropriate all that falls into his power. Or, according to another interpretation, he has the right to appropriate all that is useful to his own preservation. As a matter of fact, the objective conditions indicated by Hobbes would be sufficient in themselves to explain the misery of the state of nature. De facto equality, together with the scarcity of resources, and the right to all things, inevitably generates by itself a situation of merciless competition, which always threatens to turn into a violent struggle.

But this situation is made worse by the fact that nature has placed in this predicament beings who are dominated by passions (these too are a gift of evil nature) which incline them more to unsociability than to sociability. Hobbes does not have a flattering opinion of his fellow human beings. If we so wished, we would have ample opportunity to extract an anthology of maxims and judgments about the malice of human beings from Hobbes's works. While discussing freedom and necessity with Bishop Bramhall, Hobbes asserts that human beings resist truth because they covet riches and privileges; they crave sensual pleasures; they cannot bear to meditate; and they mindlessly embrace erroneous principles (*EW*, IV, p. 256). In a passage from *Leviathan*, after dividing human beings into those devoted to covetousness, that is, only interested in their gains, and those devoted to sloth, that is, only driven to sensual pleasures, he remarks that these "two sorts of men take up the greatest part of mankind" (XXX, p. 224). In describing the state of nature, Hobbes stresses vainglory in particular, because this is the passion "which deriveth from the imagination or conception of our *own power* above the power of him that contendeth with us" (*Elements*, I, 9, 1, p. 28). Under the broad notion of vanity we can include all pleasure of the soul, as distinct from material pleasure, (*De Cive*, I, 2, p. 5). Since there are human beings ruled by this passion, who expect to have precedence and superiority over their fellows, conflict is inevitable. In *Leviathan*, Hobbes synthetically indicates three causes of conflict: competition, which makes human beings fight for gain; diffidence, which makes them fight for security; and glory, which makes them fight for reputation (XIII, p. 81). Among the passions which generate conflict, Hobbes especially emphasizes vainglory because he deems it the most visible manifestation of the desire for power. For what drives one human being against another is the endless desire for power.

Only in *Leviathan* does Hobbes clarify the fundamental problem of political science: the problem of power (to which he devotes an entire chapter). With regard to this theme two lines are decisive: "So that in the first place, I put for a general inclination of all mankind, a perpetual and restless desire for power after power, that ceaseth only in death" (XI, p. 64). Power is defined as the means to obtain some future apparent good. There are two kinds: natural power, which depends on eminent capacities of body or mind; and instrumental power, which consists of means, such as riches, reputation, friends, apt to increase natural power. We might say that, once this endless desire for power, which ceases only with death, has been discovered, we do not need any other argument to show the misery of human life in the state of nature. But if we also consider the unfavorable objective conditions mentioned above, which stimulate rather than restrain the struggle for power, the terrifying picture of the state of nature is complete.

The state of nature is terrifying because the desire for power generates a situation which is a state of war. This happens because all are equal in their capacity to harm one another; goods are insufficient to satisfy everyone's needs; and everyone has a natural right to all things. The state of nature is the state of war of all against all. "Hereby it is manifest, that during the time men live without a common power to keep them all in awe, they are in that condition which is called war; and such a war, as is of every man, against every man" (XIII, *Leviathan*, 82).

6. The War of All Against All

We must not take literally the phrase "war of all against all." If we wish to take it literally, we should at least consider it as the apodosis of a conditioned sentence, which states in the protasis that there exists a universal state of nature. But the universal state of nature, that is, the state in which all human beings were at the beginning of history, or will be at its end, is a mere hypothesis of reason. When Hobbes speaks of the "war of all against all," he means to say that when there occur the conditions typical of the state of nature, all those who happen to live in this state are in a state of war.

According to Hobbes, the state of nature can come into existence in three specific situations which are historically verifiable:

a. In primitive societies. These comprise both contemporary savage populations, such as the natives of some areas of America, and the barbarian populations of antiquity who have now become civilized. Primitive societies live in a condition which precedes the passage from the state of nature to civil society, and is therefore *pre*political.

41

b. In case of civil war. This occurs when the state
already exists, but dissolves for various reasons. Here
there occurs the passage from civil society to anarchy.
We might call this situation *anti*political.
c. In international society. Relations among states are
not regulated by a shared power. This is a situation
which occurs *among*-political entities.[7]

Hobbes never believed that the universal state of nature was
the primitive condition in which humankind lived before it became civilized. In a passage from his polemics with Bishop
Bramhall, Hobbes says that "it is very likely to be true, that
since the creation there never was a time in which mankind
was totally without society. If a part of it were without laws and
governors, some other parts might be commonwealths" (*EW*,
V, pp. 183–84). Although he admits that a few primitive societies did live in the state of nature, he is interested in the
states of nature still existing in his time: the international system and the state of anarchy created by civil war. It is the latter
which interests him above all. The state of nature which he has
always in mind, and which he describes as the war of all
against all, is actually the civil war which has torn apart his
own country. Every time he speaks of civil war as the worst of
all evils, he characterizes it as a state of nature. When he has to
describe the consequences of the breakdown of the authority
of the state, that is, civil war, he describes it as the "war of everyone against his neighbour," in a sentence which echoes the
"war of all against all" of the state of nature. In the passage
from *Leviathan*, in which he presents examples of the state of
nature, he refers to Americans, as he also does in *De Cive*; but
he then adds a hint which could not be more explicit:
"Howsoever it may be perceived what manner of life there
would be, where there were no common power to fear, by the
manner of life, which men that have formerly lived under a

---

7. Bobbio employs three terms which contain the word state: *pre-statale, anti-statale,* and *inter-statale.* But this parallelism and the reference to the word state cannot be reproduced in translation.—TRANS.

peaceful government, use to degenerate into, in a civil war" (XIII, p. 83).

Hobbes is a realist. There is no better evidence of this than the description of the state of nature, which ends by overlapping with the description of civil war. In the end, the two become one. Hobbes's state of nature is much more realistic that that of Locke, and, of course, that of Rousseau in the *Discourse on Inequality* (which claims to be historical, but is not). Hegel, who was also a realist, and who believed not in the chattering of preachers, but in the hard lessons of history, conceived of international society as a Hobbesian state of nature.[8]

One could object that it is not realistic to speak of the state of nature as a "permanent" state of war. But, correctly, Hobbes means by state of war not only a condition of violent conflict, but also the one in which peace is precarious. In this situation, peace is ensured exclusively by reciprocal fear, by "dissuasion" as we should say today; this is the situation in which peace is possible only because of a permanent threat of war. Hobbes repeats this argument in all three works, to make sure that he is not misunderstood (*Elements*, I, 14, 11; *De Cive*, I, 12; *Leviathan*, XIII, p. 82). In the last of these, moreover, he illustrates the concept with a simile, as he usually does: "For as the nature of foul weather, lieth not in a showre or two of rain; but in an inclination thereto of many days together: so the nature of war, consisteth not in actual fighting; but in the known disposition thereto, during all the time there is no assurance to the contrary."

"War of all against all" is a hyperbolic expression. If we take away the hyperbole, it means that condition in which a great number of human beings, taken as individuals or in groups, live in reciprocal and permanent fear of violent death, because

8. This is not the only possible realistic interpretation of Hobbes's state of nature, even if it seems to me the most faithful to the majority of his texts. There have been those, such as Macpherson (see chap. 1, sec. 5, above) who have seen in some Hobbesian passages on the state of nature, especially *Leviathan*, p. 81, the description of a forthcoming bourgeois society based on competition (pp. 19ff. and 61ff.).

they lack a shared power. The hyperbole only helps us to understand that this is an intolerable condition, which human beings must sooner or later abandon if they wish to save what is most precious to them: their lives.

7. The Dictates of Right Reason

Reason comes to the help of human beings who wish to leave the state of nature. Reason is here considered as a set of prudential rules, that is, hypothetical norms, of the kind: "If you want A, you must do B." Human beings are no less beings of reason than of passion: "Reason of man," says Hobbes, "is no less of the nature of man than passions, and is the same in all men" (*Elements*, I, 15, 1, p. 57). "*True reason*," he reasserts in *De Cive*,—"is . . . no less a part of human nature than any other faculty or affection" (II, 1, p. 16).

Hobbes's reason has nothing to do with the faculty which enables us to know the essence of things. Reason is the capacity to compute, that is to calculate ("reason is calculation," *De Corpore*, I, 2, p. 3), so that, given certain premises, one necessarily derives certain conclusions. To say that human beings are endowed with reason is for Hobbes the same as to say that they are capable of rational calculations. This is another way of saying that human beings can discover which means are the most adequate to attain desired ends. They can thus act to pursue their interest, and not only to obey this or that passion. Hobbes contends that right reason is part of human nature. In saying this, he means to say that human beings have not only the capacity to know *per causas* [through causes], but to act *per fines* [in view of an end]. That is, they can follow rules which tell them the best means for reaching the desired end. (As technical rules indeed do.) What has unleashed the most divergent discussions and has maddened critics, is that Hobbes has called these prudential rules "natural laws." But he has done so only to pay homage to tradition. If we mean by law the command of a person endowed with authority, these dictates of reason are not laws at all. This holds true unless one believes, as Hobbes appears to do in order to reconcile things which are irreconcilable,[9] that these rules of human prudence are also expressions of God's will.

After saying that the laws of nature are "nothing else but certain conclusions understood by reason, of things to be done and omitted," he warns that strictly speaking they are not laws, but "as they are delivered by God . . . they are most properly called by the name of laws" (*De Cive*, III, 33, pp. 49–50). In *Leviathan*, under the label of natural laws he even speaks of "convenient articles" which reason "suggesteth" ("suggests," it is to be remarked, not "commands") in order to attain peace (p. 84). Later on, he repeats that these norms of reason are "improperly" called laws, because they are nothing other than "conclusions, or theorems concerning what conduceth to the conservation and defence of ourselves" (XVI, p. 104).

As we have already said, the state of nature is intolerable in the long run, because it does not guarantee human beings that they will the attain the highest good: life. Right reason suggests to human beings a set of rules (Hobbes lists about twenty), in the forms of laws of nature, which aim at ensuring a peaceful cohabitation. These are all subordinated, as it were, to a first rule, which Hobbes calls "fundamental," and which prescribes the seeking of peace. Since in the state of nature life is always in danger, the fundamental rule of reason and all the rules which derive from it aim at the truly primary end of the preservation of life. They attain this end by leading human beings to realize peaceful cohabitation. But since these are prudential rules, not categorical imperatives, every individual is bound to comply with them only if, by doing so, he is confident that he will reach the desired end. It so happens, however, that in most cases the end prescribed by the rule cannot be attained if the rule is not observed by all, or at least by the majority in a group. Hobbes contends that I am not bound to comply with a rule, or more correctly, I have no interest in observing a rule, if I am not sure that others do the same. In this case also, Hobbes pays homage to the natural law tradition, which speaks of laws or commands, and not of prudential

9. In Italian, "the devil and the holy water."—TRANS.

rules, by saying that the laws of nature oblige *in foro interno* [in conscience], but not *in foro externo* [in outward behavior]. However, in the state of nature, who guarantees that others will comply with the prudential rules that I am willing to respect? In other words, in the state of nature, where the supreme end is victory rather than peace, what guarantee do I have that if I act rationally, and seek peace, others will do the same? One of the first laws of nature is that one must keep one's promises. But who is so stupid as to keep a promise, if he is not certain that the other party will keep it as well?

The features of the state of nature summarized in section 5 above clearly indicate that in that condition no one can be certain that others will comply with the laws of nature. In the state of nature, the laws of nature exist, that is they are valid, but they are not effective. In simpler terms, it is the condition in which it would be most imprudent to follow the rules of prudence. Reason prescribes that human beings seek peace. But if we wish to attain peace, all, or at least most members of the group must comply with the rules that prescribe the actions addressed to such an end. This does not occur in the state of nature for one fundamental reason: if someone violates one of these rules, there is no one strong enough to force him to comply with it. It follows from this that there is only one way to make the laws of nature effective, and to make human beings act according to their reason and not their passions. This way is the institution of a power so irresistible that it makes any contrary action disadvantageous. This irresistible power is the state. In order to attain the supreme good, which is peace, we must therefore leave the state of nature and build civil society.

8. The Covenant of Union

To summarize: reason comes to the help of human beings by suggesting to them various ways to reach a state of peace. But no one of these ways is available until human beings live in the state of nature. For in this condition general insecurity dissuades everyone from acting rationally. The preliminary condition to attain peace is thus a universal compact through which human beings can leave the state of nature and institute a state that will allow everyone to follow the dictates of right reason, confident that others will also do the same. Reason alone is not enough to make human beings live in peace. If it were enough, there would be no need for the state, that is, for civil laws. (The laws of nature would suffice.) It is necessary that human beings agree to institute a state that will create the conditions for living a life according to reason. This agreement is an act of will. Thus, the state is not a product of nature, but of the human will; the state is artificial man.

Hobbes gives very precise indications concerning the nature of this compact. First, it must be a compact among many, and not few, and it must be permanent and not temporary. Second, it must not be a mere association of persons who pursue a shared end. An association of this kind would only be based on the dictates of right reason, and would thus be precarious for the reasons already considered. Hobbes decisively rejects the doctrine that founds the state on a *pactum societatis* [pact of union], and that reduces civil society to a society for mutual help. A society of this kind is unable to ensure the compliance with the rules which the association itself needs to see respected if it is to perform its role. In order to found a stable society, human beings must stipulate a preliminary agreement, thus creating the conditions which make any subsequent agreement reliable. Only through this preliminary compact do human beings leave the state of nature and found the state.

We can reconstruct the content of this compact from what we have said about the features of the state of nature and about the need to leave it. Since the state of nature is insecure, the principal aim of the agreement is to eliminate the causes of insecurity. The principal cause of insecurity is the lack of a shared power; the aim of the compact that founds the state is to constitute a shared power. The only way to constitute a shared power is for all to consent to give up their own power and transfer it to one person, be it a natural or an artificial person, for example an assembly. This person will from now on have as much power as is necessary to prevent each individual from harming others by exercising his own power.

We should include at least two essential things in the generic notion of power: economic goods and physical force. The idea that in the state of nature everyone has a right to all things ultimately means that everyone has power over all those things that he has the physical power to conquer and to defend from others. In order to constitute a shared power, all must agree to assign all their possessions to one person. This means that they transfer to that person their right to all things, and as much physical power as that person needs to resist the attacks of those who attempt to violate the compact. Individuals acquire a fundamental obligation as a consequence of this compact. This is the obligation typical of the *pactum subiectionis* [pact of subjection]: it is the obligation to obey all commands of the holder of shared power. Hobbes calls this agreement "the covenant of union," and he offers the following formulation of it: "*I authorize and give up my right of governing myself, to this man, or to this assembly of men, on this condition, that thou give up thy right to him, and authorize all his actions in like manner*" (*Leviathan,* XVII, p. 112). Unlike the *pactum societatis,* the Hobbesian covenant of union is a pact of subjection. But in the traditional *pactum subiectionis,* the parties are the *populus* as a whole on one side and the sovereign on the other. In Hobbes's interpretation, as in the *pactum societatis,* the parties are the members taken individually, who agree with one another to subject themselves to a third party who does not participate in the compact. Hobbes has merged, perhaps not completely consciously, the two contracts which are the foundations of the state according to a traditional doctrine. Hobbes's compact is a *pactum societatis,* if considered from the point of view of the agents involved; but it is a *pactum subiectionis,* if considered from the point of view of its content. In any case, the outcome is the constitution of that shared power which enables human beings to leave the state of nature and enter civil society.

This power comprises the supreme economic power [*dominium*], and the supreme coercive power [*imperium*], as in the traditional conception of sovereignty. Political power is the sum total of the two. "There is no power on earth," says the verse from the book of Job which describes the monster Leviathan, "which is equal to it."[10] The verse paraphrases the traditional definition of sovereignty: *"potestas superiorem non recognoscens."* "This is the generation of that great *Leviathan,* or rather, to speak more reverently, of that *mortal god,* to which we owe under the *immortal God,* our peace and defence" (*Leviathan,* XVII, p. 112). In his three works, Hobbes offers three definitions of the state, which are increasingly complex, but substantively similar:

a. "A multitude of men, united as one person by a common power, for their common peace, defence, and benefit" (*Elements,* I, 19, 8, p. 81).
b. *"One person,* whose will, by the compact of many men, is to be received for the will of them all; so as he may use all the power and faculties of each particular person to the maintenance of peace, and for common defence" (*De Cive,* V, 9, p. 69). (It is noteworthy that "benefit" has been eliminated from the list of the ends of the state.)
c. *"One person, of whose acts a great multitude, by mutual covenants one with another, have made themselves every one the author, to the end he may use the strength and means of them all, as he shall think expedient, for their peace and common defence"* (*Leviathan,* XVII, p. 112).

9. Sovereignty Is Irrevocable

Hobbes attributes to the covenant of union the function of making humankind pass from the state of war to the state of

10. The biblical verse to which Bobbio refers here is Job 41:24, which appears on the frontispiece of *Leviathan: Non est potestas Super Terram quae Comparetur ei.* This is the text of the Vulgate. A comparison between the Hebrew, the Latin of the Vulgate, and the English of the Standard Version (King James), shows some discrepancy. The English King James reads, for Job 41:25: "Upon earth there is not his like, who is made without fear." This renders the Hebrew *en-'al-'afar mašlo / he'asu livli-ḥat.* The Vulgate thus seems to add a phrase (*est potestas*) which was not in the original. Note, however, that the editors of the Stuttgart *Biblia Hebraica* emend the Hebrew text to *ba'al hayyot,* "[who is made] lord of the beasts." Note also that Hobbes has quoted from the Vulgate on the frontispiece, but from the King James in the parts of *Leviathan* devoted to biblical exegesis.—TRANS.

peace through the institution of the sovereign power. Hobbes devises this covenant of union so that he can characterize the sovereign power deriving from it by three fundamental attributes which are also the marks of the Hobbesian conception of the state: the sovereign power is irrevocable, absolute, and indivisible. For the sovereign power is not truly sovereign, and therefore does not fulfill the aim for which it has been instituted, if it is not irrevocable, absolute, and indivisible. To summarize, the covenant of union is

a. a pact of subjection stipulated among individuals—not between the people and the sovereign;
b. it consists in attributing to a third *super partes* all the power which everyone has in the state of nature;
c. the third party to which this power is attributed is one person—as all three definitions cited at the end of section 8 confirm.

Irrevocability ensues from the first feature; absoluteness, from the second; and indivisibility, from the third.

Hobbes constructs the original covenant as a covenant among individuals, not between individuals already constituted as a people and the beneficiary of the act of subjection. One reason for this choice is his stated aim of avoiding the danger which the traditional pact of subjection faced, namely that the covenant could be revoked. For if one interprets the covenant as a relationship between principal and mandatory, the content of that covenant is the conferral of the office of government as a trust with certain conditions and for a limited time. Hobbes offers two reasons in favor of an irrevocable covenant of union: a difficulty de facto, and an impossibility de jure. According to the traditional interpretation of the *pactum subiectionis*, if one of the parties is the people, that is a *universitas* [incorporated body], rather than a *multitudo* [multitude], a majority suffices to rescind the contract. But if the contracting parties are all the members of civil society, *uti singuli* [as individuals], that is, as a multitude, not a people, then the contract can only be rescinded if all agree. That is, unanimity is necessary, not only a majority. And since it is implausible, says

Hobbes, that all citizens should simultaneously agree to overthrow the sovereign, ergo "there is no fear for rulers in chief, that by any right they can be despoiled of their authority" (*De Cive*, VI, 20, p. 90).

The impossibility—de jure—derives from Hobbes having conceived the covenant of union as a contract in favor of a third party. That is, as a contract in which the contracting parties assume an obligation not only toward one another, but also toward the third person in favor of whom they have stipulated the contract. This contract is such that it may not be rescinded merely through the consent of the parties, but it also requires the consent of the third person toward whom the parties have assumed an obligation. This means that, once individuals have agreed to the covenant of union, their consent (already unlikely because unanimity is required) is not sufficient to rescind it, but they must obtain the consent of the sovereign himself. In *De Cive*, Hobbes interprets this contract in favor of a third person as the outcome of reciprocal compacts among the members of the association. The content of this contract is the transference of each individual's rights to one person, followed by a donation of all these rights to the person on whom all have agreed. It follows from this, explains Hobbes, that the sovereign power rests on a twofold obligation on the part of citizens. They have an obligation toward their fellow citizens; and they have another toward the sovereign. As a consequence, "no subjects, how many soever may be, can with any right despoil him who bears the chief rule of his authority, even without his own consent" (*De cive*, VI, 20, p. 92).

Hobbes offers a simpler, and perhaps even more effective version of this idea in *Leviathan*, where he remarks that a breach of contract between subjects and sovereign cannot occur, because there has never been a contract between them. For the covenant of union is a covenant among the subjects. But here Hobbes adds a fundamental point which clarifies why it is plausible to contend that there has never occurred and may never occur a covenant between subjects and sovereign. We can consider two hypotheses. The first is that this compact occurs between the sovereign and the subjects as a people. But this is impossible, because subjects are not a people before they have convened as an assembly, and if they were, they would themselves be the state. The second hypothesis is that the compact occurs between the sovereign and each of the subjects. If this were possible, the compact, once signed, would be null and void, "because what act soever can be pretended by any one of them for breach thereof, is the act both of himself, and of all the rest, because done in the person, and by the right of every one of them in particular" (*Leviathan*, XVIII, p. 114). And even if it were not null and void, there would be no one to adjudicate the controversy should the subject denounce the action of the sovereign.

Hobbes wants to reach the conclusion that it is perfectly useless to attribute sovereign power to someone through a covenant which precedes the institution of the sovereign. For the sovereign, once instituted, has no obligation to respect any previous covenant, given the kind of power which has been attributed to him. Those who want the sovereign to be bound by a compact with his subjects, do not understand the simple truth "that covenants being but words and breath, have no force to oblige, contain, constrain or protect any man, but what it has from the public sword; that is, from the untied hands of that man, or assembly of men that hath the sovereignty" (*Leviathan*, XVIII, p. 115). (Whereas it is true that only the subjects are bound toward one another.)

It is superfluous to stress the conservative and, given the times in which it was written, counterrevolutionary function of this doctrine. Even more directly linked to the struggles of the time is the parallel thesis, this also presented in *Leviathan*, that subjects may neither revoke the sovereign, that is, undo the state, nor even change the form of government, that is, transform a monarchy into a republic. Here too Hobbes offers as usual a juridical argument: "And consequently they that have already instituted a commonwealth, being thereby bound by covenant, to own the actions, and judgments of one, cannot lawfully make a new covenant, amongst themselves, to be obedient, to any other, in any thing whatsoever, without his permission" (*Leviathan*, XVIII, p. 113). In presenting this thesis, Hobbes makes a clear allusion to the parties in the revolution, when he contends with those who "pretended . . . a new covenant, made, not with men, but with God." The covenant with God is a lie, for there cannot exist pacts but with men. At the most, there may be covenants with the mediators between men and God, who are, in fact, the sovereigns.

10. *Sovereignty Is Absolute*

By holding that the sovereign power is irrevocable, Hobbes opposes the theory of trust[11] (to which Locke, among, others, will resort). And when he maintains that the sovereign power is absolute, in the strict sense of *legibus solutus* [not bound by the laws], Hobbes opposes the various and variously argued theories which favored limiting the power of the state in some way. These theories, dominant in England before and after Hobbes, were the origin of the current of political thought called "constitutionalism." Despite recent benevolent interpretations of Hobbes as a liberal, constitutionalists always considered him as one of their main adversaries. Hobbes asserts over and over again that the sovereign power is the greatest power which human beings can grant to other human beings. The magnitude of this power lies in the fact that the holder can exercise it without being subjected to any external limit: his power is absolute. In the state of nature there are no subjects and sovereigns. More precisely, each individual is a subject or a sovereign depending on the situation in which he happens to be. One can be at one moment, de jure, the most powerful of sovereigns and, de facto, the most miserable of subjects. In civil society, after the covenant of union, the sovereign is sovereign and the subject is subject. And the sovereign is sovereign because, since he alone has the right to everything which everyone enjoyed before the covenant, he is always sovereign and never subject. And he is always sovereign and never subject because his power is absolute. If someone else could limit him, this other, not he, would be the sovereign.

11. Hobbes calls it "commission," but Locke will call it "trust."—TRANS.

Antiabsolutist doctrines employed various arguments to assert the limits of the power of the state. Hobbes's work is a constant and pressing answer to those arguments. The form of the covenant itself provided a first argument against absolutism. If the covenant occurs between the people as *universitas* and the sovereign, the people can subject the transference of power to the condition that the sovereign complies with certain obligations. As we have seen, in this case Hobbes denies the assumption that there exists a compact between the people and the sovereign. Before the institution of the sovereign power there is no people, but instead a multitude, a group of isolated individuals. If a people is to be born out of a multitude, the multitude must decide to leave the state of nature. It can do so by attributing the sovereign power not to a natural person, but to an assembly which comprises or represents it (a popular assembly). But in this case the people itself is the sovereign. As the sovereign, it cannot divest itself of its rights, and its power is as absolute as that of a monarch. If there is any covenant at all between the people and the sovereign, it is merely a covenant between the holder of sovereignty and the person or persons who are delegated to exercise it. But a compact of this kind has nothing to do with the covenant of union which gives origin to civil society.

A second argument against absolutism derives from the content of the covenant, independently of its form. Whoever the parties may be, the sovereign power may be more or less extensive depending on the quantity and quality of natural rights which are the objects of transference. The supporters of limited sovereignty maintained that this transference is partial. Little by little, the opinion prevailed that some of the rights of human beings in the state of nature are inalienable. Therefore their transference is null and void, no matter how it takes place. Hobbes, on the contrary, maintains that human beings transfer nearly all of their rights. In order to give life to civil society, every individual must give up the right to all things, including the power necessary to enforce that right. Since he has given up the right to all things, the individual who has become a member of the state retains only the right to his own life. That the right to life cannot be renounced derives from the logic of Hobbes's system. Since individuals institute the state in order to escape the permanent threat of death which characterizes the state or nature, that is, in order to save their own lives, human beings must consider themselves released from the obligation to obedience, if the sovereign endangers their lives.

Chapter XXI of *Leviathan* contains, so to speak, the chart of the rights of liberty for the citizens of Hobbes's state. The most important of these rights is formulated with the following words: "If the sovereign command a man, though justly condemned, to kill, wound, or maim himself; or not to resist that assault him; or to abstain from the use of food, air, medicine, or any other thing, without which he cannot live; yet hath that man the liberty to disobey" (p. 142). The liberties which subjects enjoyed thanks to the *silentium legis* [the silence of the law] are mere liberties de facto, which can be increased, or decreased, or even suppressed "according as they that have the sovereignty shall think most convenient" (XXI, p. 143). These liberties do not represent an impairment of the sovereign's unlimited power, because "nothing the sovereign representative can do to a subject, on what pretence soever, can properly be called injustice, or injury; because every subject is author of every act the sovereign doth" (XXI, p. 139).

These first two arguments against absolutism are connected to the contractual theories of political power. The argument which classical writers adduced in favor of limiting the sovereign power is independent of these theories, and is therefore more general. It is founded on the principle that political power, no matter who holds it, is subordinated to *jus;* more precisely to the law (objective right). This principle had provided the moral foundation of the English constitutional doctrine, according to Bracton's classical formulation: "The king must not be under man, but under God and under the law, because law makes the king."[12] Hobbes immediately discards the

12. H. Bracton, *On the Laws and Customs of England,* trans. S. E. Thorne, 2 vols. (Cambridge, The Belknap Press, 1968), II, p. 33.

thesis according to which the sovereign is subject to positive law, that is, civil laws, with the old argument that no one can oblige himself. "For having the power to make, and repeal laws, he may when he pleaseth, free himself from that subjection" (*De Cive*, VI, 14, p. 83; *Leviathan*, XXVI, p. 173). Since civil laws are issued by the sovereign, the sovereign would impose an obligation on himself, if he were subject to them. But a more serious question remains: Are there not other laws, beside civil laws? Whoever wishes to defend the principle that the sovereign power is unlimited, must deal with the common law of the country and with natural law. The common law is handed down by custom, and is applied by judges. (Lawyers also hold that the common law is above the laws issued by both King and Parliament.) Hobbes is a declared and fierce enemy of the supporters of the common law, starting with Sir Edward Coke. In his later years, Hobbes wrote against Coke the *Dialogue between a Philosopher and a Student of the Common Law of England*. Here he contends that there is no law other than that issued by the king, because only the king can enforce it. But already in *Elements*, in listing the sources of the law, Hobbes does not accept any source other than the express or tacit will of the sovereign: "Custom of itself maketh no law" (II, 10, 10, p. 151; *De Cive*, XIV, 15; *Leviathan*, XXVI, p. 174).

11. Civil Laws

A lively controversy has been going on among scholars, a controversy which may perhaps never come to an end, concerning whether Hobbes offers a solution to the problem of the laws of nature, and what that solution may be. Indeed, Hobbes often repeats that the sovereign is subjected to the laws of nature (and of God). But, as we have seen in section 7, the laws of nature are rules of prudence or technical norms. Compliance with these norms depends on one's judgment about the possibility of pursuing one's aim in a given situation. Only the sovereign can pass this judgment, both in his relations with other sovereigns, with whom he lives in the state of nature, and in his relations with his subjects, toward whom he is not bound by any covenant. He has no *external* obligation toward anyone, either other sovereigns, or his subjects, to comply with the dictates of right reason. (Let us remember that the laws of nature oblige only in conscience.) Thus, de facto, the dictates of right reason do not limit the sovereign's power.

On the one hand, it is true that the aim of individuals in instituting the state is security. And Hobbes means by security the condition in which human beings can comply with the laws of nature without fear of loss. It is therefore true that individuals grant to the sovereign all powers necessary for him to turn the laws of nature into real laws, that is, civil laws. It would thus appear that the sovereign, whose main task is to enforce natural laws, should also be subject to them. But, on the other hand, it is also true that it pertains to the sovereign, and only to the sovereign, to establish what is just and what is unjust by issuing norms. As a consequence, once the state has been instituted, there exist for the subjects no criteria of just and unjust other than the civil laws.

Hobbes reasserts this idea in countless passages. This makes Hobbes's moral theory one of the most daring, though not always consistent, expressions of ethical legalism. This is the theory which holds that the sovereign (and thus God as well) does not command what is just, but that what is right is what the sovereign commands. "It belongs to the same chief power to make some common rule for all men, and to declare them publicly, by which every man know what may be called his, what another's, what just, what unjust, what honest, what dishonest, what good, what evil; that is summarily, what is to be done, what to be avoided in our common course of life" (*De Cive*, VI, 9, p. 77).[13] Or: "And to let pass, that no *law* can possi-

13. Since in recent years scholars have been arguing that Hobbes is a natural law theorist, it is worthwhile to quote another passage in which Hobbes formulates his ethical legalism with words which could not be more explicit: "Before there was any government, *just* and *unjust* had no being, their nature only being relative to some command: and every action in its own nature is indifferent; that it becomes *just* or *unjust*, proceeds from the right of the magistrate. Legitimate kings therefore make the things that they command just, by commanding them, and those which they forbid, unjust, by forbidding them" (*De Cive*, XII, p. 151).

bly be *unjust*, inasmuch as every man maketh, by his consent, the law he is bound to keep, and which consequently must be just, unless a man can be unjust to himself" (*On Liberty and Necessity*, in *EW*, IV, pp. 252–53).

One could object that civil laws establish what is just and unjust because they are nothing other than the enforcement of natural laws. Often interpreted in this way is the controversial passage of *Leviathan* in which Hobbes says that "the law of nature, and the civil law, contain each other, and are of equal extent" (XXVI, p. 174). And the passage in *De Homine*, in which Hobbes says that "once the state has been instituted, the laws of nature become part of the civil laws" (XIII, 9, p. 117). But one can reply:

a. There are some passages in *De Cive*, in which Hobbes maintains that it pertains to the sovereign to establish the content of natural laws. This means that the sovereign is in charge not only of enforcing the laws of nature, but also of establishing what they prescribe: "Theft, murder, adultery, and all injuries, are forbid by the laws of nature; but what is to be called *theft*, what *murder*, what *adultery*, what *injury* in a citizen, this is not to be determined by the natural, but by the civil law" (*De Cive*, VI, 16, p. 85 and XIV, 10; XVIII, 10). The examples which Hobbes adduces to illustrate this statement show that it is improper to say that the sovereign is subject to the laws of nature and can violate them. ("Not every killing of a man is murder, but only that which the civil law forbids.")

b. Even if we admit that the sovereign can violate the laws of nature, it remains true that the subject must obey all the sovereign's commands, except for those commands that endanger one's life. The subject's obligation to obey without reservation corresponds to the sovereign's right to give commands without limits. And to a power than which no greater can be given corresponds an obedience than which no "greater can be performed" (called in *De Cive* "simple," VI, 13, p. 82).

If we analyze in detail the two arguments (a) and (b), it is difficult to see what effective limits are imposed on the sovereign power by the fact that it has been instituted in order to enforce natural laws. More precisely, the sovereign power has been instituted in order to turn the dictates of right reason into real laws. Since it pertains to the sovereign to specify the content of natural laws, any civil law which he issues conforms to the law of nature. Although this conclusion may appear absurd, Hobbes does draw it. He insists on the idea that "though the law of nature forbid theft, adultery, etc; yet if the civil law command us to invade anything, that invasion is not theft, adultery, etc." Then he asserts: "No civil law whatsoever, which tends not to a reproach of the Deity . . . can possibly be against the law of nature" (*De Cive*, XIV, 10, pp. 190–91). At this point, the sovereign could encounter only one effective limit to his own power: the subjects' resistance to a command which they deem unjust. But the subjects have imposed on themselves the obligation to obey all the sovereign's commands. Thus, even that limit vanishes, and the sovereign power is really unlimited, both with regard to natural laws, and to the rights of the citizens.

We can find a confirmation of this in Hobbes's opinion concerning the traditional distinction between pure and corrupt forms of government. He contends that this distinction is unfounded. If the criterion of distinction is that the tyrant has broader powers than the king, then this distinction is false. "But first, they differ not in this, that a tyrant hath the greater power; for greater than the supreme cannot be granted; nor in this, that one hath a limited power, the other not; for he whose authority is limited, is no king, but his subject that limits him" (*De Cive*, VII, 3, p. 94).

A theory of the abuse of power is wholly lacking in Hobbes's works. (The abuse of power is precisely what characterizes the tyrant, at least in the figure of *tyrannus quoad exercitium*) [tyrant with respect to the exercise of his power]. Abuse consists in going beyond the established limits. Therefore there cannot be abuse where there are no limits. On the contrary, what may prompt subjects to consider themselves released from the duty of obedience is not abuse, but non-use of power, not excess but defect of power. The reason why human beings have invested another man (or a civil person) with so much power is the need for security. The sovereign who out of negligence, weakness, or incapacity is unable to prevent his subjects from relapsing into the state of nature, does not perform his task. Subjects have the right to look for another protector, if the sovereign whom they have instituted does not protect them (*Leviathan*, XXI, p. 144). So much so that the sovereign's first duty is not to divest himself and not to let others divest him of the powers conferred on him (ibid., XXX, p. 219). Thus, he must not trespass limits which *do* not exist; and he must not impose on himself, or accept limits, which *must* not exist.

12. Sovereignty Is Indivisible

In the definitions of the state, quoted in section 8, Hobbes insists that sovereignty must be attributed to one person (whether man or assembly). As Rousseau rightly saw, Hobbes's fundamental problem is the problem of the unity of power. This is the primary reason and the ultimate end of his political theory. "Of all Christian authors, the philosopher Hobbes is the only one who saw clearly both the evil and the remedy, and who dared to propose reuniting the two heads of the eagle and fully restoring that political unity without which neither the state nor the government will ever be well constituted."[14] As remarked above in section 2, two motives prompted Hobbes to devote himself to the study of politics: aversion toward the doctrines and fear of the upheavals that cause the disintegration of the state. If anarchy is to be avoided, sovereignty must not only be irrevocable and unlimited but also indivisible. Hobbes considers especially two causes of dissolution of the unity of the state, against which he fights ceaselessly: the separation among the parts of the sovereign power within the state; and the separation between temporal and spiritual power.

In Hobbes's times, those who supported the separation of

14. *Social Contract*, IV, 8, p. 180.

powers resorted to the classical doctrine of mixed government. According to this doctrine, the best form of government is the one which results from the mixing and tempering of the three Aristotelian forms: monarchy, aristocracy, and democracy. British theorists of public law usually portrayed the English state as a body politic composed of a head (the king), and the limbs (the three estates). Supporters of the prerogatives of Parliament against the Crown had appealed to the theory of mixed government. In *Elements*, Hobbes already offers an accurate description of mixed government, as the one in which "they suppose the power of making laws given to some great assembly democratical, the power of judicature to some other assembly; and the administration of the law to a third, or to some other man" (II, I, 15, p. 89).

Hobbes employs one of his typical dilemmatic reasonings in order to refute the argument that the function of mixed government is to guarantee a greater liberty to its citizens. If the three parts of the state are in agreement, their power is as absolute as the power of one person. If they disagree, the state is no longer, and anarchy ensues. This refutation gives him an opportunity to reassert that sovereignty is indivisible, "and that seeming mixture of several kinds of government, [is] not mixture of the things themselves, but confusion in our misunderstandings, that cannot find out readily to whom we have subjected ourselves" (*Elements*, II, I, 16, p. 90; and also *De Cive*, VII, 4). In *Leviathan*, he moves from the level of theoretical refutation to that of historical example, thus revealing the true target of his polemics. "If there had not first been an opinion received of the greatest part of England, that these powers were divided between the King, and the Lords, and the House of Commons, the people had never been divided and fallen into this civil war" (p. 119). He had already alluded to English events in *De Cive* (XII, 5). In criticizing as seditious the theory according to which "*the supreme authority may be divided,*" Hobbes had mentioned among others those who divide the sovereign power so that they assign the power of war and peace to one person, "but the right of raising money they give to some others, and not to him" (*De Cive*, XII, 5, pp. 155–56).

From this type of separation the following dilemma ensued. Either actual power belongs to those who dispose of finances —and in this case power is only apparently divided—or power is really divided—and in this case the state is on the path toward dissolution, "For neither upon necessity can war be waged, nor can the public peace be preserved without money" (ibid.).

Hobbes does not limit himself to criticizing the theory of mixed government. In *De Cive*, while analyzing and listing the sovereign's powers, which he calls "the sword of justice" and "the sword of war," he suggests a different approach. He remarks that these two swords must belong to the same person if they are to strike. For "no man can by right compel citizens to take up arms and be at the expenses of war, but he who by right can punish him who doth not obey" (*De Cive*, VI, 7, p. 76). As if this were not enough, the one who holds the sword must also hold the scales. For the right to punish presupposes the power to judge right and wrong. Hobbes then lists the power to make laws as one of the sovereign powers. He has thus united in one and the same person the three traditional powers of the state: the executive (the two swords), the judicial, and the legislative powers. In relation to the last of these three, he thus comments in *Elements:* "The making whereof [of laws] must of right belong to him that hath the power of the sword, by which men are compelled to observe them; for otherwise they should be made in vain" (II, I, 10, p. 87). Hobbes intends his analysis of the various powers pertaining to the sovereign to show that these powers are so interdependent that they can only belong to one person. Executive power is the power to use physical force legitimately, against both internal and external enemies. This is the mark of sovereignty itself, and it presupposes the power to judge right and wrong (judicial power). Judicial power presupposes that there be established general criteria which guide the issuing of judgments, that is, civil laws. In its turn, legislative power presupposes executive power, if laws are to be true and effective norms regulating human conduct, and not mere *flatus vocis* [mere breath]. Thus the circle closes.

13. Church and State

In condemning as seditious the theory according to which "*the supreme authority may be divided,*" Hobbes uses two examples: the doctrine of the separation of powers, and the point of view of those who divide the power of the state, so that "some divide it, so as to grant a supremacy to the civil power in matters pertaining to peace and the benefits of this life; but in things concerning the salvation of the soul they transfer it on others" (*De Cive*, XII, 5, pp. 155–56). From what immediately follows it becomes apparent why Hobbes formulates a negative judgment of this way of solving the problem of the relationship between Church and state. In countries where citizens must obey precepts different from civil laws, it may happen that they are induced to disobey the latter. "Now what can be more pernicious to any state, than that men should, by the apprehension of everlasting torments, be deterred from obeying their princes, that is to say, the laws; or from being just?" (ibid.).

For the person who believes that the indivisibility of power is the only remedy for the disintegration of the state, the most serious cause of disintegration is that there exists outside the state, and perhaps even against the state, a power as great as, if not as some believe, superior to that of the state. The danger is especially threatening if this power claims obedience to its own laws, and even maintains that obedience to its own laws must take precedence over obedience to civil laws, insofar as eternal reward and punishment are to be feared more than reward and punishment on earth. Hobbes had been a terrified spectator of a civil war which had also been a religious war. The struggle against civil power had been waged in the name, or under the pretext, of obedience to the will of God and compliance with the commandments of religious authorities hostile to one merely wordly authority or another. Despite the breakdown of religious universalism, no church had renounced the claim of the Roman Church to be the only authorized interpreter of God's law and thus superior to the state. Not the reformed national churches, nor the Anglican Church, nor the nonconformist sects would give up that claim. Hobbes detested all of them as irresponsible and fanatical instigators of civil disobedience. "The most frequent pretext of sedition, and civil war, in Christian commonwealths," he writes at the beginning of chapter XLIII of Leviathan (p. 384), "hath a long time proceeded from a difficulty, not yet sufficiently resolved, of obeying at once both God and man, then when their commandments are one contrary to the other."

Hobbes devotes an increasingly large part of his political works to the solution of this problem: two chapters in *Elements*, the third part of *De Cive*, entitled "Religio," and two parts out of four, thus about half of *Leviathan*, entitled respectively "Of the Christian Commonwealth" and "Of the Kingdom of Darkness." And since this problem presents the greatest difficulty, Hobbes attacks it with all the powers of his subtle genius. He arrives at a formulation of the terms of this problem through an exemplary biblical exegesis, which is also exemplary in its tendentiousness, and through a constant and consistent invocation of his own principles, especially the principle that human beings need a power so strong as to be able to prevent them from returning to the state of nature. Hobbes's strategy aims at demonstrating that his final thesis is the iron-clad conclusion of a syllogism.

Hobbes relies on the Holy Scriptures to establish two fundamental points. First, he elaborates an antidogmatic interpretation of Christianity, according to which all that one needs to believe to be a Christian is that Jesus is the Christ, son of God. This simplification clears the terrain of most theological controversies, thus eliminating the more frequent and insidious reasons for dissension. Second, he asserts that God's kingdom is not of this world, and that Christ has come among human beings only to teach and to preach and not to command. Jesus has left to civil authority the power to give orders, or to issue laws to which we owe obedience. So much so that even the precepts of the New Testament did not become laws, but remained mere pieces of advice which could help sinners on the path toward salvation, until the mighty of this world imposed them as civil laws. In *De Cive*, Hobbes remarks incisively: "Moreover, our Savior, hath not showed subjects any other laws for the government of a city, beside those of nature, that is to say, beside the command to obedience" (XVII, 11, p. 267; and also *Leviathan*, XLII, p. 343). As already seen, the laws of nature do not limit the sovereign power at all. For once the state has been instituted, there are no laws of nature other than the ones which the sovereign recognizes, and which he transforms into civil laws. The following passage confirms this: "It may therefore be concluded, that the *interpretation* of all laws, as well *sacred* as *secular* (God ruling by the way of *nature* only), depends on the authority of the city, that is to say, that man or counsel to whom the sovereign power is committed" (*De Cive*, XV, 17, p. 222). Moreover, in the passage just quoted Hobbes makes an even more compelling statement: he contends that natural laws can be summarized in the command to obey the state. Hobbes formulates and specifies this statement for the first time in chapter XIV, sec. 10 of *De Cive*, which is devoted to the laws and violations of the laws. (Since Hobbes does not insist on this point in *Leviathan*, we should be cautious in accepting it as his definitive thought on the argument.) "By the virtue of the natural law which forbids breach of covenant, the law of nature commands us to keep all the civil laws." Taken literally, this assertion would eliminate even the possibility of a contrast between natural and civil law.

Having shown that there is no priestly power different from civil power, and having reasserted that power can only be efficacious if it is indivisible, Hobbes does not even need to deny that the spiritual and the temporal spheres differ. He has created the conditions which enable him to deny that the difference between the two spheres corresponds to a distinction between two powers. The power to decide spiritual matters [*iura circa sacra*] pertains exclusively to the state: "But it is reason's inquisition," he explains, "and pertains to *temporal right* to define what is *spiritual* and what *temporal*" (*De Cive*, XVII, 14, p. 271). With regard to the question of who is entitled to summon the assembly of the faithful—in which the Church properly speaking consists—Hobbes answers that an assembly of

the faithful, that is, a church, may deliberate only if it first becomes a civil person. In order for a church to become a civil person, it must be legally summoned. And if it must be legally
summoned, it must be summoned by the person who has the
power to force even the recalcitrant to participate. But this person can only be the sovereign. Thus there cannot be in a state
any church other than the one that is recognized (or imposed)
by the state. There is no separation between Church and state.
Even more, Church and state are one and the same thing. They
are "termed by two names," says Hobbes, for the same thing,
which is called state "as it is made up of *men;* the same, as it
consists of *Christians* is styled *Church*" (*De Cive,* XVII, 21, p.
278). In this way Hobbes's theory of the indivisibility of the sovereign power, founded on the assumption that the sovereign
power is either one or else is not sovereign, ends by reducing
the Church to an institution of the state, and establishing a
state religion without reservations.

14. Hobbes and His Critics

In his three main political works, Hobbes devoted some of his
more pugnacious pages to the condemnation of theories dangerous to the salvation of the state. But it was his fate to be
singled out by his contemporaries as the author of one of the
most dangerous theories ever conceived for the salvation of
subjects. Hobbes recommended that the theories dangerous
for the state should be banned from any well-constituted commonwealth, while his own should be accepted and publicly
taught. But it so happened that the theories he damned continued to circulate and to struggle freely with one another;
whereas his theory was the only one execrated to the point that
no one could name it without causing scandal. He devised a
theory of the state that was supposed to please conservatives
by taking advantage of the arguments which were dear to
liberals. Both conservatives and liberals fought him fiercely:
conservatives, because of the nonchalance with which he employed the Holy Scriptures; liberals, because of his conclusions
contrary to the principles of constitutional government.

Hobbes was a supporter of authoritarian government, like the traditionalists; but also of contract theory, like the innovators. The former rejected him as irreligious; the latter, as an absolutist. His rationalism, which was lucid and consequential to the point of temerity led him to fight on the same side as the absolutists. But they rejected the alliance for fear of compromising themselves. Meanwhile, the constitutionalists had to resort to the tradition of English monarchy in order to refute him. What his contemporaries could not understand was that the Leviathan was the great modern state, arising from the ashes of medieval society. They saw Hobbes as a skeptic, a cynic, even a libertine while he was first and foremost a boldly impartial observer; a spectator, personally horrified, but philosophically unmoved by the origin of a great event, which he tried to understand in its causes and end. He was so convinced that his edifice was geometrically exact that he—as Hegel would also do—presented a description as a justification, the real as the rational, and what there was as what there ought to be. Like all realists, by mocking those who take their own desires for reality, Hobbes also, like Hegel, mistook the cruelest reality for what is most desirable.

Hobbes was haunted by the problem of the unity of power in an epoch of devastating struggles. He thus could not recognize that conflict has at times beneficial effects. He saw in every conflict, even at the level of ideals, a cause of dissolution and death. He saw in the smallest dissension a seed of discord which ruined the state; and in the variety of opinions a sign of the human passions which the state must vigorously discipline, so as not to lose its grip. Hobbes condemned as factions parties that are aroused by demagogues, and condemned the groups of dissident minorities as sects of ignorant persons dominated by exalted preachers. He believed that he had constructed the only rational theory for rational human beings. He thus detested party leaders for their eloquence which spoke to feelings rather than to reason; and religious leaders for their religious inspiration, which exalted faith in invisible things to the detriment of experience. Hobbes saw no alternative to anarchy other than the authority of the sovereign, and no alternative to a state always divided within itself, other than a monolithic and indivisible power. For a man who no longer believed in salvation through the Church, there was no other path than through political society. "Lastly, out of it, there is a dominion of passions, war, fear, slovenliness, solitude, barbarism, ignorance, cruelty; in it, the dominion of reason, peace, security, riches, decency, society, elegancy, sciences, and benevolence" (*De Cive*, X, 1, p. 127).

Hobbes's anthropological pessimism did not allow him to believe that human beings could save themselves. But his radical secularism induced him to seek a solution to the problem of salvation that was different from what was preached by the churches. In agreement with the Augustinian-Lutheran conception of the state, Hobbes thought of the state as a remedy for the corrupt nature of man. But his version was secular. The condition of corruption which human beings had to leave was not the condition of sin (in which Hobbes did not believe), but rather that of the natural passions. It was the task of philosophy to describe and classify these passions as we describe and classify the parts of the body. The state was thus not a remedy for sin, but a means for disciplining the passions. As a sound rationalist, Hobbes thought that corruption originated in ignorance more than cruelty, fanaticism more than malice, mystical exaltation more than brutality, and stupidity more than wickedness. But as a moderate, a lover of that peace which is conducive to meditation and the development of knowledge, Hobbes considered the primary cause of all evils to be the desire for power and for every instrument of power, especially riches and reputation.

Hobbes believed that the only remedy for the power of all was the power of one. He believed too little in human rationality to devise a solution to the problem of the desire for power other than in the institution of a great power which annihilates small powers. The power of one must be so great that the sum total of all small powers cannot equal it. In one word, that power must be irresistible. If the secret of salvation is the creation of an irresistible power, then it is better that this power be in the hands of one rather than of many. In discussing the three forms of government, Hobbes offered arguments (persuasive rather than demonstrative, as he remarked in the Preface to *De Cive*) which showed the superiority of monarchy to democracy and aristocracy. He contended, among other things, that if there is to be excess of power, the excess of one was to be feared less than the excess of many. Nero's crimes do not belong to the essence of monarchy. But "in a popular dominion, there may be as many Neros as there are orators who soothe the *people*" (*De Cive*, X, 7, p. 133). Since Hobbes himself did not participate in the race for power, he personally felt more protected where power was more centralized. It is difficult to avoid the impression that the following remarks contain an autobiographical reference: "Whosoever therefore in a *monarchy* will lead a retired life, let him be what he will that reigns, he is out of danger. For the ambitious only suffer" (ibid.).

15. Hobbes Interpreted

Politically, Hobbes was a conservative. He was not at all a precursor of the totalitarian state, as some chose to portray him when totalitarianism made its appearance in Europe. (As, for example, did Vialatoux, refuted even then by René Capitant.) Except for its name, Leviathan, Hobbes's state was not at all monstrous, as Carl Schmitt remarked. It was merely a great machine, the *machina machinarum*, in an age dominated by the mechanistic conception of the universe. We must go through the German idealists' organistic conception of the people, in order to arrive at the conception of the state-totality. The philosophical premise of the totalitarian state is Hegel's "ethical totality," not Hobbes's *"persona civilis."* For Hobbes, before the state there is no people, let alone a *Volksgemeinschaft*, but only a multitude. The Hobbesian state is founded on a reciprocal covenant among isolated and scattered individuals, and is therefore much more similar to an association than to a community. Hobbes also, like Hegel, calls the state "the mortal God" (*Leviathan*, XIX, p. 122). But the difference lies in the fact that Hegel's God is pantheistic, while Hobbes's God is theistic.

Hobbes was a conservative, not a totalitarian. However, he

was neither a liberal writer, nor a precursor of liberal ideas, as some have recently contended, in an attempt to react against the image of Hobbes as the cursed philosopher. (This interpretation is shared by scholars as different as Carl Schmitt, Michael Oakeshott, and Mario Cattaneo.) There are, it is true, some features typical of liberalism in Hobbes's thought. He accepts that, in extreme cases, an individual has the right to resist commands (when his own life is threatened). He values the principle of legality in the administration of justice. He wants the law to be certain; he prefers a government ruling with few, clear, and simple laws, to a government which uses too many and confused norms. He deems a moderate economic liberty useful to the welfare of the nation. And he holds that the sovereign has the duty to grant an innocuous liberty to citizens. But the ideal for which he fights is authority, not liberty.

Hobbes never had the slightest hesitation in choosing between the excess of freedom, and the excess of authority. He fears the former as the worst of all evils; he is resigned to the latter as the lesser evil. No matter what commentators say, all his system is founded on the mistrust of liberty: "But when private men or subjects demand liberty, under the name of liberty they ask not for liberty but *dominion*" (*De Cive*, X, 8, p. 135). The state of perfect liberty is the state of nature. Civil society does not arise so as to save the liberty of the individual, but rather to save the individual from liberty, which leads him to his ruin. Hobbes does speak of liberty as the liberty of the individual with regard to the state, and as the liberty which he enjoys thanks to the *silentium legis* [silence of the law]. (Hobbes would never dare to say, as Hegel would, that "true" liberty consists of obedience to the laws.) But this liberty from the state is not a right of each individual. It is a concession by the sovereign, and it can be greater or lesser, depending on the will of the person who holds power.

Hobbes does not believe in freedom of conscience. Once he has joined the state, the individual has given up his private conscience; only a public conscience exists, of which the sovereign is the only interpreter. And Hobbes does not admit free-

dom of thought. He is convinced that se
in the heads of human beings; he theref
ereign has the right to "judge what opi
enemies unto peace, and also that he fo
(*De Cive*, VI, 11, pp. 79–80) and to repr
"to root these out of the mind of men;
by teaching" (*De Cive*, XIII, 9, pp. 171–, _,
hume the liberty of the ancients,[15] but there is nothing
writings which induces us to believe that he wanted to proclaim the liberty of the moderns.

Despite persistent and often revived interpretations (first
and foremost that of Macpherson) of Hobbes as the ideologue
of the rising bourgeoisie, Hobbes was a conservative. He did
not feel materially, emotionally, or ideologically tied to the rising class. He led the life of an erudite man, at the service of a
great family of the English aristocracy. He was never tempted
to engage in different economic activities. And, unlike Locke,
he was never really interested in the study of economic problems. (He nearly ignores them in his works.) As has been
observed (by Keith Thomas, in polemics directed against Macpherson), Hobbes admired aristocratic virtues, such as
courage; he exalted the rare "generous natures" who alone do
not respect the laws out of fear (*Leviathan*, XXVII, p. 195).
Among the main causes of conflict he listed, besides competition for gain, diffidence and vainglory, which thrust human
beings against one another in defence of their reputation.
Hobbes insisted repeatedly on the importance of questions of
prestige or honor in arousing enmity and disputes. When he
wished to distinguish human beings from beasts, he said that,
unlike beasts, human beings, "are continually in competition
for honour and dignity" (*Leviathan*, XVII, p. 111).

The true mark of the bourgeois spirit is its judgment on private property. Locke lifted private property to the rank of a natural right, and conceived of the state as an association of
proprietors who wish to defend their own goods. Hobbes, on
the contrary, did not recognize private property as a natural

15. Hobbes speaks of Athenian democracy only to show its shortcomings.

n the state of nature the distinction between mine and
does not yet exist.) He maintained that property comes
o being only after the state has come into being; the sovereign is the only owner, and it is up to him to establish, together with what is just and unjust, what belongs to the one
and what to the other. Among the seditious theories, Hobbes
included that which accords to each citizen an absolute right of
property over his possessions, since property only belongs to
the sovereign and "is just so much as he will, and shall last so
long as he pleases" (*De Cive*, XII, 7, p. 157).

The conception of life that would triumph with the bourgeoisie would be competitive and antagonistic. As remarked
in the previous section, Hobbes saw only the negative aspects
of conflict. He imagined a state able to eliminate dissent
through the exercise of unlimited authority, to which subjects
had consented because of the social contract. He held a static,
not a dynamic conception of society. The supreme good which
the state was supposed to realize was neither progress attained through conflict, nor Comte's idea of progress through
order, but rather order pure and simple. A rising class has egalitarian tendencies. But Hobbes, like all conservatives, held fast
to the belief that society can only stand on a basis of inequality,
above all, the essential, inescapable inequality between the
sovereign and his subjects, between those who have the right
to command, and those who have no duty other than to obey.
Human beings are born equal, but they *must* become unequal if
they want to survive. In other words, equality is from nature,
and inequality from convention; but the rational state for rational human beings is founded on a convention.

It would be difficult to find a political thinker who, more
than Hobbes, reveals the essential traits of the conservative
spirit: political realism, anthropological pessimism, and an in-
egalitarian conception of society which is based on an opposition to conflict. To complete the picture, we might add that
Hobbes has neither an evolutionary nor a dialectical vision of
history, but rather a cyclical one. History moves constantly and
monotonously between the two poles of anarchy and civil society. History is now torn asunder by Behemoth, and then re-

stored to unity by Leviathan, to be taken apart again, in endless recurrence. Even when he allows himself to hope that peace will return after civil war, and that power will again be undivided, Hobbes predicts that the new order is destined to last only until past misery has been forgotten. "Except," he adds, "the vulgar be better taught than they have hitherto been" (*Leviathan*, XVIII, p. 119). But that "the vulgar" would have better judgment in the future was precisely what Hobbes was not willing to believe.

three

Introduction to *De Cive*

If we wish to encompass in one formula the meaning of Thomas Hobbes's political philosophy, we might say that it expresses the first modern theory of the modern state. This formula lifts Hobbes's philosophy above the level of sheer polemical writing, which is too partial a view if related to his own time, and too anachronistic if related to ours. It also acquits the great father of *Leviathan* of the charge of sinister intentions which has been attributed to him too insistently at all times, even in times close to ours. It thus helps today's readers to concentrate their attention on the essential elements of Hobbes's thought, which is of exceptional historical import, and which has recently been praised for having created "the greatest, perhaps the sole, masterpiece of political philosophy . . . in the English language."[1]

The aim of the modern state in its long and bloody struggle has been to attain unity. This unity is the fruit of a process which is at the same time one of liberation and unification: of liberation from the authority of the Church, which aspired to be universal. Since it is spiritual, this authority proclaims itself superior to any civil power. It is also a process of unification of

1. M. Oakeshott, Introduction to *Leviathan* (Oxford: Basil Blackwell, 1946), p. viii.

the lesser institutions, associations, corporations, and towns, which were a constant source of anarchy in medieval society. As a consequence of these two processes, the formation of the modern state coincides with the acknowledgment that political power ought to be superior to every other human dominion. Such absolute supremacy is called sovereignty. This means independence, in relation to the process of liberation. And it means superiority of the state's power over any other source of power existing in a given territory, in relation to the process of unification. The two attributes of the sovereign power—independence and absolute supremacy—thus reflect the struggle which the modern state has fought on two fronts. The power of the state is original, for it does not depend on any other power superior to it. And it is indivisible, for it may not be shared with any inferior power.

Thomas Hobbes is the most lucid, consequential, tenacious, subtle, and daring theorist of the unity of the power of the state. His entire political philosophy has one polemical target: to confute the doctrines, be they traditional or innovative, conservative or revolutionary, inspired by God or by the devil, that prevent the state from attaining unity. His unique goal is to offer a compelling and mathematically rigorous demonstration that political unity corresponds to the deepest aspects of human nature, and thus, like a law of nature, is absolute and inescapable. Hobbes's political philosophy is pervaded by the fundamental belief that the state is either one and indivisible or nothing. Human beings have but two alternatives: they either accept this as a supreme reason for the existence of the state, or they lose themselves in the violence of a perpetual and universal war. "Of all Christian authors," asserted Rousseau with clarity "the philosopher Hobbes is the only one who saw clearly both the evil and the remedy, and who dared to propose reuniting the two heads of the eagle and fully restoring that political unity without which neither state nor government will ever be well constituted."[2]

The years in which Hobbes was educated and then came

2. *Social Contract*, IV, 8, p. 180.

into his own were also the years of the greatest religious war in our history, the Thirty Years War. The unity of power was threatened throughout continental Europe; and in England that unity was threatened just as harshly, and was indeed destroyed. By then, a whole century had gone by since the first break in Christian universalism. This universalism had been an attempt, however uncertain and unstable, to reduce the thousand conflicting fragments of medieval society to unity. During that century the Reformation had progressively eroded a hierarchical order which until then the civilized world had accepted as valid. This order had been eroded either in the name of new spiritual powers or in the name of the natural rights of individuals. New and revolutionary political doctrines favored democratic ideas. These doctrines demolished the principle of obedience and extolled resistance and the right of rebellion, to the point of offering apologies for tyrannicide. They did so in the name of the people, as opposed to the power of princes, and in the name of a natural authority antithetical to those grounded on tradition. In the years between the assassination of Henry IV (1610), and the treaty of Westphalia (1648) and the end of the English Civil War (1649), a crisis broke out throughout Europe. Henry's assassination had aroused indignation and terror in Hobbes, for he saw in it the fruit of seditious theories. The events of 1649 forced Hobbes, the humanist and mathematician, the lover of quiet study and erudite wanderings, into a voluntary ten-year-long exile in France. This crisis of authority threw Europe into the chaos of war and anarchy, and threatened to destroy the unity of public power, without which, as Rousseau commented in the sentence quoted above, "neither state nor government will ever be well constituted."

According to Hobbes, the main obstacle to the unity of the state is the claim of religious authority, as embodied in the Roman Catholic church, the national Reformed churches, or the independent lesser Christian associations, to be legitimate holders of a power superior to the power of the state. "The most frequent pretext of sedition, and civil war, in Christian commonwealths," Hobbes says in *Leviathan*, "hath a long time proceeded from a difficulty, not yet sufficiently resolved, of obeying at once both God and man, then when their commandments are one contrary to the other."[3] Religious authority inspires theories of resistance to the commands of civil power when those commands are contrary to divine ones. Such theories advocate, depending on circumstances, passive obedience, disobedience, revocation of mandates, deposition, and tyrannicide. What other power than one which claims superiority because of direct inspiration from God can pronounce on the justness of the sovereign's command? The distinction between the Christian Church and civil power thus carries within itself a perpetual source of discord. Only by subjecting religious power to civil power can that danger be eliminated.

Hobbes's polemic is not directed against any one church in particular, but against all churches without distinction, simply because they proclaim themselves to be independent of the state. He polemicizes against the very existence in modern society, which needs unity to survive, of institutions like the churches, which preach and administer an absolute and therefore unquestionable truth.

Hobbes's attack on the Roman church is more violent, because its declared universalism makes its claim to supremacy all the more frightening. Hobbes judges it, as would a representative of the Enlightenment, to be a disseminator of ignorance and a source of superstitions which have nothing to do with Christ's message, but are rooted in pagan cults. The Roman church by means of excommunication disseminates rebellion. It professes an antiquated and empty philosophy, although it employs the well-informed political theories of the Jesuits to preach the assassination of kings to its followers. And Hobbes is no less opposed to the authoritarian, ambitious, and intolerant Reformed church, which in England planted the seed of discord through Scottish presbyterianism. In his impassioned history of the Civil War, written in his old age, with bitter tones against fanatics, and with somewhat apol-

---

3. *Leviathan,* XLIII, p. 384.

ogetic tones toward the English monarchy, Hobbes charges the Reformed church with responsibility for the catastrophe which has befallen his country.

His judgment on the Anglican church is more prudent and shows some vacillations. But even in this case Hobbes does not hide his aversion, for the Anglicans do not renounce the principle of divine investiture of bishops. Hobbes's aversion is reciprocated by the Anglican clergy, to the point that they cause his falling out of grace with the Court after the publication of *De Cive.* But Hobbes holds tight to the principle that ecclesiastical power, of whatever form, depends on the King. He is only somewhat uncertain as to whether to accept the primacy of bishops within the ecclesiastical hierarchy, for this appears to be supported by the Scriptures.

Finally, there are the Puritans, the members of independent sects, those who hold that the Church is a voluntary association without hierarchy and rituals. These people believe that they are directly inspired by God, and they go around preaching that religion is a private, not a public affair, a problem of conscience, not of obedience. It does not matter to Hobbes that among them are mystics side by side with the possessed, and apostles of freedom side by side with fanatics. For him all these free religious preachers are nothing less than dangerous madmen. In the name of a supposedly divine word, learned through who knows what supernatural ways, these preachers judge and even condemn the actions of their sovereign. They foment disorders under the pretext of freedom. They are often merely men of bad faith, charlatans, and demagogues, who invoke God in order to stimulate more easily the credulity of the people, which they turn into an instrument of their ambition.

Hobbes's position against an established church, whether Roman Catholic, Calvinist, or Anglican, betrays his obstinate anticlericalism, and his support for an uncompromising and radical secularism. But by means of his antipuritan polemics, he extends his criticism from the Church as an external fact to religion as an internal experience. He goes far beyond the dispute concerning the *jura circa sacra* [laws concerning spiritual matters], to strike at the very core of the *preambula fidei* [things

which are prerequisite to anything concerning faith] themselves. Hobbes assumes the attitude of the modern scientist toward religion, although this is mitigated by his profound
assimilation of humanistic culture. Hobbes's attitude is one of
bold impartiality, but not of vulgar disrespect, more agnostic
than destructive. It is grossly pragmatic, but not radically
negative. From a theoretical point of view, religion is simply set
aside as something which has nothing to do with creative research and demonstrative reasoning. We thus cannot have any
science of religion. In practice, on the contrary, religion is accepted for its pedagogical value, provided that it is regulated,
disciplined, and controlled by the state. For the state alone is
responsible for, and can thus dispose of, the subjects' conduct.

What Hobbes vehemently rejects is religion transformed
into superstition, the worship of God transformed into an idol-
atric cult, and faith turned into credulity. He rejects vulgar
belief in miracles, the exploitation of ignorance, and the in-
stigation of raging fanatisms. All these expressions of pernicious religiosity are, for Hobbes, the fruit of machinations of
the clergy. The most irriverent (an irreverence which borders
on mockery) part of his religious critique is thus permeated by
anticlericalism more than by antiChristian feelings.

Hobbes does not burn all bridges with Christianity, but takes
refuge in a very advanced position of antidogmatic Christianity, which is separated by only a thin veil from natural religion and Deism. Hobbes's Christianity is humanistic, as it can
be found cherished among the erudites of his time and in those
persons who believe in the irenic function of a universal religion, firmly planted in the soil of humanistic culture. This
irenic Christianity attempts to rise above factions. But in order
to do so, it must abandon one by one the principal dogmas disputed by theologians. Eventually, after freeing itself of this or
that dogma, this Christianity is reduced to the embarrassing
nakedness of one single article of faith: Jesus is Christ, the son
of God. It is a Christianity reduced to a skeleton, and divested
of all that which constitutes a positive religion, of dogmas, sac-
raments, and discipline. It is understandable that this Christianity can easily be subjected to civil power. According to

Hobbes, faith in Christ is very simple indeed. Everything which appears to make it complicated and irksome to a spirit that loves clarity is not at all essential to it, but rather the product of the quarrelsome, sectarian, and vain spirit in human beings, especially theologians. It is an expression of scholastic superficiality, not of spiritual depth. It is no wonder, then, that all disputes passed off as discussions about religious issues are merely highly human disagreements about worldly, even lowly worldly questions. And is it surprising that they can only be solved by the holder of the sovereign power on earth? No legal order distinct from that of the state, and no power separate from civil power, is necessary to a religion which has been stripped to its bones. Hobbes has thus paved the way for reducing the traditional dichotomy between religious and temporal power to unity. He has collected the good reasons that allow him to establish the unity of power which alone can ensure peace among human beings.

There is no doubt that Hobbes's main concern, not to say obsession, is to build his potential theory in such a way as to solve the problem of the relationship between Church and state. He devotes more than one third of *De Cive* and about half of *Leviathan* to this problem. It has been said that Hobbes's major political work, like that of Spinoza, is a theological-political treaty more than a political one. Indeed, in order to obtain his solution to the problem of the relationship between Church and state, Hobbes not only employs the rational arguments to which he has accustomed us, he also plunges into biblical exegesis and religious controversy. He emerges from these excursions with a personal interpretation of the meaning of the Christian message.

The fundamental point of Hobbes's scriptural analysis is that Christ's reign is not of this world. Christ has not come into this world to command, but rather to preach and to teach. Therefore, there is no reason why there should exist an authority which claims to represent Christ's reign on earth, for this reign is not to be realized. Neither is there any ground for the distinction between canonical and civil laws. For there is no authority on earth other than the temporal one, and thus no laws other than those imposed and sanctioned by the civil sovereign. As for the Church, it is, in accordance with the etymology of the term, nothing more than an assembly of persons who join together to practice a divine cult. But in this case as well, if the Church is merely an organism external to the state, there is no reason why it should have an institutional order different from that of the other associations that live within the state. And these associations have a legal personality only because the state has accorded one to them. The Church, as an association for the worship of God, is subordinate to civil power, which has the authority to summon its assembles, to appoint its ministers, and so forth. Facing the problem of the relationship between Church and state, Hobbes thus chooses to unify the two institutions, to the point of fusing them. There are not two powers, but only one: and this is the state. In contrast with the dualistic theses which held the ground throughout this centuries-old controversy, Hobbes's thesis has the merit of being so clear as not to allow for misunderstanding. This clarity could only spring from an inflexible logic, employed in the service of a rare independence of judgment, and of a proud, even scandalous moral boldness.

However, there is in England another cause of disorder and thus of dissolution of the state, one of which Hobbes never loses sight: the conflict between Crown and Parliament. This was the moment when the process of centralizing power into the hands of the king was beginning in the other European countries. A new kind of state was thus coming into being, founded on two principles: that the *princeps* is *legibus solutus* [the prince is not bound by the law]; and that the state is the only source of the law. Both principles were antithetical to the medieval ones which had established that the prince was subordinate to the law of nature and that there existed a plurality of legal orders, which limited one another reciprocally. However, unlike the constitutions of the continental states, the English constitution presented the Crown with serious obstacles to its transformation into an absolute state.

The English constitution was the final outcome of a long and slow process which had managed to balance the main political

forces of medieval society—the court, the great and petty feudal nobility, and urban classes. Jurists had handed down the
image of the English state which was by now traditional, as a
body politic composed of a head (the king) and the limbs (the
three estates). On the basis of this image, sixteenth-century
writers on public law had represented the English state as a
mixed government; it was a state founded on the principle of
the separation of powers, and as such it was antithetical to absolute monarchy, in which power is one and indivisible. Since
the beginning of the seventeenth century the English monarchy in the person of James I, who was a supporter of absolutism and the divine right of kings both in theory and in practice,
had attempted to introduce into England a monarchy of the
French type. But given the historical conditions in which this
attempt was made, it awakened the increasingly resolute opposition of Parliament. While reasserting its loyalty to the medieval constitution, and its position to the abolition of feudal
privileges, Parliament made a case for, and created the presuppositions of, what would later become the liberal state.

The opposition to the Crown was destined to break out
openly, as we have said, under the successor to James I,
Charles I (1625–49), whose reign was an uninterrupted history
of dissentions, which grew increasingly irreconcilable between Crown and Parliament. The Crown insistently, and at
times unskillfully, asserted its prerogatives, which clashed
with Parliamentary demands, especially in religious, financial,
and international matters. These dissentions culminated in the
Civil War (1642) between the royalist and parliamentary parties. The outbreak of the Civil War threatened the very existence of the state, and indicated to easy-going pacificists,
enemies of every turmoil, and lovers of order, such as Thomas
Hobbes, that a period of ferocious anarchy had begun. In a
passage of *Leviathan*, with a candor which could not have been
greater, Hobbes puts his finger on the wound and suggests the
remedy: "If there had not first been an opinion received of the
greatest part of England, that these powers were divided between the King, and the Lords, and the House of Commons,
the people had never been divided and fallen into this civil

war; . . . which have so instructed men in this point of sovereign right, that there be few now in England that do not see, that these rights are inseparable."[4]

The indivisibility of the sovereign power is one of Hobbes's *idées fixes,* and one of the pillars of the thought of the first and best-known theorist of absolutism, Jean Bodin, whose work Hobbes knew well.[5] Bodin himself had devoted a chapter of his monumental work on the state to the confutation of mixed government.[6] But Hobbes's main target is the separation of powers which ensues from attributing the faculty of imposing taxes to an agency different from the agency which has the right to decide war and peace. The allusion to the English situation could not be more transparent. Such a situation is intolerable, according to Hobbes; even worse, it is contradictory. Through a dilemmatic reasoning, which is Hobbes's favorite way of leading his reader to assent, Hobbes frames the question in extremely concise terms. Either the powers of the state are not really divided, because the person who commands is the one who has the power to impose taxes; in this case the state is no longer mixed, but absolute. Or the powers are really divided; in this case there is no state, but rather the lack thereof, anarchy and civil war. In opposition to the distinction between civil and religious power, which reflected a limit external to the state, Hobbes established the principle that there is only one holder of the sovereign power. In similar fashion, by rebelling against the doctrine of the separation of powers within the state, he established the principle that the sovereign power is one and indivisible. For Hobbes, there are thus two aspects to the problem of the unity of the state: there should be a unique source of power, and power should be internally unified.

But there was another source of limits to the sovereign power, which was specific to the English legal order, and which was a typical expression of a pluralistic society like the

4. Ibid., p. 119.

5. Hobbes cites him, in support of the thesis of the indivisibility of power, in *The Elements of Law Natural and Politic,* II, 8, 7, p. 137.

6. J. Bodin, *The Six Bookes of a Commonweale* (see chap. 1, n. 3), II, i.

medieval one. This constitutional limit can be expressed as the primacy of the common law over statute law. The common law was composed of the norms which had been handed down through custom and which had been made legally effective by the fact that the supreme jurisdictional courts recognized and accepted them. Such primacy, upheld by the common opinion of jurists, obviously impaired the legislative power of the sovereign, and infringed upon the principle of *princeps legibus solutus*, on which absolute monarchies were founded. Given the English legal order, the *princeps* found himself bound not only by natural and divine laws, but also by a system of positive laws dictated by the nature of things and approved by judges, one which was quite extensive and in constant evolution. The relevance of this issue did not escape Hobbes, who was keen on eliminating any cause of erosion of the supremacy of the sovereign: so much so that he devoted to it, besides hints in his political works, an entire book, *A Dialogue between a Philosopher and a Student of the Common Law of England*.[7]

This is one of Hobbes's least known, but not least interesting works, which shows Hobbes's logical style at its best. Here he brandishes the syllogism like a sword, and, by pruning and cutting problems at their roots, reduces the most muddled questions to their original and essential nucleus. The book was written in Hobbes's later years (around 1666), in the form of a dialogue between a jurist and a philosopher. It contains an implacable condemnation of the doctrine, espoused by Sir Edward Coke, of the supremacy of the common law over the king's law. And it asserts, on the basis of a rigidly voluntaristic conception of the law, that the only valid law of the kingdom is the law issued by the king as legislator. Consequently any other legal norm, including those of the common law, becomes valid only if approved tacitly or expressly by the sovereign. Once more, Hobbes shows himself an antitraditionalist and radical writer. His radicalism is perhaps excessively intellectualistic, and sets him apart from the most genuine current of

7. I edited the first Italian translation of this work, published in the second edition of the Italian translation of *De Cive*: T. Hobbes, *Opere Politiche* (Turin: Utet, 1959), I, pp. 393–558.

English political thought, that which inclines toward empiricism, is respectful of tradition, and loves compromise.[8]

But Hobbes, while he keeps his eyes fixed on the political situation in England, is prompted by his own rationalistic mentality, his mathematizing mind, and his aspiration to discover laws which are universally valid and acceptable to all reasonable human beings, to go far beyond the boundaries of the English tradition. He aims at outlining a conceptual model of the state as an ideal type, from which all shortcomings that make the existence of historical states so precarious would be eliminated. He intends this ideal state to serve as the abstract model for a historical reality which is bringing all countries at different speeds to the adoption of a few shared principles, those that constitute the fundamental principles of the modern state. These principles, which are independent of the political formulas of the individual states, are essentially two. The first is the principle of political unity, which is achieved through the unification of legal orders which are inferior or superior to the state, leaving only the legal order of the state itself. The second principle is that of juridical unity, which is obtained by unifying the sources of norms, leaving the only source which is appropriate to organized political power, that is, the law of the state. Upon close examination, we can see that Hobbes uses his polemics against the English constitution to express these two processes which characterize the modern state: political unification, attained by eliminating the dualism of Church and state and the contrast between King and Parliament, and juridical unification, attained by proclaiming that the norms of the common law depend on legislative laws.

To be sure, this way of seeing the state was not new. The conception of the state as the sovereign legal system formed the nucleus of Bodin's political work, which had been influential in England. Furthermore, the doctrine of the divine right of kings, which had arisen and developed in France, and had found its major supporter in England in James I, was the ex-

8. G. P. Gooch defines Hobbes as "the first, the most original, and the *least English* (emphasis added) of our three great political thinkers" ("Hobbes," *Proceedings of the British Academy* 25 [1939]: 3).

pression of the historical process of the unification and liberation of the state. It was the great monarchies which, perhaps
without being fully aware, were working in that direction.
They were jealous of their independence and thus hostile to
any interference from other powers; and they trusted their
own ability to govern their own countries, to the point of al-
lowing no one else to share their political authority. Nonetheless, the supporters of the divine right of kings had disguised
this fundamental need for unity by hiding it under the principle of the divine origin of kingly power. But this disguise did
not match the efforts which thinkers were making at the time
to leave what Hobbes himself called "the kingdom of darkness." The doctrine of the divine right of kings was a medieval
formula superimposed on a new historical situation, in which
needs antithetical to those of medieval society were arising.
The significance of Hobbes's political theory lies in his attempt
to justify rationally this great process of political unification out
of which modern history began, and to elaborate, so to speak,
a new form for new contents, thus building a system adequate
to a new historical situation. A Hegelian writer would say that
in Hobbes's thought the modern state acquires for the first time
full consciousness of itself. Or, if one prefers, Hobbes's political theory is the self-consciousness of the modern state.

Until Hobbes's times, the resort to authority had been the prevailing method in political science. To teach his prince how to
acquire and preserve the state, Machiavelli acknowledged that
history was the supreme authority from which to draw teach-
ings and examples. Supporters of the divine right of kings appealed to the supernatural authority of the Holy Scriptures to
justify the foundation of monarchic power *ex jure divino* [by divine right]. The great Bodin had resorted to both. Hobbes, on
the contrary, is the first to introduce a rationalistic method into
the study of political phenomena, and to abandon the method
based on authority. This is his innovation with regard to
method, of which he himself is most proud. Hobbes's aim,
constantly declared and pursued, is to apply to the moral and
political disciplines the same methodical rigor from which ge-

ometry and the natural sciences in general had profited. In this respect, which all seventeenth-century natural law theorists have in common, Hobbes is fully aware of being an innovator, and does not hesitate to declare it: "I shall deserve the reputation of having beene the first to lay the grounds of two sciences: this of *Optiques,* the most curious, and that other of *Natural Justice,* which I have done in my book *De Cive,* the most profitable of all other."[9]

Hobbes does not disdain basing his arguments on authority, but does not employ authority as a main source of justification. Authority merely corroborates demonstrations carried out through rational procedures. He is always ready to find a passage from the Scriptures to support any assertion, in particular the most daring. And we are not far from the truth when we say that he was as subtle, albeit less fortunate, a biblical interpreter as he was a formal logician. But he engages in this retrospective inquiry into the Scriptures more to silence his adversaries than out of a need to ascertain the truth. Hobbes neglects almost completely any reference to the authority of history, even though he was, as he tells us in his autobiography,[10] a passionate reader of ancient and modern history, especially in his formative years, when he was influenced by Bacon's work.[11] His passion for history even led him to translate the entire work of one of the two great historians of ancient Greece. And he does, of course, make a few historical references, as when he cites Americans or people who live by raiding. But these are only sporadic cases. However, we should not forget that, although Hobbes does not mention it, the contemporary history of his own country is always present in his mind, as a continuing drama which he lives intensely. This history is the experimental corroboration of his theory, one which cries out so loudly that he does not even have to mention it. But in his writings he makes no reference to history "not to define

9. This is the finale sentence of: *A Minute or First Draught of the Optiques* (1649), of which there are two fragments in *EW,* VII, p. 471.

10. *Opera philosophica quae latine scripsit omnia* (hereafter *OL*), II, p. LXXXVIII.

11. As L. Strauss has emphasized, *The Political Philosophy of Hobbes, Its Basis and Its Genesis* (Oxford: Clarendon Press, 1936), pp. 79ff.

aught which concerns the Justice of single nations,"[12] so as not to violate the principle of scientific objectivity.

The scientific method which Hobbes intends to apply to the study of political problems is the same which has enabled the natural sciences to make such continuous and lasting progress: the method of composition (synthesis), and resolution (analysis). It is the method which allows us to inquire into causes starting from known effects, or into effects starting from known causes. Through analysis a notion is resolved into its constitutive elements; through synthesis a notion is recomposed into unity, starting from its constitutive elements. We may remark that these two processes of synthesis and analysis can be assimilated to the two arithmetical operations of addition and subtraction. We thus can draw the conclusion that scientific reasoning is a calculation, and that science is therefore mathematics applied to natural phenomena.

Even political science, which Hobbes calls civil philosophy, as the distinction between science and philosophy had yet to come, must participate in this mathematization of scientific thought, where we may see Hobbes's full adherence to the cultural climate of the century of Descartes. Civil philosophy can employ both the synthetic and the analytic methods. We rely on the former when, proceeding from the first principles of philosophy, we attain knowledge of the human passions, and, on this basis, we understand the causes for the constitution of states. We rely on the latter when, after asking whether an action is just or unjust, we resolve step by step the notion of injustice as that of acting against the law; and then the notion of law as that of the command of the person who has the power to coerce; and finally we reach the first cause for human beings' desire for there to be a person who has coercive power, and can thus issue a law.

In his political works, Hobbes resorts to both methods. In the introduction to *De Cive* he declares that in order to know a thing we must know the elements of which it is composed. He

12. *De Cive*, preface, p. xxii.

gives as an example the clock, whose workings cannot be fully understood if it is not dismantled. The state, this object of political science which human beings have studied for too long without rigorous criteria, in obedience to the passions rather than to the rule of truth, he thus compares to a mechanism. The comparison itself is evidence of the scientific approach which Hobbes adopts to analyze the state, in contrast to the ethical and humanistic approach which had prevailed in political studies up to him. Individuals are the elements that compose the state, that is, they are the gears of this mechanism. A doctrine of the state which aims at being scientific must therefore study individuals, their characteristic passions and their fundamental needs. It is the opposition between these passions, which lead human beings toward war, and their needs, which irresistibly drive them toward peace, that prompts individuals to subject themselves voluntarily to a unique and absolute power, that is, the state. The study of the state is thus a *scire per causas* [to know through causes], and is therefore true science.

It goes without saying that the research must be founded upon a universally recognized principle, upon which all may agree, and beyond which we need not look. This principle, which in the introduction to *De Cive* Hobbes says is "by experience known to all men and denied by none," is that all human beings naturally mistrust one another and are thus willing to harm one another whenever they can. This is the principle which we can summarize in the well-known saying *homo homini lupus* [man is a wolf to man]. But to this principle we must add at least a second, rooted no less than the first in human nature, as can easily be seen. Human beings are at the same time hostile toward their fellow human beings, and incline by natural instinct to preserve their own lives or, more precisely, to avoid death. To put it in elementary terms, human beings are afraid of dying; above all they are afraid of violent death. It is from these two principles, based upon the observation of the human spirit, that politics as a science is born; that is, there arises a construction of the state built with a scientific method. The state of nature precedes the constitution of any organized society, and is the condition in which human beings act following only their own natural inclinations.

We can only imagine this state of nature as a condition torn by the incurable conflict between two drives. One is the inclination to harm others which generates the war of all against all, and constantly threatens human beings with violent death. The other is the instinct of self-preservation which prompts human beings to employ any means in order to avoid the death which is incumbent upon them because of their antisocial nature. The state of nature is thus an intrinsically contradictory situation, that is, a situation in which human beings cannot live, and which they absolutely must leave behind. We might more correctly say that the state of nature is presented as an absurd situation, so that the reasonableness of civil society, which is opposed to the state of nature, may by contrast be enhanced. So much so that to leave the state of nature means to resolve its intrinsic contradiction. This can be done only in the following way: by hindering or at least moderating the inclination to harm others, so that human beings can be liberated from the fear of death. The state is the institution destined to resolve the contradiction inherent in the state of nature. It consists of a power superior to the power of individuals, that is, a power endowed with sufficient force to hinder the individual use of force. The state is the antithesis of the state of nature. It replaces the reign of war with the reign of peace. It is a rational construction based on the reasonable hypothesis of the state of nature.

If the state is a work of reason, it is apparent that civil philosophy acquires its rigorously scientific character from its reproduction of the rational process through which the state is instituted. But civil philosophy is not just one science among many. It is *the* science by definition, more than physics, for example, and on a par with geometry. And this is so for a reason which cannot fail to bring to mind Vico and the method he used to demonstrate the scientific value of history, the human science par excellence.

Hobbes distinguishes between demonstrable and nondemonstrable sciences. Demonstrable sciences are those in which the first causes are in our power, since they are the expression of our will, or more simply, since they are produced by us. Nondemonstrable sciences are those in which first causes do not depend on us, but on the divine will.[13] Physics is a typical example of this latter category. Of the former, the best examples are geometry and civil philosophy: "Geometry therefore is demonstrable," he writes, "for the lines and figures from which we reason are drawn and described by ourselves; and civil philosophy is demonstrable, because we make the commonwealth ourselves."[14] Civil philosophy, like geometry, thus aims at knowing an object which we ourselves have produced. We still have to ask: in what sense can we say that we produce the object of civil philosophy, or, in Hobbes's own words, that we form the state? The state, he answers, is not by nature but by convention. It is because the state fulfills a fundamental need of human beings that human beings themselves want it and give it life through a reciprocal agreement.

Hobbes thus poses a contractual hypothesis as the basis of the state. The contract which gives origin to the state stipulates what follows. A number of human beings decide to give up the unlimited right to all things which belongs to them in the state of nature. They also decide to transfer it to a third person (which may be not a natural person, but an assembly). Their twofold aim is to take out of their own hands the main weapon through which they can harm one another, and to entrust it to someone who can use it in defense of all. As a matter of fact, if human beings must be able to will all of the above, then we must presuppose a third principle of human nature, to be set alongside the two already cited. Hobbes does not even mention this third principle, for it does not even cross his mind that one could doubt it. That is, we must start from the assumption that human beings are reasonable. They can realize, with a calculation which only reasoning beings are capable of making, that war ensues from the unlimited right to all things, and

13. *EW,* VII, pp. 183–84. Hobbes deals with this argument more clearly in *De Homine* (*OL,* II, 10, 4).

14. *EW,* VII, pp. 183–84.

that only by giving up such an unlimited right can war be avoided.

It is not easy to imagine how this reasoning, perhaps utilitarian, but formally rigorous, may take shape in the human beings driven by instinct such as those whom Hobbes describes. The implausibility of this assumption has often been charged against him, especially by those who mistake his rational construction of the state for an inquiry into its historical origins. But there is no doubt that it is reasoning which leads Hobbes's human beings to found the state. While war is the product of a natural inclination, peace is a "dictate of right reason," that is, of that faculty which allows human beings to derive certain consequences from certain premises, or to reconstruct first principles starting from factual data. It is also true that if we begin with such a desolate conception of man as the one which Hobbes outlines for us in his portrait of the state of nature, we may wonder how this passionate, violent, instinctive, and selfish being can abandon his natural inclination in favor of reason. But Hobbes's work is not a historical inquiry into society, aimed at giving a general overview of the phases of social evolution. It is a demonstration, which claims to be rigorous, of the nature of the state. With this demonstration Hobbes aims at persuading his contemporaries to choose the road which he considers right, and to abandon the wrong one. This project is in itself a sign of trust in human reasonableness. Hobbes is convinced of the persuasive strength of good reasoning because he starts from the assumption that human beings are reasonable. If it were not so, he would himself resort to authority. He is thus not concerned to ascertain whether primitive human beings were ever able to follow their reason to the point of agreeing on the institution of the state. The individuals whom he addresses are his contemporaries, even better, his fellow countrymen, led astray by false doctrines; and the state of nature which they must leave is the religious and political strife occurring in his country which is leading to civil war. He wishes to explain that the state is made by human beings, more precisely by the will of human beings as reasonable creatures; if you like, by the rational will of human beings.

Man thus cannot *not* will the state, except at the cost of either contradicting himself, or of giving up one of his eminent characteristics: reasonableness.

Hobbes appeals to the rational part of human nature in his attempt to show that the basic feature of political society is obedience to the sovereign. All of Hobbes's doctrine consists of an iron chain of logical propositions aiming to demonstrate that we must obey the sovereign, whatever he commands, provided that he does command. At the core of Hobbes's political writings is a preaching about obedience, which tries the path of reason rather than of the heart. His preaching is intelligent rather than vehement, astute rather than warm. Gooch has rightly remarked that if "the *Prince* is a manual of statescraft, *De Cive* [is] a grammar of obedience."[15]

Hobbes's politics, beginning from the thesis of the unity of power, and guided by the thread of an exceptionally rigorous reasoning, weaves one of the most radical theories of obedience that the history of political doctrines has ever known. In comparison with this theory, even the doctrine of the divine right of kings, which was employed in Hobbes's time to support absolutism, that is, the state founded on obedience, could be considered moderate. This doctrine admitted at least passive obedience. That is, it acknowledged that one could disobey the civil law when this went against the divine law, provided that disobedience was, as it were, compensated by the voluntary acceptance of the punishment which would follow transgression of the law. Hobbes does not allow passive obedience, indeed he condemns it severely as a mistake. The consequential logician leaves only one way open to subjects, active obedience. The subject must obey in any case except when his life itself is threatened. Hobbes provides two formidable arguments as the foundation for obedience. The first is that the individual is obliged through the covenant of union to obey all of the sovereign's commands. In other words, the individual has acquired an obligation to obey independently of

15. G. P. Gooch, *Hobbes*, p. 17.

the content of the command, and has thus lost any right to judge whether the command is just or unjust. The second argument is that the sovereign may not, even if he so wishes, command actions contrary to religion, for no one but the sovereign determines religious matters.

Here the consequential logician is at an advantage because of his rationalistic and antitheological assumptions. So much so that Hobbes, in order to support his demonstration, employs the argument provided by his adversaries, who ground the sovereign power on a human convention. In the eyes of his subjects, a monarch by divine right may not be able to free himself completely of his own subjection to the supreme authority which has invested him with power. (It is from this that theorists of the divine right of kings find the need to leave the door open to passive obedience.) On the contrary, it is easy to conceive of a power absolutely independent of any ethical or religious constraint, when this power derives from the will of the individuals over whom it is exercised. For these individuals not only grant to its holder his legal title, but they also free him of any responsibility. But this solution works only if one can show that the agreement among subjects is, once stipulated, irrevocable.

It is precisely in discussing this issue that Hobbes engages all his acumen, and succeeds in devising the most surprising of his formulas, the one which constitutes the key to his whole system. The convention on which the state is founded is not a contract between subjects and sovereign, as imagined by contractual writers of democratic persuasion. It is, further, not a contract which subjects may rescind when the sovereign has not complied with the obligations he has assumed. The contract is among the subjects themselves, which they stipulate with the goal of giving up their natural rights in favor of a third party. Only the unanimous consent of all parties (but how can unanimity obtain?) together with the beneficiary's consent (but why should he make this concession?) can rescind such a contract. The contract which supporters of the right of resistance had employed to break the chains of absolutism is employed by Hobbes to reinforce them. He destroys the theory of the right of resistance with its own weapons. And he defends the theory of obedience with the very arguments that had been used to destroy it.

Hobbes appreciates that the most effective way to demolish adversaries and convince the hesitant is to turn arguments against their own supporters. His contractual theory is an ingenious and shrewd game of turning the tables, which we can view today with wonder as a masterpiece of demonstrative and dialectical art, independent of its historical meaning. Hobbes could attain this result only thanks to the methodological clarity which his scientific education had imposed on him. Even the famous writings of his immediate predecessors, for example Bodin's *Six Bookes of a Commonweale*, are full of historical quotations and references, which are complex and heavily erudite. But if we compare Hobbes's work with these, we realize that for European culture the *Discourse on Method* was not written in vain. Not by chance, Hobbes is a wicked and impertinent enemy of the scholastic method. He misses no opportunity for shooting poisoned arrows at the Aristotelians' ponderous tomes. Hobbes wants to aim precisely and directly at his target. The result is *De Cive*, which is a model of clarity, conciseness, intelligence, and passion, but is also controlled by an iron logic and an unbroken pace. *De Cive* is a work which imposes admiration even on those who reject its conceptual content, and captures even its most prejudiced readers so that they forget or forgive all that is paradoxical, excessive, disconcerting, and repulsive in it.

Nonetheless, we must not let Hobbes's dialectical game overcome us to the point of thinking that his theory of obedience is simply the harmonious conclusion of fortunate reasoning. The principle of obedience is rooted in Hobbes's vision of man and the world, and is therefore, much more than the conclusion of a line of reasoning, a direct expression of his philosophical personality. We cannot grasp the meaning of that principle if we do not understand that it is firmly grounded on two constitutive principles of Hobbes's moral philosophy: his ethical conventionalism and his anthropological pessimism.

Hobbes's ethics acknowledges no absolute values, either in the sense of a transcendent morality or in the sense of an immanent one. Values are neither eternal truths which hold even for the divine will, nor are they natural truths which impose themselves on the human will. The source of every value, and therefore of every criterion of evaluation of good and evil, just and unjust, is the human will itself. More precisely, it is the agreement of human wills, that is, a convention, obtaining in the social condition in which human beings are forced to live, thus abandoning the inhuman state of nature. This moral conventionalism is a consequence of Hobbes's logical nominalism. One might contend that this nominalism is not always present in Hobbes's most theoretical works, and that it is not very consistent, if one accurately analyzes Hobbes's logic. But one may not dismiss its explicit and insistent formulation and its function in Hobbes's political works: "*Truth* is the same with a *true proposition*," Hobbes asserts in *De Cive*, "but *the proposition is true* in which the *word consequent*, which by logicians is called *the predicate*, embraceth *the word antecedent* in its amplitude, which they call *the subject*. And to *know truth* is the same thing as to *remember* that it was made by ourselves by the very usurpation of the words."[16]

To offer a concrete example, with regard to the proposition, two and three is five: "And to know this truth is nothing else, but to acknowledge that it is made by ourselves. For by whose will and rules of speaking II is called two, III is called three, and IIII is called five; by their will also it comes to pass that this proposition is true, *two and three taken together make five*."[17] What is valid for the truth in logic is also valid for justice in politics: there is no eternal or natural justice. "Just" is what human beings have agreed to call by this name. In order to leave the state of nature, human beings have agreed to subject their wills to that of a third person, who is the beneficiary of their agreement. "Just" is therefore, in the last instance, what the sovereign wills.

16. *De Cive*, XVIII, 4, pp. 303–4.
17. Ibid.

Ethical conventionalism, supported by logical nominalism, thus leads Hobbes to elaborate a voluntaristic conception of the law. Only in the dogmatics built by positivist jurists of the nineteenth century for the use of legislators, can we find a version as rigid as Hobbes's. This conventionalist and therefore antinaturalistic conception of justice (justice is by convention, not by nature) produces a voluntaristic and antirationalistic construction of the law [*stat pro ratione voluntas*]. With regard to obedience, this choice has two important consequences. First of all, the individual, once he has become a member of a state, no longer has the right (for he does not have the power) to decide himself what is just and unjust. His only duty is to subject himself to the sovereign, for only the latter has the right to distinguish just and unjust, having been granted the power to do so by shared consent. Second, since the sovereign is by shared consent the only holder of the right and the power to decide what is just and what is unjust, there cannot exist any just action other than the one commanded by the sovereign, and any unjust action other than the one prohibited by him. As a consequence, all that the sovereign commands is just merely because it has been commanded; and all that he prohibits is unjust merely because it has been prohibited.

In a conception of the world in which nothing is measured against absolute values, even man, as such, has no absolute value. In Hobbes's man there is no trace of moral conscience, which might reveal man to himself and others as a moral person, and no trace of moral feeling, which might reveal to man the presence of absolute values. Man is a creature of nature, determined by mechanical laws, dominated by inborn and overpowering passions, which irrevocably define his position in the world. Vanity is perhaps, in Hobbes's anthropology, man's most characteristic passion.[18] It is vanity more than interest, that is, the pleasure of being respected and honored by others, more than the pleasure of deriving advantage from them. For vanity is the pleasure of the soul, whereas interest is

18. L. Strauss has emphasized this point in *The Political Philosophy of Hobbes*, pp. 11ff.

the pleasure of the senses. Vanity and interest are in any case aspects of amour-propre and thus evidence of the selfish nature of man. Vanity is the love of one's own natural capacities. Interest is the love of one's own material welfare. Both of these dominant passions make man an antisocial being by nature. Man seeks the company of other human beings not out of a natural and spontaneous inclination, but rather to satisfy his desire for honors and material goods.

Only one passion is stronger in man than amour-propre: the fear of dying. Man is not only vain and selfish, but also cowardly. Amour-propre assumes the forms of pride, ambition, vainglory, arrogance, and the pursuit of the useful, in the presence of which there exist no absolute, but only instrumental values. But amour-propre is defeated by man's attachment to his own life. Love for one's self finds a limit in love for life. Life thus becomes the greatest good of this ethics of power which is constantly turned upside down, and becomes a statement of impotence. Only the fear of death convinces man to give up the honors and advantages of the state of nature, and accept civil society. This unsociable being becomes sociable out of fear. Kingdoms are thus founded on fear, not justice.

In such a vision, what do liberty, dignity, knowledge, and beliefs represent? All that matters to man is to save his own life in this war of all against all, which is the original human condition. Only a master can make him feel secure. Only the state, that is the power founded on the consent of all, can guarantee it. We must therefore entrust ourselves to the state, and obey it. If the preservation of life is man's first great instinct, and if life becomes the greatest good, we can sacrifice all other goods to it, even those that a naive or hypocritically optimistic anthropology calls moral goods. Among these there are dignity and liberty. But what is dignity for Hobbes except a consequence of the excessive evaluation of ourselves, and thus of vanity? And what is liberty, except a pretext for indulging our desires without limits? What do we then sacrifice to the state, except our misery, weakness, errors, and instincts? If in exchange for this sacrifice of our negative qualities we receive assurance that our life, which is the only thing which counts, is safe, why should we not accept the state, despite its absolute power and our absolute obedience?

There really is something cynical in this conception of man. For man is divested of all the ornaments with which a long tradition of scholastic and academic ethics had generously dressed him. But Hobbes's cynicism reveals man's meanness more than wickedness. It perceives the ridiculous rather than the tragic in human passions. It uncovers the bloated emptiness which underlies the tawdry coat of presumption, and the cowardice which lies at the bottom of the drive to harm others. But this shows that Hobbes had absorbed the satirical aspects of humanistic anthropology, which pervades all his works, more than the edifying one. There is also in Hobbes a healthy cynicism, which at least rescues traditional philosophical thinking from the taste for rhetoric and idealistic optimism, and from the tendency to schematize moral issues. This remains true even if a thought so disrespectful toward all traditions is destined, in a highly traditional philosophical environment, to arouse scandal. It is also destined to be isolated, like a person carrying a contagious disease, under the pretext of atheism, heresy, and immorality. The weapons used against Hobbes were in fact typically those used by persons who do not have the whole truth, but who replace the truth as the criterion of judgment and condemnation with the consensus of those who do not want to think, or do not not want others to think.

It is apparent that starting from an attitude which is so suspicious of human beings, Hobbes could only build an inhuman state. This was also the result of his radicalism, which knew no compromise, but only the alternative between yes and no, and responded to extreme events with an extreme rationalism. We have remarked that Hobbes conceives of the state as an antidote to the state of nature. There is a page in which Hobbes presents this contrast with exasperated rigor, concluding that "out of it [the state], there is a dominion of passions, war, fear, poverty, slovenliness, solitude, barbarism, ignorance, cruelty; in it, the dominion of reason, peace, se-

curity, riches, decency, society, elegancy, sciences, and benevolence."[19] The state represents the unity of the will over
against the multiplicity of wills in the natural condition; it represents objective norms over against subjective rights, obligation against *arbitrium* [arbitrariness], and authority against
liberty. But there is no dialectical relationship between the two
terms of each pair of concepts. Thus, if the state of nature is
complete liberty and nothing but liberty, the state must be
complete authority and nothing but authority. The *esprit de géométrie* does not admit half-measures.

Hobbes portrays the state of nature as the human condition
of licence and chaos; the state, as the condition of discipline
and order. In this violent antithesis, we cannot be surprised if
the state, which is *machina machinarum*, that is, a mechanical
model built with skill by a rationalist philosopher, acquires
more and more threatening features. Under our own eyes we
see it turn into the monstrous Leviathan, of which it is said in
the book of Job that "there is no power on earth which is equal
to it." But a monster is indeed an inhuman creature, at least as
inhuman as the wolf man of the state of nature. But the
Leviathan is inhuman because it is more than human, while
the wolf man is inhuman because it is less than human. The too
consequential rationalist has opposed one monstrous condition to another. Hobbes has not realized that, in the end, he
has skipped over man, that is, the human person. It was this
person who right in Hobbes's own country was demanding
freedom, religious tolerance, and freedom of thought. These
were the formulas which were destined to untie the old knots
which absolutism had tried to cut, not knowing how to untie
them. They represented a compromise between the state of
nature, characterized by the natural rights of individuals, and
civil society, characterized by the exercise of power over individuals. But Hobbes saw in liberty merely a cause of disintegration, and therefore suppressed it. He saw freedom of thought
as the sower of discord, and therefore wanted it checked and
humiliated. He saw religion as the main source of disobe-

19. *De Cive*, X, 1, p. 127.

dience and the dissolution of states, and therefore diminished it, to the point of turning it into a mere instrument of obedience to civil power. Finally, he saw man as the being who is always afraid, and thought that fear could only be opposed by fear. This is why Hobbes's state has such threatening features; it is the response of organized fear to unbridled fear. But fear is its essence.

And yet, Hobbes had only followed with his merciless logic in the steps of the merciless formation of the modern state, which was being built as the unifying principle of dissolving medieval society. Neither traditionalists who saw a threat to the independence of religious authority, nor innovators who considered the state an obstacle to individual liberties, could grasp the meaning of that process. Both the former and the latter fought against it as a calamity. But now we are in a position to understand it well. We can see the ineluctable, though not always peaceful, process of the realization of political and juridical unity, and its necessary, though not always beneficial, results. Hobbes's edifice is not so paradoxical as may appear at first sight. If we understand this, we can also understand its persuasive force and its lasting value. The modern state is truly the monstrous power and the enormous machine which Hobbes described, and to which he gave a name. As Hobbes saw it, it is truly both the Leviathan which devours human beings, and the *homo artificialis* which turns them into gears without souls. The history of humankind knows this might, which is human and superhuman at the same time, too well to miss the fact that the value of Hobbes's thought consists in offering an exact perception of the nature of the state, and an eloquent warning of its power.

The problem of politics was central to Hobbes's concerns throughout his long life as a thinker. He offered a systematic treatment of this problem in three different works, composed in his mature years:

1. *Elements of Law Natural and Politic,* written in 1640, and published as two distinct treatises, entitled

respectively, *Human Nature or the Fundamental
Elements of Policy,* and *De Corpore Politico or the Elements
of Law, Moral and Politic,* in 1650.[20]

2. *Elementorum Philosophiae Sectio Tertia De Cive,* written
in the first year of his French exile (1641), published
anonymously in a small edition in Paris in 1642,
reprinted in Amsterdam, in 1647, and edited by
Samuel Sorbière. To this were added explicatory and
polemical notes, and it was prefaced with a
dedicatory epistle to William Cavendish, Earl of
Devonshire, dated 1 November 1646, and an
important methodological preface to the readers.[21] It
was faithfully translated into English by the author
himself in 1651, with the title *Philosophical Rudiments
concerning Government and Society.*[22]

3. *Leviathan or the Matter, Forme and Power of a
Commonwealth Ecclesiastical and Civil,* written in the
last part of his stay in France at the end of the civil
war, in 1649, and published in London in 1651. It later
appeared in Amsterdam, in 1688, in Latin, mutilated
and mellowed, in the first complete edition of
Hobbes's Latin writings.

Hobbes conceived of *De Cive* as the third and last part of his
philosophical system, which was to include the elements of
natural philosophy (*De Corpore*) in the first place, and then the
elements of ethics (*De Homine*). But as he explains in his "Preface to the Readers," while he was systematically elaborating
his system, his country was shaken by very serious political

20. In the edition of Hobbes's *Opera Omnia* by Sir William Molesworth, distinct in two series entitled *English Works* and *Opera Philosophica quae Latine Scripsit Omnia,* this work constituted the first part of vol. VI of the first series (229
pp.). It was reprinted in its original form, that is, as one work and with the
original title, revised directly from Hobbes's manuscripts, by F. Tönnies (Cambridge: Cambridge University Press, 1928).

21. In Molesworth's edition, it is with *De Homine* in the vol. II of *OL* (pp. 133–
423).

22. In *EW,* II. A French translation by Sorbière had been published two years
before, in 1649, which was dedicated to the Danish Earl Ulfeld, brother-in-law
of King Christian IV.

problems, which would in a short time lead it into civil war. Hobbes therefore deemed it better to put off the definitive draft of the first two parts, which would appear much later (the first in 1655, and the second in 1658), in order to set himself to work on the third, which would offer an original solution to the political and religious controversies of the day. He wrote *De Cive* right after his arrival in France, where he had gone into voluntary exile at the end of 1640, before the beginning of the Long Parliament. As a supporter of the royalist party, he feared persecution and outrages on the part of the Parliamentarians. While still in England, he had written his first political work, which he had not yet published. In this work he supported the principle of absolutism against the principle of limited or mixed monarchy, which was maintained by the Parliamentarians. He had thus attracted the attention of the adversaries of the royalist party. He therefore had good motives for fearing serious consequences, should the Parliamentary party triumph. Hobbes himself tells us that his life would have been in danger, had the king not dissolved Parliament. (This was the Short Parliament, which lasted from April to May 1640.) Whether this danger was real or not, Hobbes left the country and found safe shelter in France, even before the beginning of the Long Parliament. There he set as his immediate goal the systematic reelaboration and publication of those ideas which might further the cause of the King in England. The result was *De Cive*, written at a crucial moment of English history, between the beginning of the Long Parliament and the outbreak of the Civil War. It appeared like a warning to those led astray by seditious literature, and as a prediction of the even greater evils which actually did ensue.

When *De Cive* appeared and was made public, although in a narrow circle, the Civil War had already broken out. Hobbes could thus sarcastically reply to those who accused him of a book that was seditious and born to increase disorder [*rebus permiscendis natum*], that his book had been published while "the Civil War was being waged throughout England, so that matters, which then were already in a state of confusion, could not be [further] confused by that book."[23] His book was not a new seed of dissension thrown into an environment of heated passions. It was rather an indictment of errors, and an accusation against the sowers of disorder, and therefore a contribution to peace. Elsewhere Hobbes added that he had written *De Cive* "to the end that all nations which should hear what you and your Con-Covenanters were doing in England, might detest you, which I believe they do."[24]

Hobbes was in any case more concerned with the cause of peace than with that of the King. His aim was the end of the war, no matter how it might end, as events surrounding the second edition showed. In 1645, after matters worsened for the royalist army, the Prince of Wales took shelter in France, where Hobbes became his mathematics teacher (October 1646). Sorbière, who had succeeded in extracting an annotated text of *De Cive* from him, in order to promote a second edition of the work in Holland, had the following words engraved under the portrait of the author: "Teacher of the Prince of Wales." Hobbes would have nothing of it. In his letter to Sorbière of 22 March 1647, Hobbes remarked that he was not the teacher of the Prince of Wales, and not a member of his household. Hobbes let Sorbière know that he did not want to compromise himself too much with the monarchy, and added with his usual nonchalance: "I do not see any reason why I should not return, if the country somehow finds peace."[25] The second edition was published, as we have said, in Amsterdam in the same year. It appeared without the contested caption, but with a preface which emphasized that, insofar as obedience was concerned, aristocracy and democracy were on a par with monarchy. In a few years, when the English Civil War had ended with the tyrannicide (1649), that is, with the act which *De Cive* seemed intended to execrate, Hobbes wrote the third

23. *OL*, I, p. XLIX. *"Bellum civile per Angliam geretur, ita ut res, tum permistae, permisceri ab illo libro non potuerint."* [Translation mine—Trans.]

24. *Consideration on Reputation, EW,* IV, p. 415. (He addresses a contender who impersonated someone in the rebel party.)

25. F. Tönnies, *Thomas Hobbes: Leben und Lehre* (Stuttgart: F. Frommann, 1925), p. 30. [Translation mine—Trans.]

of his political works. His specific aim was not to cut off all chances of going back to his country, where he returned after ten years of absence. By then he had fallen out of grace with the Court, and at the beginning of 1652 he went back to England as a faithful subject of Oliver Cromwell.

Among Hobbes's political works *De Cive* is the most organic and homogeneous. The first thirteen chapters of the first part of *Elements* contain a short treatise on human nature. *Leviathan*, besides the opening treatise on human nature (the first twelve chapters of the first part), contains a fourth part devoted to biblical and philosophical criticism. *De Cive* is divided into three parts, in which Hobbes does not inquire into any matter other than the state, seen in its origin, structure, and relation with the Church. This small work is certainly at an advantage for having been conceived as an integral part of a philosophical system. In comparison with the other two, it is much more systematic, and therefore also more concise and at times clearer.

Leviathan is by far a richer and more vigorous work. But compared to it, *De Cive* acquires in precision and rigor what it loses in complexity. *Leviathan* better reveals Hobbes's greatness and personal ingenuity. *De Cive* shows the acumen of his intelligence, his passion for exactness, and his subtly logical mind. *De Cive* succeeds, in the end, in being sharper and more persuasive, because its various parts are symmetrical and measured, and because its arguments are concise and rapid. *De Cive* is truly a triumph of exact argumentation, of close reasoning, and of *l'esprit de géométrie*. In the author's intention, *De Cive*, as a part of a philosophical system, was addressed to the learned of all nations; while *Leviathan* was addressed to Hobbes's fellow countrymen. Both books reveal rather clearly the signs of these different intentions. As *De Cive* is more controlled and well-ordered than *Leviathan*, so *Leviathan* is richer in historical references and experiences. In the works of a writer who assigned great importance to method, to the point of believing that he had founded a new science, *De Cive* remains an unsurpassed model of methodological wisdom. For this reason, it has maintained until today its irreplaceable position in the history of political doctrines. This is so even if we compare it with Hobbes's subsequent work, which reshapes the same matter with greater freedom and richness.

Hobbes's contemporaries often preferred this small, concise volume to his fundamental work. Pufendorf, with his treatises on natural law which spread throughout Europe, became the first and greatest herald of Hobbes's work. In his first work, written a few years after the publication of *Leviathan*, in mentioning the debt of gratitude which tied him to Hobbes, Pufendorf already cited Hobbes's minor work rather than his major one. "We declare that we owe much to Thomas Hobbes, whose thesis in the book *De Cive*, while it may taste somewhat of the profane, nonetheless contains matter which is acute and sound."[26] In his great treatise on natural law, nearly all Pufendorf's very frequent quotations from Hobbes refer to *De Cive*, in which Hobbes's greater methodological accuracy bestows a more precise paradigmatic value to its theses. When Hobbes himself, with his characteristic confidence bordering on arrogance, presented the achievements which formed the basis of his claim to glory, he considered the most important of these his having been the founder of political science; and he was understandably pleased to the highest degree with *De Cive*. Here his systematic efforts had been much more successful. In his *Vita carmine expresso* he could thus write rather emphatically that *De Cive* "pleased the learned and was entirely new; it was translated into several languages, and was read with praise, so that my reputation grew extensively."[27]

Although this peculiar and very famous work has been very important both in the evolution of Hobbes's thought and in the history of political thought, it was not so widely known in Italy. Mario Vinciguerra's complete translation of *Leviathan* for the publisher Laterza in Bari (1911–12) met with great success. It attracted the attention not only of scholars, but also of educated readers, students, and politicians to Hobbes's more pop-

---

26. Preface to *Elementorum Iurisprudentiae Universalis Libri Duo* (Aia, 1660). "Nec parum debere nos profitemur Thomae Hobbes, cuius hypothesis in libro *De Cive*, etsi quid profani sapiat, tamen caetera satis arguta et sana." [Translation mine—Trans.]

27. *OL*, I, p. XC.

ular, and, given its famous title, more sensational work. But P. D'Abbiero's diligent and faithful, albeit incomplete translation of *De Cive*, produced in 1935 for the publisher Carabba in Lanciano, was nearly ignored. I tried to compensate for this unjustified neglect with my first edition of *De Cive*, published in 1948. This offered for the first time to the Italian public a complete translation, which had been made from the Latin text and checked against the English version,[28] and was accompanied by an apparatus of interpretative and historical notes. It is true that in the meantime a new translation of *Leviathan* was published.[29] But the fact that after about ten years this translation of *De Cive* is being reprinted makes me think that the enterprise was not useless. Even this less famous work, which is, however, as worthy of attention as *Leviathan*, must have found in Italy a few more than the usual twenty-five readers.[30]

Appendix: Introduction to *A Dialogue between a Philosopher and a Student of the Common Law of England.*

Hobbes's minor work *A Dialogue between a Philosopher and a Student of the Common Law of England* was as unfamiliar to Hobbes's contemporaries and to posterity as *De Cive* was familiar to them.[31] I have added this work to this second edition of *De Cive*

28. For both I followed the already cited edition by Molesworth, see notes 21 and 22 above.

29. *Il Leviatano*, translated and edited by R. Giammanco, 2 vols. (Turin: Utet, 1955). A third translation was published in 1976, edited by G. Micheli, for La Nuova Italia. The same publishing house published the first translation of *Elements* in 1968, edited by A. Pacchi. Editori Riuniti published in 1979 a new translation of *De Cive* edited by T. Magri.

30. A line taken from Manzoni's Introduction to *The Betrothed*.—TRANS.

31. It was known, as a matter of fact, by the great jurist Sir Matthew Hale (1609–76) even before it was published. He wrote on it some important considerations, which however remained in manuscript and were only published by

to provide a more complete image of Hobbes's political and juridical thought. Hobbes wrote this dialogue in his old age (about 1666, when he was seventy-eight years old) and left it unfinished. It was published in 1681,[32] and since that time, for all I know, it has not seen the light again but twice. The first time was in the 1750 edition of Hobbes's moral and political works; the second, in the often-cited edition by Molesworth.[33] And it has not yet found any translator so foolhardy as to engage in the risky and thankless effort of transferring into an-

---

W. S. Holdsworth in the Appendix to vol. V of the *History of English Law*, London: Methuen & Co., 1904, pp. 500–513, with the title *Reflections by the Lord Chief Justice Hale on Mr. Hobbes His Dialogue of the Law*.

32. Together with the *Art of Rhetoric*, in the volume *The Art of Rhetoric*, with *A Discourse of the Laws of England*, by Thomas Hobbes of Malmesbury, London, printed for William Crooke at the Green Dragon without Temple Bar, 1681. In a brief preface to the reader, the publisher presents it with these words: "The other piece is a discourse concerning the laws of England, and has been finished many years. Herein he has endeavoured to accommodate the general notions of his politics to the particular constitution of the English monarchy: a design of no small difficulty, wherein to have succeeded deserves much honour; to have perchance miscarried, deserves easy pardon. It has had the good fortune to be much esteemed by the greatest men of the profession of the law, and therefore may be presumed to contain somewhat excellent. However it is not to be expected that all men should submit to his opinions, yet it is hoped none will be offended at the present publishing of these papers; since they will not find here any new fantastic notions, but only such things as have been already asserted with strength of argument by himself and other persons of eminent learning. To the public at least this benefit may accrue, that some able pen may undertake the controversy, being moved with the desire of that reputation which will necessarily attend victory over so considerable an adversary" (*EW*, VI, p. 422). Although the editor says that the dialogue had been finished many years before, the work is certainly unfinished. It ends suddenly and without a conclusion. Moreover, if Hobbes's plan was originally to write a critical comment to the four volumes of Coke's *Institutions*, the dialogue, as it has been handed down to us, mostly refers to volumes II and III. Only in the last pages does Hobbes begin to comment on volume I which is also, given its theme (the rights of property), the longest and most complex. Right at the beginning of this last part, Hobbes says: "Then let us consider next the commentaries of Sir Edward Coke upon Magna Charta and other statutes" (p. 545). But the dialogue stops after a few pages, and the announced comments never appear.

33: *EW*, VI, pp. 3–161.

other language Hobbes's discourse, which bristles with the terms of English juridical language.

Sir James Fitzjames Stephen, who shared Hobbes's severe judgment of Coke, praised the work, and spoke of this nearly forgotten work as "the most powerful speculation on the subject to which it refers before the days of Bentham and Austin."[34] Nonetheless, even the most recent historiography on Hobbes, which has been growing increasingly broad and deep, has not taken it into account. But there are signs that more fortunate days may be approaching. (Times ripen even for historical criticism.) After such long silence, two Italian scholars have in these last years devoted their attention to it.[35] And by a curious coincidence, while I was finishing the present edition, a well-informed and documented study, the first to my knowledge, has appeared precisely on this dialogue, and on Hobbes's relations with the English Common Law.[36]

The idea of the *Dialogue between a Philosopher and a Student of the Common Law of England* arose in Hobbes's mind from his wish to write an *apologia pro se,* as apparent from the first lines ("Which was enough, for me, that meant not to plead for any but myself").[37] The plague which broke out in the winter of 1664–65, and above all the subsequent fire of the days 2–6 Sep-

34. *A History of the Criminal Law of England* (London: Macmillan, 1883), II, p. 106, note 4. Regarding Coke, Stephen writes: "A more disorderly mind than Coke's and one less gifted with the power of analyzing common words it would be impossible to find" (ibid., note 1). Of the same author, see also *Horae Sabbaticae,* second series (London: Macmillan, 1892), especially chap. III, "Hobbes's Minor Works," p. 46, where he says: "The *Dialogue of the Common Laws* is probably the first attempt ever made in English to criticize the law of the land in anything like a philosophical spirit."

35. T. Ascarelli, "Interpretazione del diritto e studio del diritto comparato" (1954), in *Saggi di diritto commerciale* (Milano, Giuffrè, 1955), p. 489; and B. Leoni, in a series of lectures given in the summer of 1958 at Claremont College, especially in the fourth lecture, now in the volume B. Leoni, *Freedom and Law* (New York: D. van Nostrand, 1961), pp. 92ff. The *Dialogue* was published in the original in T. Ascarelli, *Th. Hobbes e G. W. Leibniz,* with a comment by G. Bernini (Milan: Giuffre, 1960), pp. 73–195.

36. E. Campbell, "Thomas Hobbes and the Common Law," *Tasmanian University Law Review* (1958): 20–45.

37. *EW,* VI, p. 3.

tember 1666, which had destroyed two thirds of the capital, and the bad direction taken by the war with Holland, had rekindled rancors which were dormant, but not yet extinguished. People increasingly lent their ears to those who, looking for scapegoats, accused Presbyterians, atheists, and Catholics, in turn, of being the causes of so many calamities. A few days after the fire, on 21 September, a few members of Parliament, aiming to express their indignation, and at the same time to silence the rumors against those presumed to be responsible for it, presented a bill of law against atheism. The *Journal of the Commons* of 17 October gave news of the order that "the committee entrusted with the bill against atheism and profanation, is authorized to gather information regarding books which incline toward atheism, cursing, and profanation, or are contrary to the essence and attributes of God, in particular the book published in the name of a White,[38] and the book of Mr. Hobbes called *Leviathan,* and to convey their opinion to the House." Fortunately the charge did not go very far, for the bill, approved by the House of Commons, was dropped by the House of Lords. But Hobbes, under the threat of being accused of heresy, had begun, despite his old age, to study the history of the crime of heresy in English law, so as to be ready to defend himself. He immediately wrote a short essay, entitled *An Historical Narration Concerning Heresy and Punishment thereof,*[39] which ended with the statement that the crime of heresy had been extinct for a long time in English law, despite the relentless attacks of bishops and Presbyterians against *Leviathan.*

But what did the great jurists think of the issue? Sir Edward Coke's fame must have been formidable, for he was the defender and restorer of the English common law. His four great volumes of the *Institutes* had been published between 1628 and 1641 and reprinted several times. They were the encyclopedic *summa* of all juridical matters, extending from private law to

38. This Thomas White was a Catholic priest, friend, and admirer of Hobbes. The incriminated work was the book *Of the Middle State of Souls* (English ed. 1659, Latin ed. 1682), which called into question the immortality of the soul.

39. *EW,* IV, pp. 385–408.

public law, and from criminal law to procedural law. The *Institutes* were undoubtedly the major juridical work of the century, and are still considered milestones in the history of the formation of the common law. It was natural for Hobbes to resort to them, in order to be well-armed for his role. Besides, he knew them and had already had opportunities to consult them.[40] He must have been annoyed by the fact that Coke, in the third volume of his *Institutes,* had put the crime of heresy before that of high treason (p. 527). Hobbes was very dissatisfied with this. Coke was a great expert on legal texts. But in a field such as heresy, which required historical and theological knowledge, Coke was a fish out of water. He could not even say what heresy consisted of (p. 495), whereas when he dealt with other crimes, he began immediately with a definition. Neither had he realized that the last condemnations of guilt for heresy, which had been executed in the reigns of Elisabeth and James I, were illegal. On the contrary, he had justified them, with subtle, but hairsplitting arguments, mistaking historical narratives and precedents for laws (p. 508).

Hobbes's disagreement with Coke did not merely concern this or that solution. It was rather a disagreement founded on principles. Hobbes was the most rigorous theorist of the position wherein all law is reduced to the command of the sovereign. Coke was the restorer of the common law against the claims of James I. He had been exempted by the King from his high function as a magistrate for having ignored the royal prerogative, and for having been the instigator of the claims of Parliament in the first phase of the struggle. Coke was an adversary with whom Hobbes had wanted to contend for a long time. Coke's erroneous and annoying opinions on heresy were very likely a pretext for beginning the battle, which had always been put off, but never forgotten.

We have no reason to doubt that Hobbes was induced to go deeper in his study of law by his reading of Bacon's work, *Elements of the Common Law of England* (published in 1630).

40. See three quotations of Coke's work in *Leviathan*, XVIII, p. 119, XXX, pp. 222 and 229.

Hobbes's friend and first biographer Sir John Aubrey, who had given him the book as a gift in 1664, tells us so himself.[41] This episode is accepted by subsequent biographers. But we cannot assign too much weight to it, for there is no trace left of Bacon's influence in Hobbes's *Dialogue,* although the best-known works of English law are cited in it.

The *Dialogue* is a continuous and pressing discussion with Sir Edward Coke. Hobbes denies him, at times with harsh words, the skills of a good reasoner, of a good grammarian, and even of an intelligent jurist. In this work, Hobbes takes the opportunity to reassert the theses dearest to him, regarding sovereignty, the nature of the law, of justice and equity, the supremacy of the written law over the common law, of the King over Parliament, and of the commands of the King over the decisions of the judges. Hobbes exalts the monarchical form of government, ridicules old and new demagogues, and, above all, presents his own interpretation of the common law. He identifies the latter with natural reason, that is, with equity, and reasserts that its only authorized interpreter is not the judge, but the sovereign. Hobbes thus does not leave any other positive law, as the common law was considered by jurists, side by side with the written law. (And I think that this is the core of his reasoning.) Only the law of nature survives, but this acquires legal validity only through the will of the sovereign. The historical value of the dialogue lies in the fact that Hobbes adopts this position. This position springs from the confrontation with a consolidated legal doctrine which would remain the dominant doctrine of English jurists, despite Hobbes's criticism. Hobbes's dialogue is thus the last testimony of a line of thought which he had consistently pursued throughout the three decades which are among the most decisive in the civil and intellectual history of England.

If someone were to ask me what prompted me to engage in this new effort, I could only answer by repeating, with even

---

41. J. Aubrey, *Brief Lives,* ed. Andrew Clark (Oxford: Clarendon Press, 1898), I, p. 341.

greater justification, what I wrote at the end of the introduction to the first Italian edition. There I remarked that I never forgot that when Gassendi wrote to Sorbière urging him to publish products of Hobbes's genius other than *De Cive*, he said: "Heaven grant that you succeed in extracting from him other things which he has written, and that by bringing these to the light, you may thus cause the happiness of the entire nation of philosophers." I fully shared Gassendi's opinion, and the penetrating judgment of Hobbes which he expressed when he wrote: "I know of no one who in philosophizing is more free of prejudice, and who has inquired more deeply into things."[42]

42. *OL*, I, p. XXXIV. [Translation mine—Trans.]

four

Natural Law and Civil Law in the Political Philosophy of Hobbes

1.   Thomas Hobbes belongs, de facto, to the history of the natural law tradition. There is no text on the history of legal and political thought which does not mention and analyze his philosophy, as one of the typical expressions of natural law theory. On the other hand, Hobbes belongs, de jure, to the history of legal positivism. His conception of the law and the state is indeed a surprising anticipation of nineteenth-century positivist theories. In these we find expressed most radically the anti–natural law tendencies of Romantic historicism. When people speak of Austin, they usually recollect that he had an (isolated) precursor in Hobbes. Natural law theory and legal positivism are two antithetical currents, which constantly polemicize with one other. One represents the negation of the other. How can Hobbes belong to both at the same time? Historians of natural law theory consider the author of *Leviathan* as one of the four great natural law theorists of the seventeenth century, together with Grotius, Spinoza, and Pufendorf. If the historians are right, how can the founders of legal positivism, whose success has lasted without interruption for nearly a century, and who were fervent adversaries of natural law theory, consider Hobbes's theory as their historical model? And if the legal positivists are right, has the time not come for us to revise the traditional histories of natural law theory, and delete the name of Thomas Hobbes from them?

It is well known that the history of modern natural law theory requires a profound revision. A good example is offered by the laborious exegesis which has been performed in recent years on Grotius, on the one hand, and on the natural law theory of the Catholic Counter-Reformation, on the other. Scholars have emphasized Grotius's ties with the medieval tradition, and the influence of the Catholic Counter-Reformation on subsequent natural law theorists. This revision has blurred the image of Grotius as an innovator and a precursor, which had been established by his followers Pufendorf and Thomasius, and which since then has been mechanically and faithfully repeated and obstinately reproduced. But the problem of Hobbesian exegesis may not be at all a problem of historical criticism. Hobbes does belong to the natural law tradition, and he does initiate the school of legal positivism. The Hobbesian paradox is genuine—if we can still use a term, "paradox," which historians have partially worn out. To understand this paradox, we must patiently enter into Hobbes's vast and apparently air-tight system through detailed analyses. We must carefully observe its most delicate joints, test its buttresses, and uncover the reasons why it has taken the shape which it has. In my opinion, one of the fundamental problems which allow us to touch the most sensitive points of Hobbes's clever and systematic mechanism, is the problem of *the relationship between natural law and civil law*. First, this problem is fundamental for any natural law theory. Second, as we shall see, in Hobbes it acquires so many facets that we may consider it as one of the most vexed questions in all of Hobbes's juridical and political work.

2.   We can briefly formulate the question of the relationship between natural law and civil law as follows. Hobbes developed one of the most typical and rigorous conceptions of legal justice which has ever been held. By legal justice is meant that conception which maintains that justice consists in compliance

with one's obligations, whatever the content of the obligation may be. If we consider a particular kind of obligation (those of the citizen toward the state), justice consists in obeying the law, whatever the content of the law may be. Hobbes presents this conception in well-known passages, when he states that we can only be unjust toward the person with whom we have stipulated a compact or to whom we have made a promise. Justice thus means to comply with, and injustice not to comply with, the terms of a compact or a promise.[1] It follows from this definition that we cannot speak of just or unjust actions[2] in the state of nature, where human beings are not bound by any compact. But once civil society has been instituted, through the intersubjective covenant of union, a just action is one which conforms to the law, while an unjust action is one which does not conform to the law. The law, in its turn, derives from the will of the sovereign, on the basis of the conditions established by the social contract. This is, as anyone can see, a clear formulation of the legalistic conception of justice, which is a feature of a conception which looks at justice from a merely formal point of view.

The essential characteristic of a legalistic conception of justice is to consider the law as the only and insuperable criterion of just and unjust, for it is the command of the only person who has the legitimate power to command. What is commanded is just, merely because it is commanded by the person who has the power to command. What is prohibited is unjust, merely because it is prohibited. It is clear that the legalistic conception of justice provides the ideological framework for legal positivism. Legal positivism is the juridical conception which considers positive law as the self-sufficient criterion of what is just and what is unjust. Such a conception eliminates any reference to natural law, taken as the set of principles or norms of conduct which should allow us to approve or disapprove of positive law. And yet here lies the interpretative problem regarding Hobbes's theory, for his entire legal system rests on his

1. *De Cive*, III, 4, pp. 31–32.
2. But only of useful or harmful actions.

acknowledgment that there exist laws of nature, to which he devotes, as is well known, a specific and exhaustive analysis in his political books.[3] The question thus arises: how can a system which begins by accepting laws of nature be a typical expression of a formal conception of justice?

We face the same difficulty if we ask the question in another way. The aim and outcome of Hobbes's system is the theory of the absolute state, that is, of a state endowed with a power which is as free from constraints and limits as humanly possible. One of the salient features of Hobbes's inquiry is his systematic hunting down of everything that can constitute a constraint or a limit to the power of the state. Hobbes engages in this hunt with skill, rigor, and rational passion. At its end, Hobbes has succeeded in giving us a conception of the state which has driven the process of monopolization of the law by the state to its extreme consequences. Hobbes has eliminated all sources of norms (especially the common law) other than the law, that is, the will of the sovereign; and all legal orders other than that of the state (in particular those of the Church, of the international community, and of minor associations). However, we cannot say that the state has a complete monopoly of the law if we let the law of nature survive side by side with positive law, and side by side with the various forms which positive law may assume. In other words, we cannot say that the power of the state is absolute, that is, without constraints, if we recognize the existence and legitimacy of the laws of nature. For these are indeed, by their inner constitution superior to positive laws, which must conform to natural laws. And yet Hobbes, as remarked above, placed his state on the traditional pedestal of natural law. Furthermore, whenever he had a chance, he set natural law side by side with positive law. He constantly refers to it, and mentions it in countless passages, besides analyzing it specifically in the chapters cited in note 3. A question analogous to the previous one thus arises: how can the power of the state be absolute if the will of the sovereign must measure itself against natural law? Why should

3. *Elements*, XV, XVI, XVII, XVIII; *De Cive*, II, III, IV; *Leviathan*, XIV, XV.

Hobbes eliminate every source of norms other than the state, if he then lets natural law survive, which is the most dangerous adversary of every positive law? We can finally present this fundamental antinomy of Hobbes's thought in the following terms: Hobbes's inquiry begins with natural law. Therefore natural law theorists rightly consider him one of their own. But Hobbes ends with the solid construction of a positivistic conception of the state. Therefore legal theorists rightly appropriate him. There is an apparent contrast between Hobbes's starting point and his point of arrival. Hobbes's theory is known above all for the strength of its construction, and the rigor of its logic. Along what path does Hobbes develop his analysis, so that he can move from a premise, which is certain, to a conclusion, which is as certain, but which contradicts the premise? This essay aims at analyzing all of the road which Hobbes followed, and answering this question, which we consider crucial to our historical understanding of Hobbes's legal philosophy.

3. Hobbes offers a definition of the law of nature which does not formally differ from traditional definitions. For Hobbes the law of nature is a dictate of right reason.[4] As such, the law of nature is different from positive law because the latter is produced by the will. What distinguishes Hobbes's definition from the definitions offered by other natural law theorists is the different meaning which *reason* has for him. For Hobbes reason is a calculation through which we draw consequences from names on which we have agreed in order to express and denote our thoughts. Reason has only a formal, not a substantive value. It does not reveal essences to us, but it enables us to draw certain consequences from certain principles. Reason is not the faculty through which we learn the evident truth of first principles, but the faculty of reasoning. It has been said, even recently, that Hobbes's reason does not have any ontological meaning, but only a methodological one.[5] Reasoning does not

4. *De Cive*, II, I, p. 16; see also *Elements*, I, xv, 1, pp. 57–58; *Leviathan*, XIV, p. 84.
5. R. Polin, *Politique et philosphie chez Th. Hobbes* (Paris: Puf, 1952), p. xii.

consist of learning evident principles, but is rather a method for thinking. Hobbes's concept of reason is not metaphysical, but instrumental. He himself adds this remark to the definition of natural law quoted above: "By right reason in the natural state of men, *I understand not, as many do, an infallible faculty,* but the act of reasoning, that is, the peculiar and true ratiocinations of every man concerning those actions of his, which may either redound to the damage or benefit of his neighbours."[6]

A fundamental difference between Hobbes's conception and traditional conceptions of natural law ensues from this different meaning of reason. For other natural law theorists, *naturalis ratio* [natural reason] or *recta ratio* [right reason] prescribes what is good or evil in itself. For Hobbes, on the contrary, reason indicates what is good or bad in relation to a given end: "But those which we call laws of nature . . . are nothing else but certain conclusions, understood by reason, of things to be done or omitted."[7] And even more clearly: "For they are but conclusions, or *theorems* concerning what conduceth to the conservation and defence of themselves."[8] Besides, there cannot be principles true in themselves in a nominalistic philosophy such as Hobbes's, according to which "true and false are attributes of speech, not of things. And where speech is not, there is neither *truth* nor *falsehood.*"[9]

Since, according to Hobbes, the law of nature indicates what is good or evil in relation to a given end, the fundamental problem in understanding the law of nature has shifted to locating and understanding what that end is. Here the gap broadens between the Hobbesian conception and the traditional one. From Hobbes's utilitarian point of view, the supreme end of human beings is peace. For other natural law theorists, the supreme end is the (moral) good. Therefore, for traditional natural law theorists natural law prescribes what is good, and prohibits what is evil, independently of the utility or harm which we can derive from complying with the law. This is why

6. *De Cive,* II, 1, p. 16. Italics mine.
7. Ibid., II, 33, p. 16.
8. *Leviathan,* XV, p. 104. Italics mine.
9. Ibid., IV, p. 21.

we can speak of something which is good or evil in itself. For Hobbes, the law of nature indicates what is convenient or inconvenient to the attainment of the end, which is peace, and which represents the supreme utility. Therefore the fundamental law of nature prescribes *seeking peace.* All other laws of nature derive from this fundamental law, considered to be the first principle of practical reason. Hobbes calls them "derived," in order to show that his system is deductive, in conformity with the canons of the nonmetaphysical rationalism which is the fruit of his acquaintance with the mathematical sciences. He reproaches his predecessors for "they could not observe *the goodness of actions to consist in this, that it was in order to peace, and the evil in this, that it related to discord,* they built a moral philosophy wholly estranged from the moral law, and unconstant to itself."[10] Let us keep in mind that even the knowledge of the ultimate end, peace, is not an immediate perception, which we might draw from a *naturalis ratio,* capable of apprehending self-evident truths. Even that knowledge is, in conformity with Hobbesian epistemology, drawn from a reasoning which procedes from principles to consequences. According to Hobbes, we know that peace is man's end because it is the conclusion of our positive study of human nature. This study shows that man, who is dominated by the instinct of self-preservation, considers *life* as the supreme value.

This is not the place to discuss whether Hobbes was right or wrong in considering life as the supreme value. (Besides, such a discussion would be inconclusive, if conducted in these terms.) What matters is to emphasize that Hobbes frames the problem of natural law in a way which is methodologically correct. (Natural law is for him, as for other natural law theorists, identical with the moral law.) Natural laws, or moral laws, coincide with the set of prescriptions deriving from the good which is considered to be the supreme good. This is the good to which all others are subordinate, as means to the end. We are aware today that every moral system is a system of norms

10. *De Cive,* III, 32, pp. 48–49. Italics mine.

which prescribe actions for the attainment of the end considered supreme by human beings. And we have realized that
moral systems differ in that each of them poses a different end
as the supreme end. In the sentence quoted, Hobbes declares
"the goodness of actions *to consist in this, that it was in order to
peace, and the evil in this, that it related to discord."* We can reproach him for having considered peace as the ultimate end.
But we cannot avoid admiring the clarity with which he posed
the problem of the law of nature, which had tormented natural
law theorists. For Hobbes, the crucial problem is not so much
the unsolvable (because badly formulated) problem of discovering what is good and evil in itself. It is rather the solvable
problem (although solvable in different ways) of establishing
what conduct human beings ought to adopt, once an end has
been given and accepted as the supreme end.

4.   Let us keep in mind these two points: (1) Natural laws do
not prescribe actions that are good in themselves, but rather
actions that are good in relation to a given end. (2) This end is
peace (or the preservation of life). Both these assertions help us
to understand how Hobbes, by modifying the traditional notion of law of nature, could reach a positivistic conclusion,
even though he started from a premise derived from natural
law theory. Having posited peace as the end,[11] Hobbes derives
from this the first law of nature, which prescribes that *"The
right of all men to all things ought not to be retained; but that some
certain rights ought to be transferred or relinquished".*[12] But by giving up their right to all things, and by transferring this right to

11. Hobbes considers peace to be prescribed by the fundamental law of nature.
12. This is the formulation offered in *De Cive*, II, 3, which is, in my opinion,
the most authentic. In *Leviathan*, we can read the following formulation: *"That a
man be willing, when others are so too, as far-forth, as for peace, and defence of himself
he shall think it necessary, to lay down his right to all things; and be contented with so
much liberty against other men, as he would allow other men against himself"* (XIV,
p. 85). In *De Cive* there is also a more precise distinction between fundamental
and derived laws of nature. This distinction disappears from *Leviathan*, and the
law quoted above is presented as the second law of nature.

others, human beings leave the state of nature and institute civil society. The first law of nature thus prescribes the institution of the state. This means that the state is the most effective means for attaining peace (and realizing the supreme value of preserving life). But if the state is the most effective means for attaining peace, this means that human beings can realize the end posed by the first law of nature by instituting the state, which is the agency in charge of issuing positive laws. The state is thus founded on the law of nature itself. The issuing of positive laws is the reason why the state arises; but positive laws draw their justification from the law of nature. In other words: the law of nature states that human beings must let positive laws govern them, if humankind are to attain the end prescribed by the law of nature. This is a declaration of impotence on the part of the law of nature. So much so that, leaving aside any other consideration, the law of nature only obliges *in foro interno* [in the domain of conscience]. That is, it does not oblige at all, given Hobbes's utilitarian conception. And this declaration is, at the same time, an abdication, which recognizes the strength of positive laws.

We can express what has just been said in a more radical form. The law of nature is the dictate of reason which suggests to human beings that they obey only positive laws if they want to attain peace. This first approach to Hobbes's system leaves us with the impression that the law of nature has no function other than to provide a justification for the birth of the state, and therefore of positive laws. It is as if the law of nature had appeared, only to disappear a moment later. Its function would thus not be to establish a code of behavior for human beings, which is valid without and above positive laws. (This is the traditional interpretation of the function of natural law.) The only function of the law of nature would be to provide a rational foundation to the system of positive law, that is, to the state. One is tempted to say that Tarantino is right, when he remarks that the laws of nature contained in Hobbes's system are destined never to be in force. This is so both in the state of nature, because *inter arma silent leges* [when arms speak, the laws are silent]; and in civil society, where positive laws replace the laws of nature, as constraints imposed on the behavior of citizens.[13]

Hobbes has thus relied on the law of nature only as a device, which is all the more effective because of its long-standing and authoritative use in the tradition of political thought. Hobbes employs it to provide an acceptable foundation for the absolute power of the sovereign, and thus to ensure the undisputed supremacy of positive law. But since Hobbes uses it merely as a device, he has emptied it of content and deprived it of prestige. It is worth remarking, albeit in passing, that one of Hobbes's most astute tactics is to use his adversaries' categories in order to demonstrate a thesis contrary to theirs. And this tactic is one of the most brilliant and attractive features of his vocation as a controversialist. We have only to think of the theory of the social contract, which was the principal argument of democratic writers. Hobbes successfully transforms it into the main pillar of an absolute system. In similar fashion, the interpretation of the law of nature which I offered in the first part of this essay suggests that Hobbes used it with the specific intent of appropriating one of the most formidable arguments which his adversaries had at their disposal for limiting the power of the state.

Supporters of a limited state relied mainly on two arguments: the state has a contractual foundation, and the law of nature has primacy over positive law. Hobbes rejects neither the contract or the law of nature. He does not take the easy path of simply denying one way and taking another as defenders of monarchy, such as Filmer, did at the time. Hobbes takes the more difficult path, which is however much more seductive, that of using the same ingredients as his adversaries but combining them so as to obtain the opposite result. He tries to show that the law of nature is not the foundation of the right of resistance, as liberals, radicals, and anarchists contended, but that it is the foundation of absolute and unconditioned obedience. If he succeeds, he will have helped the cause of absolut-

13. G. Tarantino, *Saggio sulle idee morali e politiche di T. Hobbes* (Naples: Giannini, 1900), p. 116.

ism much more skillfully and effectively than those who, in attempting to attain the same end, exhume old doctrines and ancient texts which have lost all their power of insight and persuasion. Do his adversaries contend that the sovereign power is revocable by definition, because it is founded upon a contract? Like a skillful lawyer, Hobbes manipulates the terms of the question in such a way as to show that the compact through which citizens institute the sovereign power cannot be revoked by the citizens themselves, without the consent of the sovereign. Do his adversaries contend that the law of nature, by being above positive law, legitimates the citizens' right of resistance to oppression? Hobbes is so successful in turning the tables that he is able to show that absolute and unconditional obedience is the first and fundamental dictate of the law of nature itself.

5.   But this is not the only function which natural law plays in Hobbes's doctrine. Several other laws follow the one which prescribes that human beings give up the absolute rights that they enjoy in the state of nature. These other laws have in common the feature of prescribing behavior that is necessary to maintaining or restoring peace. Of all these laws only the second, which prescribes the "keeping of promises" and is therefore a corollary of the first, refers, like the first, to the institution of civil society. The others prescribe types of behavior which are approvable in themselves, independently of the institution of civil society. If we wish to classify them, we can divide them into two groups. The first group comprises the laws that prescribe virtues indispensable to peace. Using the numbering found in *De Cive*, these are gratitude (3d), sociability (4th), mercy (5th), moderation (9th), and impartiality (10th). This group includes the laws that condemn vices caused by discord or war: revenge (6th), lack of generosity (7th), and arrogance (8th). We might call all of these *substantive* laws. The second group comprises the laws that prescribe actions and attitudes necessary for restoring peace when it has been violated. We might call these *procedural* laws. As such they regard

mediators of peace (14th), arbiters (15th, 16th, 17th, and 19th), and witnesses (18th). (The laws 11, 12, and 13 can be considered corollaries of the tenth which prescribes impartiality.)[14]

However a problem arises. Are these laws, which prescribe types of behavior independently of the institution of civil society, also valid outside civil society? If the answer were yes, it would undermine the rigid positivistic construction presented above. Those who consider Hobbes a natural law theorist would thus be right. Let us now try to deal with this new difficulty.[15]

There is, first of all, a general characteristic of the laws of nature which weakens their strength; they only oblige in conscience.[16] It is true that this characteristic is not specific to Hobbes's doctrine, but is shared by all natural law theories, even those which preserve the primacy of the laws of nature. But this characteristic acquires particular value in Hobbes, because of the utilitarian foundation of his moral doctrine. It greatly modifies, and even dissolves the usual meaning of limiting obligation to one's conscience. For natural law theories which have an ethical and religious origin, natural law expresses absolute moral values. Obligation in conscience is an unconditioned obligation. It is, as such, stronger than external obligation, which is proper to positive laws. The latter only oblige to a behavior conforming to the prescribed conduct, without requiring perfect correspondence between internal attitude and external behavior. But if the command of the law of nature refers to a divine order of the world, the sanction, although not immediate, is such that no one can escape it. The sanction of a divine law depends on an infallible justice; whereas it is possible to elude the sanction of civil power, which accompanies the violation of merely external obligations. Indeed, it can be shown that for traditional natural law

14. Polin has recently presented a differente classification, *Politique et philosophie*, pp. 200–201.

15. This difficulty has been remarked by G. Bianca, *Diritto e stato nel pensiero di T. Hobbes* (Naples, Casa editrice libraria Humus, 1946), chap. III, pp. 73–103.

16. *Elements*, I, 17, 10, pp. 71–72; *De Cive*, III, pp. 45–46; *Leviathan*, XV, p. 103.

theorists obligation *in foro interno* is stronger than obligation *in foro externo*. They hold as shared opinion that positive laws[17] also oblige in conscience. In other words, they think that obligation in conscience, which is linked to the unavoidable sanctions of an infallible judge, helps to reinforce external obligation, which can only be imposed by the avoidable and fallible civil power.

Hobbes, on the contrary, turns the relationship between internal and external obligation upside down. The obligations which are for Hobbes unconditioned are those that the citizen assumes toward civil power. His position on this point is known. Once the sovereign power has been instituted, the citizen owes absolute obedience to the state. That is, he owes obedience to the command of the sovereign, merely because it is a command, independently of any judgment on the content of the command. The most significant passage in this respect is section 23 of chapter XIV of *De Cive*, in which Hobbes refutes the theory of passive obedience. This was widely supported by absolutist doctrines, like his own, which however gave a divine foundation to kingly power.[18] Hobbes holds on the contrary that the citizen owes active obedience to the state. And he supports this thesis, let us not forget, by asserting that positive law is not a hypothetical norm which would leave the citizen free to choose between following the precept and subjecting himself to the sanction. It is rather a categorical norm, which unconditionally prescribes that the citizen must comply with the precept.[19]

Hobbes thus wishes to show, on the one hand, that positive laws hold unconditionally. On the other hand, he does not want to leave any doubt regarding the opposite thesis, which maintains that laws of nature merely hold conditionally. That the laws of nature only hold in conscience means, for Hobbes,

17. At least most of them, with the exclusion of penal laws.

18. On passive obedience as a feature of the theory of the divine right of kings, see the well-known book by J. N. Figgis, *The Divine Right of Kings* (Cambridge: Cambridge University Press, 1922), pp. 208ff.

19. This passage from *De Cive* has no equivalent either in *Leviathan* or in *Elements*.

that they prompt us to *desire* their implementation. We move from the desire for implementation to implementation only when we are sure that we can implement the laws of nature without harming ourselves. This means that the laws of nature hold conditionally, that is, provided that their implementation is not harmful to us. The utilitarian principle of Hobbes's ethics thus plays a role in this respect too. The laws of nature do not prescribe actions good in themselves, and do not at all refer us to divine sanction, but are merely means to attain a specific, vital end (peace). It would therefore be contradictory if the person who complies with them should derive harm rather than utility. In other words, since the laws of nature are not absolute, but only relative to an end, the obligation deriving from them is not unconditioned, but conditioned to attaining that end. And when does man find himself best situated for acting in conformity to natural law without being harmed? When he is sure that others will do the same. "For he," explains Hobbes in a passage of *Leviathan*,[20] "that should be modest, and tractable, and perform all he promises, in such time, and place, where no man else should do so, should but make himself a prey to others, and procure his own certain ruin, contrary to the ground of all laws of nature, which tend to nature's preservation." But we can only attain this security in civil society, that is, in that situation wherein the actions of human beings are no longer imposed conditionally, but unconditionally. This means that I am obliged to perform the commands of the laws of nature only when these laws of nature have been transformed into civil laws. It is clear at this point that the laws which I obey from now on are no longer natural laws, but rather civil laws. Once again, the path that Hobbes assigns to the laws of nature ends with, and even plunges into, the state. Once the state has been built, the laws of nature no longer have any raison d'être.

6.   They no longer have any raison d'être as laws, that is as dictates that anticipate and regulate behavior. But one could object that they remain valid because of their content, that is,

20. *Leviathan*, XV, p. 103.

because of what they prescribe. Let us consider, for example, the law of nature which prescribes that arbiters or judges must be impartial. This obliges, it is true, only because it has been accepted by civil power, which alone has the right to issue laws and enforce them. But from where does civil power derive the dictate of impartiality if not from the law of nature? In other words: positive law provides the form, and natural law provides the content of the norm.

If we accept this objection, natural law is not at all deprived of authority, but rather preserves a function which is both relevant and irreplaceable. If we push this approach—that the laws of nature prescribe the types of behavior that positive laws make obligatory through the coercive apparatus of the state—to its extreme logical consequences, we should draw the conclusion that Hobbes's system does not differ at all from that of Locke. For Locke, individuals institute civil power mainly with the aim of guaranteeing the peaceful implementation of the laws of nature. The characteristic feature of Locke's state is that it is based on natural rights and duties, which precede the rise of the state. The state has as its main, if not exclusive task the implementation of this set of natural rights and duties, through the exercise of coercive power. But the liberal state is by definition the limited state. It is limited in that it presupposes the laws of nature, from which it derives the content of its legislative activity. How can we reconcile Hobbes's plan to give life to an absolute state[21] with this theory of the relationship between natural and positive law, which lays the premises for a theory limiting the powers of the state?

It is indeed dangerous for a thinker who inclines toward a rigorously positivistic doctrine to accept the laws of nature. Once he has done so, it is difficult for him to get rid of them. On this point, even Hobbes reveals some hesitations, which come close to endangering his whole system. That is, he appears overwhelmed by the logic of natural law theory, which is

21. As is well known, his political works are full of polemical attacks on the theorists of limited political power.

grounded on the dualistic assumption that there exist two orders of laws, one superior to the other. He writes in a passage from *De Cive:* "The exercise of the natural law is necessary for the preservation of peace, and . . . for the exercise of the natural law security is no less necessary."[22] The meaning of this passage is that the function of civil power is to ensure security, that is, to enforce the laws of nature. According to this, the laws of nature would thus provide positive laws with the content of norms. Positive laws would be formally and materially norms, while natural laws would be only materially norms [*ratione materiae*].

Positive laws should always be, so to speak, natural from the point of view of their content. We find the same statement in *Leviathan*, in a broader and therefore more problematic formulation. Hobbes goes so far as to say: "The law of nature, and the civil law, *contain each other, and are of equal extent.*" And more synthetically: "Civil, and natural law are not different kinds, but different parts of law; whereof one part being written is called civil the other unwritten, natural."[23] If we are not mistaken, we can assign only one meaning to these two sentences, which are far from being clear. By themselves, the laws of nature do not oblige to compliance; only positive laws oblige. If the laws of nature are to become obligatory, they must be imposed by a civil law. It therefore follows that it is the civil law which makes a natural law obligatory. In other words, the law is positive from a formal point of view, for it is issued by an authority legitimated to create binding legal norms. But the law is natural from a material point of view, since it draws the content of its rules from the precepts of the law of nature. Only on these grounds can one say, as does Hobbes, that natural law and civil law are coextensive, and parts of the same law. Civil law contains nothing more and nothing less than natural law does. And they are parts of the same law because positive law constitutes the form of the law, and natural law its content. It

22. *De Cive*, V, 3, p. 64.
23. *Leviathan*, III, p. 17. Italics mine.

thus appears that here Hobbes has completely inverted the relationship between natural and positive law in comparison with traditional natural law doctrine. This is indeed true. For a natural law theorist, positive law is binding only because it conforms to natural law; whereas for Hobbes natural law is binding only because it conforms to positive law.

7.   Despite these statements, I believe that we should proceed very cautiously in claiming that Hobbes has made more concessions to natural law than the frame of his system would have required. According to the excerpts quoted above, especially those from *Leviathan*, we should draw the conclusion that Hobbes has not expunged natural law from his system, since, by turning it into the content of positive law, he has assigned it an essential role. But according to other passages, and the spirit of his system, it is evident that positive law does not merely attribute legal validity, as we should say today, to the laws of nature, and that it does not remain at all extraneous to determining the content of norms. The laws of nature are generic. They do not precisely determine all forms of behavior and all procedures which civil authority needs if it is to establish and maintain civil peace. The laws of nature are empty formulas, which civil power alone can fill with specific content. In some passages from *De Cive* Hobbes gives us a sense of what the sovereign can do in order to manipulate the pliable laws of nature to his liking and advantage. He writes:

> Theft, murder, adultery, and all injuries, are forbid by the laws of nature; but what is to be called *theft*, what *murder*, what *adultery*, what *injury* in a citizen, this is not to be determined by the natural, but by the civil law. For not every taking away of the thing which another possesseth, but only another man's goods, is theft; but what is our's, and what another's, is a question belonging to the civil law. In like manner, not every killing of a man is murder, but only that which the civil law forbids; neither is all encounter with

woman adultery, but only that which the civil laws prohibit.[24]

It seems to me that here Hobbes's campaign against natural law reaches its highest intensity, or, if you like, its greatest wickedness. What is left of natural law after he has posited the problem of the relationship between natural and positive laws this way? Up to this point, it had looked as if natural law provided positive law with its content. It is now clear of what that relationship really consists. Natural law prescribes that we must not commit murder, but civil law establishes what we mean by murder. It establishes, for example, that killing an enemy in war is not murder. Therefore, it does not prohibit killing an enemy in war. The relationship which natural law seemed to have with civil law is thus cancelled. Through this approach, Hobbes arrives, without even realizing it, at a purely positivistic conception. For there is also implicit in his position a critique of the fact that the so-called laws of nature are too generic to be useful at all. At first it looked as if he were only saying: the laws of nature exist, but they are not binding. But now he pushes his devaluation much farther. The laws of nature exist, but are so indeterminate as to be inapplicable. By saying that laws of nature are not binding, Hobbes has deprived them of effectiveness; by saying that they are indeterminate, he has made them useless. To say that it is civil law that must determine what is theft, murder, and adultery, means to say that civil law determines its content by itself, without drawing it from natural law. There is no better example of this than the one which Hobbes himself provides: "The Lacedaemonians of old permitted their youths, by a certain law, to take away other men's goods, they commanded that these goods should not be accounted other men's, but their own who took

24. *De Cive*, VI, 16, pp. 85–86. There are passages analogous to this in other chapters of *De Cive*. One is in chap. XIV, 10, p. 191: "For though the law of nature forbid theft, adultery, &c; if the civil law command us to invade anything, that invasion is not theft, adultery, &c." Another is in chap. XIV, 17, p. 196: "But we demand not whether theft be a sin, but what is to be termed theft; and so concerning others, in like manners."

them; and therefore such surreptions were not theft."[25] What does this example show except that only civil power determines what is permissible and what is impermissible, without depending on any superior law? The most rigorous theorist of contemporary legal positivism, Hans Kelsen, could fully subscribe to this position. For Kelsen, there is no content prior to positive law, but any behavior can be prohibited or authorized, provided that this is done according to established forms.

8. It goes without saying that we should be as cautious in seeing in Hobbes's theory a rigorously positivistic system *tout court*, which is still centuries away, as we have been in admitting that his system leaves a space open for the laws of nature. It is worthwhile to add a few more reflections on this point. The thesis we analyzed in the previous section holds only for *De Cive.* Not only does Hobbes expunge it from *Leviathan,* he also assigns a much greater role to natural law. Even if we cannot say that Hobbes has changed course, we must recognize that he inclines more toward the traditional theses of natural law theory. In *Leviathan,* Hobbes deals with a question that reveals the complexity of the relationship between natural law and positive law. This is the question of the gaps in a legal order.

As is well known, a genuine positivist has a ready-made solution for this question. A gap in the legal order must be filled without leaving the positive legal system. One can follow two well-known methods: analogy, and appeal to the general principles of the law in force. This solution is unthinkable for Hobbes, because even if he was a positivist in his aims, he was a natural law theorist in choosing the foundations of his system. There is a fundamental difference between him and a nineteenth-century legal positivist. For a nineteenth-century positivist, the positive legal system is self-sufficient. For Hobbes the positive legal system is legitimated by a preexisting natural (or rational) order. Having been compressed up to this point, this preexisting natural (or rational) order nec-

25. *De Cive,* XIV, 10, p. 191.

essarily reemerges in case the positive order is lacking. This is what happens with the gaps. Hobbes has no doubt that the judge must resort to natural law in order to find a solution to issues that have not been foreseen by the positive legal order.[26] A further consequence which Hobbes formulates clearly only in *Leviathan*, ensues from this statement: the laws of nature are binding whenever positive laws are silent.

This point is important because, in my opinion, it helps us to show as clearly as possible the difference between a rigorously positivistic legal theory and Hobbes's theory. Hobbes's theory is the most serious attempt to reduce law to positive law which was ever made in a cultural environment in which no one had ever contested the existence and validity of natural law. A legal positivist holds that there is the so-called empty legal space where positive law has not yet extended its control: that is, in that space there is a more or less broad freedom of action. Hobbes, on the contrary, holds that natural laws are in force when positive law has not yet issued its commands. There is thus a space filled with norms different from positive norms. This is the logical consequence of the fact that, for Hobbes, the positive legal order incorporates the laws of nature. We have seen that the function of the positive legal order is to make the laws of nature valid. We now understand better what this means. It means that the laws of nature oblige *in foro externo*, not only *in foro interno*, only when they are comprised within a positive legal order. That is, they are binding only for those who have become members of a state through a compact. In other words: the laws of nature are not binding in the state of nature, because human beings cannot comply with them without harming themselves. But they are binding in civil society, because the sovereign is held to enforce them if they have been violated.

A few passages from *Leviathan* confirm that this indeed is Hobbes's conception. There is nothing comparable to them in Hobbes's previous works. But they do not represent a retraction on his part; they show that Hobbes has become fully

26. *Elements*, II, 10, 10, p. 151; *De Cive*, XIV, 14, p. 194; *Leviathan*, XXVI, p. 183.

aware of the foundations of his own system. While discussing the principle that the law must be made known in order to be binding, Hobbes remarks that there are laws that "*oblige* all the subjects without exception," without requiring any publication or promulgation. These laws are the laws of nature.[27] And furthermore: "Ignorance of the law of nature excuseth no man; because every man that hath attained to the use of reason, is supposed to know, he ought not to do to another, what he would not have done to himself."[28] It thus seems that there are two sources of legal obligations for subjects. One source of obligations is constituted by positive laws, which are the products of the express or tacit will of the sovereign.[29] The other source is constituted by natural laws, which, if violated, might be punished as positive laws are. According to the excerpt quoted above, the laws of nature would penetrate the stronghold of positive law, to the point that positive law must protect them, thus turning them into binding norms. Another passage might confirm this point: "But if an unwritten law, in all the provinces of a dominion, shall be generally observed, and no iniquity appear in the use thereof; that law can be no other but a law of nature, equally obliging all mankind."[30] This passage implies that these unwritten laws, which are the laws of nature, are binding in the same way as, and side by side with, written laws.

It thus appears that the laws of nature are in force in the same way as, and alongside with, positive laws, but only within a specific positive legal system. If this is true, it is then the laws of nature that provide juridical solutions to cases which positive law has not expressly regulated. Neither do we need an explicit reference to them. It is the logic of Hobbes's system which leads us to this conclusion. Once the state has been instituted, the laws of nature become laws as are the laws

27. *Leviathan*, XXVI, pp. 176–77. Italics mine.

28. Ibid., p. 191.

29. Laws in the strict sense of the term are the products of the expressed will of the sovereign; while those norms that the sovereign tacitly accepts are those belonging to the common law.

30. *Leviathan*, XXVI, p. 175.

of the state. For it is precisely the task of the state to enable citizens to comply freely with the dictates of right reason, through the creation of a peaceful legal order. Therefore, in cases when the state has not legislated, everyone is bound to make his conduct conform to the laws of nature. This implies that it is perfectly legitimate for a judge to evaluate a subject's behavior by applying the dictates of the law of nature—if positive law does not help him to decide. Let us take an example, chosen at our discretion. One of the laws of nature accepted by Hobbes forbids me to insult my neighbor. Independently of whether there is a law in the positive legal order, I am bound not to proffer insults, because the law of nature is fully in force. If I do not conform my behavior to this law, the judge can punish me.

But can we be completely sure that this principle does homage to the law of nature, and is a constraint imposed on positive law? If such were the case, we should moderate our initial thesis, which emphasized Hobbes's legal positivism. We have, however, good reasons for believing that in this case also Hobbes's homage is only superficial, and conceals on the contrary a devaluation of the laws of nature.

The law of nature, which is supposedly in force alongside positive law, cannot be applied to a concrete case that has not been regulated by positive law[31] without being interpreted. But who is entitled to interpret the law of nature? There is no doubt that, according to Hobbes, the state is entitled to interpret it, through the person of the judge. Hobbes explains that the interpretation of the laws of nature is not based on books of moral philosophy, for these only express the personal opinion of philosophers, which are often contradictory. It is "the sentence of the judge constituted by the sovereign authority, to hear and determine such controversies"[32] which establishes the correct interpretation of the law of nature. Therefore it pertains only to the judge, that is, to the sovereign, to decide whether a concrete case which is not regulated by a positive

31. For only in this case are the laws of nature binding.
32. *Leviathan*, XXVI, pp. 180–81.

law is regulated by natural law. And it pertains only to the judge to decide which law of nature should be applied, and what it dictates. It is thus entirely at the judge's discretion to identify and specify the law of nature. But this means that it is the sovereign who puts a law of nature in force, and attributes to it one content rather than another. He does so by performing the double operation of identifying and specifying the content of the law. We thus discover that, in filling the gaps of a positive legal order, the judge has the same power of manipulating the laws of nature that the sovereign exercises in determining their content. We might say that the sovereign, as the legislator, deprives the laws of nature of any meaning when he creates positive laws. And that the sovereign, as judge, deprives them of any meaning, when facing an issue which the legislative power has not regulated.[33]

9.   What we have said until now holds when we consider the relationship between the laws of nature and the behavior of individual citizens. But Hobbes's political doctrine mainly considers two subjects (or persons): citizens and sovereign. We now have to explore the relationship between the law of nature and the behavior of the sovereign. In this respect, too, Hobbes formulates the issue in the most orthodox terms of natural law theory. He contends that the sovereign is bound to respect the laws of nature. This statement sets back on their feet the laws of nature which we had taken to be definitely felled. The laws of nature have ceased to exist in the relationship between individuals and sovereign. But this does not mean that they have been completely eliminated from human relations. In civil society, the sovereign has interposed himself between the original laws of nature and the actions of citizens, because of the

33. We can follow the same reasoning in analyzing the statement according to which customs must not be contrary to the laws of nature if they are to be "very laws" (*Leviathan*, XXVI, p. 186). But who is entitled to judge of their conformity? Clearly the sovereign, as we can infer from the following passage: "And our lawyers account no customs law, but such as are reasonable, and that evil customs are to be abolished. But the judgement of what is reasonable, and of what is to be abolished, belongeth to him that maketh the law, which is the sovereign assembly, or monarch" (*Leviathan*, XXVI, p. 174).

well-known covenant of renunciation and transference of natural rights. From the moment when the contract comes into force, the sovereign becomes the only person entitled to issue legal norms. If citizens are only subjected to positive laws, is the sovereign also subjected to the same laws? On this point Hobbes's answer could not be clearer. The sovereign is not bound to comply with civil laws; he is, following the ancient formulation, *legibus solutus* [not bound by laws].[34] Does this mean that the power of the sovereign is not bound by anything, and is therefore arbitrary? To this question also Hobbes's answer is very clear. The sovereign is bound to observe natural laws. The laws of nature are thus silent for citizens, but they hold for the sovereign.

An orthodox natural law theorist would have no qualms in following Hobbes when he progressively deprives of authority the laws of nature within the state, provided that these have been assigned a place of honor among the prince's duties. It thus finally appears that Hobbes does greatly value those laws which up to now he has mistreated. For he assigns to them the fundamental and irreplaceable function that was most relevant to natural law theory: that of limiting and correcting the sovereign power. With his dialectic Hobbes has been corroding the doctrine of natural law theory to the point that it looks like an empty shell, a name without substance, or a name with another substance. Now he is about to deal the decisive blow. After having gone so far, will he retrace his steps and follow in the path of his predecessors? Are the laws of nature the code of conduct for princes, for Hobbes as well? A moral code, if one wishes, rather than a legal one, but nonetheless a code which is binding in conscience and before God, if not in human courts. The list of natural laws which Hobbes makes at the beginning of his inquiry is thus not a superfluous show. The dictates of right reason are at least binding for sovereigns.

Let us look at things a bit more closely. Hobbes repeats several times that sovereigns are bound to respect the laws of na-

34. *De Cive*, VI, 14, pp. 83–84. Hobbes lists among seditious theories the opinion that the sovereign is subjected to civil laws. *Elements*, II, 8, 6, p. 136; *De Cive*, XII, 4, pp. 153–54; *Leviathan*, XXIX, pp. 212–13.

ture. But he does this in passing, as something which is obvious but of secondary importance. In *De Cive*, in a footnote, he says with respect to the question whether the sovereign may perform illegal acts: "First, though by right, that is, without injury to them, he may do it, yet can he not do it justly, that is, without breach of the natural laws and injury against God."[35] In *Leviathan:* "[The sovereign] never wanteth right to any thing, otherwise, than as he himself is the subject of God, and bound thereby to observe the laws of nature." And elsewhere: "It is true, that sovereigns are all subjects to the laws of nature; because such laws be divine, and cannot by any man, or commonwealth be abrogated. But to those laws which the sovereign himself, that is, which the commonwealth maketh, he is not subject."[36] Hobbes never devoted a specific analysis to this issue. But if we accurately study Hobbes's system, we realize that this is only an apparent problem.

10. The sovereign establishes two kinds of intersubjective relationships: with other sovereigns and with his subjects. When we say that the sovereign is bound to respect the laws of nature, we mean that he should have this obligation both toward other sovereigns and his subjects. But we can repeat for international relations the same reasoning that Hobbes developed for the relationships among individuals in the state of nature. We can say that the sovereign is bound to respect the laws of nature only if he can do so without harming himself. He will not be sure of that until he and the other sovereigns have instituted a power superior to all of them, and capable of exercising coercive power over a sovereign who does not comply with such laws. But in the meantime, while the state of nature lasts in international relations,[37] the sovereign is not bound to endanger his own life and the preservation of the state, by subjecting himself unilaterally to the sublime but inconvenient dictates of reason. The law of nature is thus not effective with

35. *De Cive*, VI, 13, p. 80.

36. *Leviathan*, XXI, pp. 139, and XXIX, 212.

37. Hobbes considers international relations to be a typical example of the state of nature.

regard to the behavior of the sovereign in his relations with other sovereigns.

Is the law of nature more effective in relations between the sovereign and his subjects? If we wish to assign a legal meaning to the duty of the sovereign to respect the laws of nature, we must admit that the subject has the right not to obey, that is, to resist any command of the sovereign that is contrary to the laws of nature. But if we accept this consequence, we also renounce, on the one hand, the theory of the absolute state, and, on the other, a positivistic conception of the law, and a legalistic conception of justice: that is, those theories that Hobbes has tried to support with every possible device, at least judging from what we have been able to make out up to now.

But even in this case, Hobbes does not fall into the trap which natural law has prepared to undermine the solidity of the absolute state. Hobbes's doctrine is clear in this respect. The violation of a law of nature on the part of the sovereign does not authorize the subject to disobey. The fundamental argument which he uses to support this thesis is the following: by signing the social contract, every subject has bound himself to do all that the sovereign commands, and not to do all that the sovereign prohibits. That is, every subject has granted to the sovereign the power to determine what is just and what is unjust. For the consequence of the contract has been that every subject considers the sovereign's actions as his own. It follows that all that is commanded is just merely because it has been commanded. The sovereign therefore cannot commit a wrong or an injustice toward his subjects. If the sovereign violates a law of nature—for example, by sentencing an innocent person to death[38]—he commits a wrong toward God, but not his subject. Since no wrong has been committed toward the subject, the latter has no right of resistance, which is the just and legitimate reaction to an action which is considered unjust and

38. As in *Leviathan*, XXI, p. 139. Hobbes explains in another passage that the punishment of subjects who are innocent constitutes the violation of three laws of nature: the law that prescribes aiming for a future good, by taking revenge; the law that forbids ingratitude; and the law that commands equity (ibid., XXVIII, p. 207).

illegal. Here is how Hobbes articulates this delicate point, without leaving any doubt about his position:

> It is true, that a sovereign monarch, or the greater part of a sovereign assembly, may ordain the doing of many things in pursuit of their passions, contrary to their own consciences, which is a breach of trust, and of the law of nature; but this is not enough to authorize any subject, either to make war upon, or so much as to accuse of injustice, or any way to speak evil of the sovereign; because they have authorized all his actions, and in bestowing the sovereign power, made them their own.[39]

It is true that there is a well-known exception to this. The duty of obedience ends when the sovereign's order endangers the subject's life. This means that the subject must obey every command, except those that endanger his own life (for example, a death sentence). The rationale for this objection is obvious if we keep in mind the premise of Hobbes's system. For man the fundamental value is life. Human beings institute the state with the sole aim of suppressing the state of nature, in which life is constantly threatened by universal war. Every individual accepts the hard discipline of the state in order to save his own life. He gives up all the rights he possesses in the state of nature, except his right to life. As a consequence, he is no longer bound to the compact of obedience, if the state endangers his life. We could say, employing a Rousseauian terminology, that there is for Hobbes a natural right, that is, the right to life, which is inalienable. It is inalienable in the same way and with the same consequences as those that characterize the right to freedom for Rousseau. But let us not forget that the subject's right of resistance does not at all correspond to the sovereign's duty not to condemn to death a subject who, in the sovereign's opinion, deserves it.

Cesare Beccaria shared Hobbes's starting assumption, but he reached the conclusion that the death penalty was unacceptable. "Is it conceivable," he asked, "that the least sacrifice

39. Ibid., XXIV, p. 162.

of each person's liberty should include sacrifice of the greatest of all goods, life?"[40] Hobbes, on the contrary, merely concedes that the subject can legitimately resist those who execute the sentence. But Hobbes does not deny the sovereign the right to convict the subject and to enforce that conviction against a subject who is (even legitimately) recalcitrant. The sovereign's right clashes with the equal and contrary right of the subject. How can we explain what happens in this case? We can remark that the covenant between sovereign and subject has been broken. Both are back in the state of nature, that is, in that condition in which everyone has as much right as he has power. The subject who has been condemned to death has the right to use force to avoid the execution of the sentence. The sovereign has the right to use force in order to see his order carried out. As in the state of nature, the stronger of the two wins. The subject's rebellion is justified by the first law of nature, which enjoins that we "must seek peace." But the same law of nature does not at all constitute an obligation for the sovereign. Once more we can see to what degree the law of nature is a mere *flatus vocis* [a mere breath]. As already remarked, the law of nature is not in force in civil society, because it is completely replaced by positive laws. Neither is it in force in the state of nature, because there no other law is in force except the laws of utility and force. Since there is no third condition in which human beings may live, the law of nature has no specific domain of implementation. It does not yet exist in the state of nature; it no longer exists in civil society. For the law of nature, the present does not exist in any place and at any time.

11.   At this point it would appear that the problem of the validity of the law of nature no longer exists. This law is not yet in force in the state of nature, and is no longer in force in civil society. But now we have to see what happens in the passage from the state of nature to civil society, at the very moment when the state is instituted. It is Hobbes's genuine teaching that, once the sovereign has been instituted, only the norms

40. *Of Crimes and Punishments* (New York: Bobbs-Merrill, 1963), XVI, p. 45.

issued by his authority are valid.[41] But what is the source of the sovereign's authority? In other words, what grounds the validity of the norm that binds subjects to obey the sovereign?

Here we agree with Kelsen[42] who contends that a norm must either be evident in itself, or have some ground for its validity. The ground of validity of a norm can only be another norm, which is therefore called superior. In Hobbes's system, the norm prescribing that subjects must obey the sovereign is either evident in itself, or must be grounded in a norm that is superior to it. Hobbes chooses the latter solution. According to him, the norm establishing that subjects must obey the sovereign derives its validity from the fact that subjects, through the social contract, have given up their rights and transferred them to the sovereign, thus authorizing him to issue legal norms. The norm prescribing that subjects must attribute to the sovereign an absolute power to command is thus the norm which provides the ground of validity to the norm which prescribes obedience. But for Hobbes this norm is a law of nature. More precisely it is, according to the text of *De Cive*,[43] the first law of nature, from which the others derive. It thus follows that a law of nature provides the ground of validity of the whole positive legal system.

Hobbes fought obstinately against the remnants of natural law theory in his conception; he elaborated a concise and consistent positivist theory of law; but he could not avoid asking himself what provides the ground of validity of the whole positive legal system. Inferior positive norms refer to superior norms, which are themselves positive. But we must reach the point where we find the supreme norm. No other positive norm provides the ground of validity for that norm, which is in its turn the ground of validity of all other norms. This supreme norm is the ultimate ground of the positive system. It therefore cannot be a positive norm itself, for it may not have the same

41. And this is also true legal positivism, as we have remarked.

42. *General Theory of Law and State* (Cambridge: Harvard University Press, 1945), pp. 110–11.

43. In *Leviathan* this norm is mentioned as the second law of nature, XIV, p. 85.

ground that is the foundation of the norms which derive from it.

A modern legal positivist, who has openly rejected, or at least temporarily set aside in his inquiry any reference to natural law theory, would only say that this supreme norm is the fundamental norm of a specific legal system. He would also remark that the fundamental norm is no longer a norm which is absolutely valid, but rather a hypothetical norm, which allows us to build an objective science of positive law. Hobbes, on the contrary, is a legal positivist by inclination and way of reasoning, but is by necessity a natural law theorist. He thus considers the supreme norm that supports the positive legal system to be a law of nature. Although he eliminates all interference from the law of nature as soon as the positive legal system has been instituted, he cannot avoid positing the law of nature at the basis of that system. That is, he falls into the arms of natural law theory just when he seems to have definitely escaped from it.

We can summarize the consequences of this position, compared with that of the modern legal positivist, as follows. The modern legal positivist considers the particular legal system that is the object of his inquiry as one of the possible legal orders, because he sees the supreme norm as a hypothetical norm. Hobbes considers the legal system that he has described to be the only possible legal system because he sees the supreme norm as a law of nature. And a law of nature carries within itself universalistic and absolutist features which are alien to a hypothetical norm. This difference should not surprise us. For behind the legal positivist there is the relativistic conception of contemporary science; behind Hobbes, the absolutist conception of science which is proper to seventeenth-century rationalism. The modern scientist is not concerned with the premises of his inquiry; he accepts them as possible guidelines for his research. But despite his conventionalism and nominalism, Hobbes espouses the rationalistic vocation of his times, and has the ambition of establishing a political system which is absolutely valid, as valid as geometry; that is, to be more precise, as valid as people thought geometry was. But he had only one way to give absolute validity to his system. He had to place it on the pedestal of natural laws, that is, on a law which was either evident in itself like a mathematical axiom, or rationally deductible from another law of nature evident in itself.

12. For Hobbes, the fundamental norm of the state, which establishes that individuals agree in giving up their sovereign rights and transfer them to others, has absolute validity. It possesses this absolute validity because this law is the logical consequence of another natural law, the first and supreme law of nature, which prescribes that human beings seek peace.[44] Hobbes does not, however, present the first and supreme law as self-evident. Rather he justifies it through his study of the selfish nature of man. This study prepares the well-known description of the state of nature, and leads Hobbes to the conclusion that this condition is intolerable, making it necessary for human beings to pass from the state of nature to civil society.

We may say that Hobbes, unlike the modern jurist, was concerned with the presuppositions of his inquiry. So much so that he constructed a rational system of natural laws which could provide a ground for a positive legal order. But we could also say that he makes as small a concession as a rationalist could make to the laws of nature. An authentic natural law theorist does not merely see the question of the law of nature as the question of the foundation of positive law, which regards the issue of whether positive law is founded on universal (natural) laws, or on principles of limited validity, or even on conventions. For a natural law theorist the question is much more important, and regards the issue of whether there exists another law side by side with positive law, that is equal, if not superior to the latter, and to which the citizen, the judge, or another authority can appeal if positive law contradicts it. It is this conception of natural law that Hobbes does not accept, as

44. The way in which the second law of nature derives from the first is different from the way in which a positive law derives from another positive law. In the latter case, following Kelsen's terminology, the derivation is formal, or by delegation. In the former case, the derivation is substantive.

we have tried to show. Hobbes does not accept that there exist two laws; that is, that there exists, side by side with positive law, which is for him the only law in force, a binding natural law, as today's surviving and rejuvenated natural law theorists would say. Hobbes does not accept the law of nature except as the foundation of positive law. But in doing so, he attributes to the law of nature no function other than that of justifying the absolute value of his own conception of positive law. We may say that for Hobbes the law of nature is not itself a legal norm, but only a logical argument. The law of nature does not shape conduct, but demonstrates rationally the reasons why we must behave in one way rather than another.

This last remark brings us back to where we started. For Hobbes, the laws of nature are not laws, but rather theorems. More precisely, they are not legal norms, but rather scientific principles. They do not command, but rather demonstrate. They do not oblige (or coerce), but rather aim to persuade. They do not belong to the sphere of what ought to be (to adopt Kelsen's terminology in this case also), but rather to the sphere of what is. The laws of nature are not binding legal norms, but rather demonstrate the validity of a system of legal norms. But this means, once again, the dissolution of the law of nature in the classical sense of the term, that is as a system of valid legal norms. Nonetheless, even if Hobbes reduces the system of natural laws to a system of scientific statements which have demonstrative rather than normative value, the positive legal system must have a normative foundation, and not merely a rational justification. As for Kelsen, so for Hobbes, the legal order refers to a fundamental norm. For Hobbes, this fundamental norm is not merely a normative hypothesis, but rather a law of nature. This means that the reduction of the laws of nature to theorems is not complete, and that the law of nature has normative value at least at one point, which is the pivot of Hobbes's whole system.

This fundamental law of nature establishes a contract in favor of a third person as the normative foundation of the legal order of the state. We may add that the validity of this norm implies the validity of another norm, which establishes that

promises must be kept [*pacta sunt servanda*]. Hobbes consequently considers this norm as the second of the derived natural laws.[45] According to an authoritative doctrine in the field of
international law, a legal order composed of peers cannot do
other than acknowledge as its foundation the norm *pacta sunt
servanda*. Hobbes accepts a contractual conception of the state's
legal order, which is composed of peers. The scientific tradition of theorists of international relations has considered such
a ground-norm as a principle of natural law, as did Hobbes. Today, however, a consistent legal positivist who accepts this
norm, would try to show that even this norm is a norm of positive law. But the norm *pacta sunt servanda* cannot derive its validity from an agreement among parties—that is from positive
law—since it is itself the foundation of the validity of the agreement. A positivist would thus contend that the validity of this
norm derives from custom. But we may not ask a philosopher
and jurist of the seventeenth century, even one so daring as
Hobbes, to think like today's boldest and most consistent legal
positivist.

For Hobbes, both the norm that establishes the covenant of
union and the norm *pacta sunt servanda* are laws of nature. This
is confirmed by the fact that Hobbes considers the crime of
lèse-majesté, which consists in breaking the original covenant
rather than in disobeying laws, as he presents it in a passage
from *De Cive*, as a sin against the law of nature: "That sin,
which by the law of nature is treason, is a transgression of the
natural, not the civil law."[46] As a consequence, the person

45. *De Cive*, III, I, pp. 29–30. In *Leviathan*, this norm is introduced as the third
law of nature, XV, p. 93.
46. *De Cive*, XIV, 21, p. 201. Hobbes does not deal with the crimes of lèse-
majesté in *Leviathan* on purpose. He lists them as crimes which are especially
serious in a paragraph in which he compares various crimes in relation to their
consequences (XXVII, p. 200). But he does not emphasize as their characteristic
that of being violations of the law of nature, perhaps because such a statement
would seem to contradict what he asserted in the same chapter. We can call
crime only a violation of civil law; while the violation of natural law, however
much it may incur guilt, may not be called a crime (XXVII, p. 190). We should
analyze separately what relation there is between this version and the overall
political revision of Hobbes's major work, because of the changing conditions
of the country and the defeat of the royalist party.

guilty of lèse-majesté will not have to be punished according to civil law, but rather according to natural law, that is, not as a bad citizen, but rather as an enemy of the state.

13. We are now better equipped to understand the implications of what we said in section four. No decisive argument against Hobbes's legal positivism ensues from the thesis that the fundamental norms of his system are laws of nature. On the contrary, this feature reinforces Hobbes's legal positivism.

We asked first of all: How can we reconcile Hobbes's formal conception of justice with his assertion that the laws of nature are valid because they are substantively just? We can now answer that this reconciliation is not difficult, since the laws of nature which survive do not prescribe any specific content. They only prescribe that we must build a positive legal order which alone and by its own strength will have a specific content.

Second, we asked ourselves: How can we reconcile the theory of the absolute state with the acknowledgement that there are laws of nature which precede the state? In this case too we can answer that reconciliation is possible, because Hobbes neutralizes the laws of nature, whenever they impose themselves, with positive legal norms. In Hobbes's system, the laws of nature finally have no other role than that of providing the ground of validity for a state that only recognizes positive law.

As for the final question: Is there not a contrast between the starting point of Hobbes's system, which is constituted by a system of natural laws, and the point of arrival, which is the construction of a positivist system of law? We can once more confidently reply, even if it seems paradoxical, that there is no contrast, because Hobbes's natural law has no function other than that of convincing human beings that there is no law other than positive law. In Hobbes's own words, this paradox reads as follows:

> *By the virtue of the natural law which forbids breach of covenant, the law of nature commands us to keep all the civil laws.* For where we are tied to obedience before we

know what will be commanded us, there we are universally tied to obey in all things. Whence it follows
that no *civil law whatsoever . . . can possibly be against the
law of nature.*[47]

In our words, there can be no contrast between civil and natural law, because the law of nature, while commanding obedience to all civil laws, also commands obedience to those
which are contrary to natural laws. There is no contrast between the two laws, not because a civil law may not be in contrast with a natural law, but because the fundamental law of
nature prescribing obedience to the state is in force above all
particular natural laws. That is, the fundamental natural law
tells us that all natural laws cease to be binding, once the state
has been instituted.

Hobbes's itinerary is complete. But we had to follow it all
the way before we could understand what at the beginning
seemed a contradiction or paradox. We now realize that there
is neither contradiction nor paradox, for the true function of
the natural law, and the only one that cannot be eliminated, is
to provide the most absolute ground to the norm according to
which there is no other valid law than positive law. All that
Hobbes manages to squeeze out of the traditional doctrine of
natural law is thus an argument in favor of the state, and of our
absolute obligation to obey positive law. Hobbes does accept
natural law, but at the service of a coherent and consistent
theory of positive law. If you like, Hobbes employs natural law
as a device to justify the absolute validity of positive law with
an argument which no historical argument could provide.
Natural law theory was, before Hobbes, and would be, after
Hobbes, a doctrine which recognizes two distinct legal spheres,
albeit connected to one another in various ways. With Hobbes,
natural law theory results in a monistic conception of law,
which denies that natural law is a system of law superior to the
system of positive law.

47. *De Cive,* XIV, 10, pp. 190–91. Italics are mine. We can read another version of this paradox in XVII, 10, p. 267: "Our Saviour hath not showed subjects
any other laws for the government of a city, beside those of nature, that is,
beside *the command of obedience.*" Italics are mine.

five

Hobbes and Natural Law Theory

1. It is commonly held that the history of natural law theory should be divided into two periods. The first includes classical and medieval natural law theory; the second, the modern version. But it seems to me that in recent years there has been a shift in the evaluation of when this change occurred, even if supporters of the two natural law theories have not been fully aware of it. Until a few years ago the prevailing doctrine, already firmly in place at the end of the seventeenth century and the beginning of the eighteenth through the work of Pufendorf, Thomasius, and Barbeyrac, was that Grotius was the initiator of the modern theory of natural law. The perspective has now changed. The conviction is spreading that modern natural law theory begins with Hobbes rather than Grotius. Two things have happened. On the one hand, Grotius's philosophical originality has been called into question, and scholars have studied more carefully and confirmed his links with the premodern tradition, in particular with the philosophy of late scholasticism. On the other hand, Hobbes's legal thought has come out of quarantine and is being studied with curiosity and with the growing conviction that it constitutes an illuminating anticipation of theories which are, rightly or wrongly, considered innovative.

Let us take into consideration the criteria which are most frequently used by both sides to establish and justify a distinction between medieval and modern natural law theory.[1] All these criteria pass a rigorous historical test only if their point of reference is the philosophy of Hobbes. If we test them against Grotius's natural law theory, they almost completely lose their argumentative strength and become unacceptable. We might say in jest that, in the dispute between old and new natural law theorists, an irresistible and inevitable *reductio ad Hobbesium* of all possible arguments has occurred.

I take into consideration the four criteria that are most frequently used. They can be classified according to whether they are employed to argue for or against the superiority of medieval over modern natural law theory, and whether they rely on ideological or methodological arguments. We shall label these four criteria 1a and 1b, and 2a and 2b. The former two are more frequently employed by defenders of medieval natural law theory; the latter two, by defenders of modern natural law theory. In both pairs, the first argument is mostly methodological (1a and 2a), while the second is mostly ideological (1b and 2b).

1a.   Medieval natural law theory is superior to the modern version because it has never attempted to build a complete system of prescriptions, which might be deduced *more geometrico* [in geometric fashion] from an abstract human nature, established once and for all. The natural law of medieval natural law theory consists of a few general principles, or even of one principle (*bonum faciendum, male vitandum* [that good is to be done and evil avoided]), which must be historically completed or specified.[2] Modern natural law theory is the fruit of an abstract rationalism, which does not make any concession to the histor-

1. It is better to leave classical natural law theory aside, for it can be employed to support both the medieval and the modern versions, depending on the situation.

2. Through secondary natural law or human positive law. Rommen speaks of natural law as providing a frame for norms, which does not make human legislators superfluous. *Lo stato nel pensiero cattolico* (Milan: Giuffrè, 1959), pp. 78–79.

ical development of humankind; while medieval natural law theory is the fruit of a moderate rationalism which, by conceiving the truth as the on-going adaptation of human reason to universal reason, accepts and justifies historical development. The most war-hardened Catholic natural law theorists do not accept defeat and are, on the contrary, again on the offensive more than ever in these years. We know well how insistent they are in asserting that modern natural law theory is anti-historical and that scholastic natural law theory, which is reconciled to history, is more modern than the doctrines that proclaim themselves modern.

If we consider this argument, we may say that the first thinker who attempted to build a deductive legal system deriving secondary prescriptions (the derived natural laws) from an original ethical postulate (the fundamental law of nature), was not Grotius, but rather Hobbes. In his *Prolegomena* (section eight), Grotius did not aim at formulating an eternal code, but merely at drawing a broad and flexible list of common rules such as abstaining from things that belong to others, returning what belongs to others, keeping promises, repairing damage done, and subjecting one's self to the punishment for transgression of laws. In the second and third chapters of *De Cive*, and the fourteenth and fifteenth of *Leviathan*, on the contrary, Hobbes, with much confidence and some presumption, presents real tables of the laws of nature, among which he even lists, in *De Cive*, the prohibition against drunkenness. No matter what people say of eighteenth-century abstract rationalism and its claims to fix natural rights once and for all, I do not know of any thinker who has been more audacious than Hobbes in taking upon himself the ungrateful role of universal legislator.

1b.   Modern natural law theory no longer starts from the assumption that human beings are social by nature, but emphasizes their selfishness, and takes into consideration the individual isolated in the state of nature, rather than the individual in society. Medieval natural law theory is thus superior to its modern counterpart, because the latter has expressed a conception of man which is narrow, particularistic, atomistic, and so forth. And it has given life to a particular political theory, that is, liberalism, which is everywhere in decline. Supporters of scholastic natural law theory present it as an ethics of the person, in opposition to an ethics of the individual, which is typical of the Enlightenment and utilitarianism. They represent it as a communitarian conception of society, in opposition to the atomistic conception. And they contend that such a conception provides a view of human beings and history more in tune with the tasks of the modern state, which are positive, and no longer merely negative.

From this point of view, and even more clearly than with respect to point 1a, it is Hobbes, and not Grotius, who represents the moment of change. If we consider this criterion of distinction between medieval and modern natural law theory, Grotius is clearly irrelevant, while Hobbes is fully relevant. Grotius's scarcely rigorous starting assumption was that of *appetitus societatis* [desire for society]. This was a vaguer version of the notion of Aristotle and Thomas's *zoon politikon* [political animal], still shared by the scholastics of the sixteenth century. Hobbes starts with the asocial individual of the state of nature, who lives with the constant suspicion of being deceived and offended by others, who does not comply with the laws of nature for fear that others may violate them before he does, and who is perpetually moved by the will to harm others (quite the opposite of *appetitus societatis!*). Hobbes says all this, as usual for him, from the first pages of *De Cive,* while replying in a note to the second edition to the chorus of objections which the traditionalists had made to him: "For they who shall more narrowly look into the causes for which men come together, and delight in each other's company, shall easily find that this happens not because naturally it could happen no otherwise, but by accident."[3]

2a.   Modern natural law theory is superior to the medieval one because the former relies on a new concept of reason,

3. *De Cive,* I, 2, p. 3.

which is more pliable and suitable to the new conception of man in the universe. It also relies on a new conception of nature, which is no longer the universal order created by God, but is simply the set of environmental, social, and historical conditions which individuals must take into account in order to regulate their social life. It has been said that, with the change in the concepts of reason and nature, "natural law ceases to be the path through which human communities can participate in the cosmic order or contribute to it, and it becomes a rational technique of social life."[4]

Such a criterion of distinction between old and new natural law theory might not have been conceived, had Hobbes's philosophy not existed. Once more, Hobbes is the obligatory step. Hobbes is the first to construct a theory of reason as calculation. In particular, reason is, for human beings in society, a calculus of utilities, which induces us to join with others through a compact, and to form civil society. It is a calculation which induces us to create the conditions for transforming natural laws, which are indeed good, but ineffective, into positive laws, which are good, that is advantageous, merely because they are at least effective, and ensure the implementation of the supreme value of peace. Hobbes is the first thinker who does not merely ascribe very general precepts to the law of nature, as his predecessors, including Grotius, had done. But he draws a long list of natural laws, which he derives mostly from the law of war. He thus tests his thesis that the laws of nature are nothing other than the product of the calculus of utilities,[5] and devices made by reason in order to make peaceful social life possible. In Grotius's work there exists no theory of reason, except as a pale reflection of the discussions going on at that time. Even the famous sentence *"etsi daremus non esse Deum"* [even if God did not exist], is a scholastic saw, as Fasso has successfully shown. As for the law of nature, this was still for Grotius the major bulwark against utilitarianism and moral

4. N. Abbagnano, *Dizionario di filosofia* (Turin: Utet, 1961), s.v. "Diritto," p. 254b.

5. And it is in this new sense that they are *dictamina rectae rationis* [dictates of right reason].

skepticism. For he saw it as a reflection of an unchangeable rational order, in which man participates. In Grotius's eyes, the correspondence of the law of nature to a nature understood as divine order,[6] ensured its universal validity in comparison to the historical validity of civil law.

2b. Modern natural law theory is superior to medieval natural law theory, because the latter considers the law of nature almost exclusively from the point of view of the duties which derive from that law; whereas the former considers the rights which that law grants.[7] All accept that the function of natural law theory has always been that of setting limits to the sovereign's power. But according to the traditional conception, natural law theory fulfilled this function by stating that the sovereign was bound not to violate the laws of nature. Modern natural law theory, however, recognizes to subjects, at first, the right to resist a sovereign who has violated the laws of nature, thus transforming the sovereign's duty from an imperfect to a perfect one, from an internal to an external one. At a later stage, modern natural law theory no longer considers the sovereign's duty to respect the laws of nature as the original foundation of the limits of the power of the state. Instead that foundation is provided by a greater or lesser set of individual rights which precede the rise of the state. These are the so-called natural rights, which are seen as the reason why the sovereign has the duty to respect the laws of nature.

Scholars agree unanimously on this point. The theory of natural rights is born with Hobbes. There is no trace of it in Grotius. When Grotius discusses sovereignty, the presumed founder of natural law theory is mainly concerned to refute the opinions of those who hold that sovereignty always has a foundation in the people. In order to deny this thesis, Grotius resorts to all

6. Even if this order was created by divine reason rather than divine will.
7. See L. Strauss, *Natural Right and History* (Chicago: University of Chicago Press, 1953), pp. 182–83, and the authors cited therein. See also Alessandro Passerin d'Entrèves, *La dottrina del diritto naturale* (Milan, Edizioni di Comunità, 1954), pp. 76ff.

sorts of arguments, including the one which Aristotle used to justify slavery. In a famous passage from *De Cive,* repeated in *Leviathan,* Hobbes faced without qualms the question of the distinction between *lex* and *jus,* by observing that "law is a *fetter,* right is *freedom;* and they differ like contraries."[8] The sphere of liberty, which is opposed to the sphere regulated by laws (here to be taken as civil laws), is the state of nature. This condition is therefore characterized by the existence of rights, not duties. Prominent among these rights are the rights to life and to all things which are indispensable to preservation. It is true that with the institution of civil society the individual is forced to give up his natural liberty and most of his natural rights. But this is a problem which for the time being must not concern us. What matters, if we are to show that Hobbes is an innovator,[9] is that he is the first to elaborate a complete theory of the state of nature. This condition would become the main device for those who wished to ground the theory of the limits of sovereignty on the perfect rights of citizens, rather than on the imperfect duty of the prince.

If we wish to draw all the consequences of the theses which we have presented and briefly discussed, we should conclude that Hobbes and only Hobbes is the initiator of modern natural law theory. Nonetheless, there is an interpretation of his thought and position in the history of legal theory which considers him to be the precursor of legal positivism. If I am not mistaken, this is also the prevailing interpretation.[10] Modern natural law theory would thus pass through a thinker in whom there also begins the dissolution of natural law theory. This would indeed be a rather embarrassing predicament, out of which we might follow two paths. We can either maintain that the so-called modern natural law theory no longer has any-

8. *De Cive,* XIV, 3, p. 186.

9. And his innovation will have many consequences, even if contrary to the ones at which he aimed.

10. For a detailed history of the historiography on Hobbes's legal theory, see M. Cattaneo, *Il positivismo giuridico inglese: Hobbes, Bentham, Austin* (Milan: Giuffrè, 1962), pp. 46ff. The author of this essay emphasizes that Hobbes is a natural law theorist, but in the end considers him "the first representative of British legal positivism" (p. 46).

thing to do with medieval natural law theory; the former is rather the antithesis of the latter. (This is the path recently taken by Piovani.) Or we can show that Hobbes, despite a few concessions to legal positivism, which are more substantive than formal, is a strong defender of natural law theory. He is substantively a natural law theorist more than people are usually willing to believe. (And this path is followed authoritatively by Warrender.) I incline toward the less drastic conviction that we can solve the problem when we realize the following:

1. The concepts "natural law theory" and "legal positivism" are quite ambiguous terms. (As are, by the way, all terms that label great currents of constantly recurring ideas.) There are various ways of being a natural law theorist or a legal positivist, which are not all antithetical to one another.
2. Despite his splendid conceptual armor, Hobbes is more vulnerable to inconsistency than would seem at first sight. And he is more vulnerable than I myself believed or have led my readers to believe in previous studies.[11]

I call "natural law theories" those conceptual systems in which at least the two following statements are recurrent:

1. Besides positive law (which no philosopher has ever dared to deny) there is natural law.
2. Natural law is superior to positive law. (In the sense that I shall specify below.)

I think that, from a historical point of view, we can find these two essential conditions in three different philosophical and juridical systems. They can be distinguished from one another because they conceive the relationship of superiority between

11. Cattaneo is right in saying: "Hobbes's thought contains a few basic contradictions—in particular the conflict between the natural right to self-preservation and sovereignty, principles which are both tendentially absolute. It is also so complex that it becomes impossible to draw from it extreme and unilateral conclusions" (ibid., pp. 119–20).

natural and positive law in different ways. I therefore think it necessary, in order to avoid confusion and misunderstanding, to distinguish three kinds of natural law theories, by formulating three broad theses:

1. Natural law and positive law are in the relation of the starting point to the conclusion (or of general maxims to applications).
2. Natural law determines the content of legal norms, while positive law makes them effective, by making them binding.
3. Natural law constitutes the foundation of validity of the positive legal order, taken as a whole.

These three possible theories of natural law rest on different understandings of how natural law is *superior to* positive law. A law[12] can be said to be superior to another law either in the sense of a static theory, or in that of a dynamic theory, according to Kelsen's well-known terminology. That is, the inferior law draws from the superior one either its content (as a logical conclusion follows from an evident premise), or its validity. In both cases the inferior norm does not have the power to abrogate the superior one. But in the former case, the inferior norm that is incompatible with the superior one is said to be unjust; in the latter case, it is said to be invalid. We may distinguish the three kinds of natural law theories depending on whether natural law is superior to positive law because it provides both content and validity to the latter (system 1); because it only provides the content (system 2); or because it only provides the ground of validity (system 3).

1. In St. Thomas, human law is conceived as a conclusion reached from the general maxims of natural law, and it draws both content and the ground of its validity from natural law.[13]
2. In a system which attributes to positive law the func-

12. By "law" I here refer both to one norm and to an entire legal order.
13. The case of human laws conceived as *determinationes* of the law of nature is different: for these only does Thomas say that "they derive their validity from the human law alone" (*Summa Theologica*, I, II, q. 95, art. 2).

tion of ensuring that the norms of natural law are effective,[14] the individual norms of positive law derive their content from natural law, but not their ground of validity.

3. Finally, in a system in which natural law provides the ground of validity of the legal order as a whole, natural law is superior to positive law because, unlike in system 2, positive law does not depend on natural law for its content, but rather for its validity.

As already remarked, Hobbes's thought is far from being simple, and contains on the contrary much roughness under its smooth surface. Nonetheless, the letter of Hobbes's system nearly always—and its spirit, in my opinion, always— prompts me to interpret it as a natural law theory of the third type. I have illustrated this thesis on another occasion.[15] But I have deemed it opportune to revive this discussion by adding some clarifications and also some nuances,[16] because recent interpreters such as Warrender and, within limits, Cattaneo have reevaluated Hobbes as a natural law theorist.

2.   Hobbes's main aim in elaborating his political theory is to give solid foundations to civil power. The ideological import of natural law theory was at the time very vigorous. Hobbes therefore thought that the best way to found civil power was to show that the obligation to obey the sovereign was a duty derived from a law of nature. He stated that the main theme of his work was the law of nature, although in it he aimed to justify a maximum of sovereignty together with a minimum of resistance. But his entire discourse on the law of nature could be reduced to the assertion that the obligation to obey the sovereign is established by the laws of nature. Consequently, once the state has been instituted, there is no natural (or moral) duty for subjects, except for cases which are exceptional and cir-

14. We can consider Locke's theory as an example of this case, although with a certain approximation.

15. See the previous chapter.

16. For which I am grateful to those who think differently from me.

cumscribed, other than that of obedience. In this respect, at least two passages from *De Cive* are irrefutable: "By the virtue of the natural law which forbids breach of covenant, the law of nature commands us to keep all the civil laws" and "Our Saviour hath not showed subjects any other laws for the government of a city, beside those of nature, that is to say, beside the command of obedience."[17]

Even the most important work on Hobbes's political thought which has appeared in recent years confirms this thesis.[18] Howard Warrender's aim is not to assign Hobbes either to the tradition of natural law theory, or to legal positivism, which would be a futile enterprise. It is rather to show that the law of nature plays an indispensable function in Hobbes's thought. More precisely, Warrender's aim is to refute those interpreters who have repeatedly noted in Hobbes's system the lack or ineffectiveness of a natural (or moral) obligation, as distinct from a civil obligation. Nonetheless, Warrender's favorite argument in support of his thesis is that Hobbes's entire theory of political obligation would have collapsed, if he had not accepted a moral obligation preceding and independent of civil obligation. Moral obligation derives from the law of nature that prescribes keeping one's promises, first and foremost the promise made in the compact from which political obligation derives.

In Hobbes's works, there are also hints and passages which may induce us to interpret Hobbes's natural law theory as a theory of the second type, that is, as a theory in which the law of nature provides the content of the norm, and positive law guarantees that the norm will be effective. Hobbes begins his discussion as follows: The laws of nature exist in the state of nature, but they are usually ineffective because of the condition of insecurity which characterizes relations among individuals. We thus need a firm and unquestioned power which makes it possible for human beings to carry out the laws of nature, thus ensuring their safety. This beginning would justify

17. *De Cive*, XIV, 10, pp. 190–91; XVII, 11, p. 267.
18. H. Warrender, *The Political Philosophy of Hobbes: His Theory of Obligation* (Oxford: Clarendon Press, 1957).

us in believing that Hobbes aimed to construct a legal system in which the laws of nature would constitute the substantive or primary norms; whereas positive law constitutes the set of the secondary or sanctioning norms. We can interpret in the same fashion Hobbes's version of the theory which maintains that the gaps in the legal system can be filled by resorting to the laws of nature.[19] In the case where a positive norm is missing, the law of nature reemerges. If this is true, it is argued, this is a sign that the law of nature has never been superseded by a positive law. On the contrary, a norm of the law of nature underlies, or must underlie every corresponding norm of positive law. Indeed, remarks Hobbes, "the *civil law* . . . also punisheth those who knowingly and willingly do actually transgress the *laws of nature.*"[20]

Hobbes thus leads us to understand that the laws of nature are always in force, as substantive norms regulating conduct. This is so even if the laws of nature cannot oblige *in foro externo*, and are thus ineffective, unless the legislator acknowledges them once and for all; or unless the judge acknowledges them, in case of a gap, that is, if there is a case which the legislator did not foresee. From the point of view of the letter of Hobbes's text, there is one passage which is highly complicated and has created problems even for Warrender (even if for other reasons), and is especially favorable to this interpretation. This is the passage from chapter XXVI of *Leviathan* in which Hobbes says that the law of nature and the civil law contain one another and are coextensive. He then goes on to remark that the laws of nature are not really laws until the state exists, "for it is the sovereign power that obliges men to obey them." He concludes: "Civil, and natural laws are not different kinds, but different parts of law; whereof one part being written, is called civil the other unwritten, natural."[21]

In my opinion, there are, however, more decisive reasons for believing that Hobbes's version of natural law theory is

---

19. *De Cive*, XIV, 14, p. 194; *Leviathan*, XXVI, p. 183.
20. *De Cive*, XIV, 14, p. 194.
21. *Leviathan*, XXVI, p. 174.

ultimately of the third type. There is, first of all, a general argument, which we can infer from the spirit of Hobbes's system. The conception of natural law theory of the second type is historically the ideology of the limited or liberal state, and of the theories of resistance. But Hobbes aims with all his energies at supporting the reasons for the absolute state. This is a state in which power encounters as few limits as possible in the rights of others; and it is the state where absolute obedience reigns, that is, an obedience than which no greater can be given.[22] As we shall see, the version of natural law theory of the third type serves very well the purpose of rationally founding the ideology of the absolute state. The essential feature of the third type consists of rejecting the law of nature as a source of prescriptive content, and of accepting it exclusively as the source of the content of norms.

We can easily document Hobbes's aversion to the law of nature as a set of substantive norms, which are valid as such even after the institution of civil society. The decisive passage is in *De Cive*, on the basis of which we could legitimately count Hobbes among the purest representatives of ethical positivism. This is the doctrine according to which the law is just merely because it is the law.

> Since therefore it belongs to kings to discern between *good* and *evil*, wicked are those, though usual, sayings, *that he only is a king who does righteously,* and *that kings must not be obeyed unless they command us just things;* and many other such like. Before there was any government, *just* and *unjust* had no being, their nature only being relative to some command: and every action in its own nature is indifferent; that it becomes *just* or *unjust,* proceeds from the right of the magistrate. Legitimate kings therefore make the things they command just, by commanding them, and those which they forbid, unjust, by forbidding them.[23]

22. *De Cive*, VI, 13, p. 80.
23. Ibid., XII, 1, p. 158. In *Leviathan:* "It is manifest, that the measure of good and evil actions, is the civil law; and the judge the legislator, who is always representative of the commonwealth" (XXIX, p. 211).

This statement is so serious that it may induce us to seek moderating hints. Hobbes appears to be referring to all possible actions. Nonetheless, we might contend that the sovereign's power to establish what is good and what is evil only regards indifferent actions, that is, those actions that are neither commanded nor prohibited by the laws of nature. This would be confirmed by another passage:

> That which is prohibited by the divine law cannot be permitted by the *civil*; neither can that which is commanded by the *divine law*, be prohibited *by the civil*. Notwithstanding, that which is permitted by the *divine right*, that is to say, that which may be done by *divine right* doth no wit hinder why the same may not be forbidden by the *civil laws*; for *inferior laws* may restrain the liberty allowed by the *superior*, although they cannot enlarge them.[24]

However, against this thesis we can adduce the curious and provocative thesis of *De Cive*, which Hobbes often repeats, and which concerns precisely necessary actions, that is, those that are commanded or prohibited by the law of nature. This thesis shows that for Hobbes it pertains only to the sovereign to establish the legality or illegality of actions, even if these are already regulated by the law of nature. "Theft, murder, adultery, and all injuries, are forbid by the laws of nature; but what is to be called *theft*, what *murder*, what *adultery*, what *injury* in a citizen, this is not to be determined by the natural, but by the civil law."[25] From this premise Hobbes draws the marvellously

24. *De Cive*, XIV, 3, pp. 185–86. Cattaneo offers another interpretation. Wishing to acquit Hobbes of the charge of ethical positivism, he draws arguments from the definition of law given in *Leviathan*, at the beginning of chap. XXVI, and from a few other passages, in order to show that Hobbes employs "just" and "unjust" instead of "legal" or "illegal" (*Il positivismo giuridico inglese*, pp. 106ff.). It seems to me that Cattaneo's thesis is acceptable for the definition offered in *Leviathan*, but cannot be applied to the passage which I have quoted in the text, and which Cattaneo does not take into consideration.

25. *De Cive*, VI, 16, pp. 85–86. Thus in XIV, 10, pp. 190–91; XVII, 10, pp. 265–66.

bold conclusion that "no civil law whatsoever, which tends not to a reproach of the Deity . . . can possibly be against the law of nature."[26] If we take this statement literally,[27] we should interpret it as meaning that the sovereign never errs, and is always right, no matter what he commands or prohibits. The laws of nature are so general, and the sovereign's freedom to interpret them so absolute that every civil law always conforms to the law of nature.

In brief, according to the second version of natural law theory, civil law incorporates the law of nature, and therefore depends on it. But according to this passage from Hobbes, civil law *shapes* the law of nature, thus subjecting it to its own ends. In the former case the sovereign resembles more a mechanic who starts a machine that is already perfect; in the latter case, he resembles more a sculptor, who makes the statue out of raw material.

But it is not the thesis cited above (which disappears from *Leviathan*) that offers the strongest argument in favor of the thesis that the civil law is substantively independent of the law of nature. It is rather the argument that derives from Hobbes's theory of obedience, which is one of the essential elements of his system. In several places Hobbes calls the obedience which the subject owes to the sovereign "simple obedience." Absolute sovereignty is not an unlimited power (only God's power is), but rather the power "than which a greater command cannot be imagined."[28] In the same way, simple obedience, which Hobbes also calls absolute, is not an unlimited obedience, but it is the one than which "a greater cannot be performed."[29] By simple obedience Hobbes means the obedience owed to the command as command, independently of its content. Such obedience is founded on our promise to do, without questioning, all the commands of the person to whom we have transferred the right to command. It is the same obedience that the

26. Ibid., XVII, 10, p. 190.
27. But we shall have to accept a few exceptions.
28. Ibid., VI, 6, p. 75.
29. Ibid., VI, 13, p. 158.

slave owes to the master,[30] and Adam and Eve to God in the Garden of Eden.[31] This type of obedience, by the way, distinguishes the law as command from advice: "Now when obedience is yielded to the laws, not for the thing itself, but by reason of the advisor's will, the law is not a *counsel*, but a *command*, and is defined thus: *law is the command of that person, whether man or court, whose precept contains in it the reason of obedience.*"[32]

One of the salient and typical features of traditional natural law theory is the thesis that a positive law is valid only if it conforms to the law of nature. In St. Thomas's famous words: "There does not seem to be a law which is not just, for insofar as it participates in justice it also participates in virtue."[33] Hobbes's theses which we have illustrated above all appear to negate this theory. First: it pertains to the sovereign to establish what is good and what is evil, so that what is commanded is just, and what is prohibited is unjust. Therefore, the law is just not because it conforms to a law which is different and superior, but merely because it has been issued by the legitimate sovereign. Second: if no civil law can be contrary to the law of nature, there can be no disagreement between civil law and the law of nature. Only such disagreement would allow us to consider a civil law invalid, independently of whether it was issued legitimately or not. Third: if the subject must obey the sovereign's commands as commands, independently of their content, it follows that the sovereign's commands, that is his laws, are valid independently of their conformity to the law of nature. Should we therefore draw the conclusion that for Hobbes, once the state has been instituted, its laws are all valid, even those contrary to the laws of nature? And should

30. "For he who is obliged to obey the commands of any man before he knows what he will command him, is simply and without restriction tied to the performance of all commands whatsoever" (ibid., VIII, 1, p. 109).

31. "In that precept of not eating of the tree of *the knowledge of good and evil* . . . God did require a most simple obedience to his commands, without dispute whether that were *good* or *evil* which was commanded" (ibid., XVI, 2, p. 228).

32. Ibid., XIV, 1, pp. 182–83. See also *Leviathan*, XXV, p. 166.

33. *Summa Theologica*, I, II, q. 95, art. 2.

we conclude that the subject is bound to obey all civil laws, even those contrary to the laws of nature? But if we can answer this question in the affirmative, can we still speak of Hobbes as a natural law theorist? Should we not count him among the most radical supporters of legal positivism, indeed of that radical form of legal positivism represented by ethical legalism?

I believe that we can give a direct answer to this question by pointing to the third version of natural law theory, and illustrating all its implications. This appears to be the version closest to Hobbes's thought. As already stated, the specific feature of this third version of natural law theory is to acknowledge that, once the state has been instituted, only one law of nature survives. This is the law that imposes on human beings the obligation to obey civil laws. The logic of this theory prompts us to conclude that the general law of nature, which founds the legitimacy of civil power, preemptively resolves any future conflict between the laws of nature and civil laws. And this is so independently of Hobbes's particular thesis that it pertains to the sovereign to determine the content of natural laws. If a conflict were possible between civil law and natural law, the citizen who obeyed the latter rather than the former would violate the general law of nature which prescribes obedience to civil laws. One could answer that the general law prescribes obedience only to those civil laws that are not in contrast with the laws of nature. But if this were the case, the general law of nature would be meaningless, for it would be enough to establish a duty of obedience to particular laws of nature. In other words: if the citizen had an obligation to obey only those civil laws that conform to the laws of nature, there would be no need to resort to the law of nature that establishes the duty to obey civil laws. It would be sufficient to assert the duty to obey the laws of nature, in order to obtain the obedience required by civil laws.

The interpretation offered here presents the third version of natural law theory as a theory which aims at ensuring the legal system as a whole against the disobedience of individuals, by formulating a law of nature which legitimates positive law. If this interpretation is correct, we can consider the third version of natural law theory as a transition between traditional natural law theory and legal positivism. This interpretation would also explain why some commentators can maintain that Hobbes is still a natural law theorist with the same confidence with which others maintain that he is already a legal positivist.[34] And they can hold these different interpretations, although they substantively agree in their interpretations of Hobbes's thought.

What prompts us to count Hobbes's system among natural law theories is that both conditions which we believe characterize every possible version of natural law theory are present in his thought: the existence of natural law besides positive law, and the superiority of the former to the latter. Vice versa, what suggests that we can consider Hobbes's theory close to positivistic theories is the way in which the attribute of superiority functions. In the first two versions of natural law theory, natural law is superior to positive law in the sense that a positive norm contrary to natural law is not valid. In other words, the conformity of norms to natural law is the criterion of validity for every single norm of positive law. This is so in both versions. In the first version, positive norms are deductively derived from the general principles of natural law, while in the second version, positive laws guarantee the effectiveness of the corresponding natural laws. In both cases, the consequence is that a positive norm is valid only if it conforms to natural law. In the third version of natural law theory, it is legitimate to say that the law of nature is superior to positive law, because the former founds the legitimacy of the latter and makes it obligatory. But the consequence of this position is that natural law founds the legitimacy of, and makes obligatory the positive legal order as a whole, not the individual norms

34. "It is interesting to note that one of Hobbes's theses—that is, the fact that the law of nature is merely the foundation and justification of positive law—prompts Bobbio, on the one hand, to identify Hobbes as the initiator of legal positivism, and prompts Kelsen, on the other hand, to consider Hobbes as a natural law theorist, and to confirm his [Kelsen's] conviction that the main aim of natural law theory is to attribute an absolute and sacred foundation to positive law" (Cattaneo, *Il positivismo giuridico inglese*, p. 49).

which comprise it. Civil power is instituted on the basis of a law of nature. But once civil power is instituted, the individual norms of the system derive their validity from the authority of the sovereign, and no longer from particular laws of nature. Individual norms may thus be valid without conforming to the laws of nature. What holds for this principle of legitimation of the legal order also holds for the principle of efficacy in Kelsen's system. The principle of efficacy constitutes the criterion of validity of the legal order as a whole, not of its individual norms. There may thus be individual norms which continue to be valid without being effective. In the same way, Hobbes's principle of legitimation provides a criterion of validity for the whole legal order, not for individual norms. There may thus be norms which are valid even if they are contrary to the law of nature.

I mention the principle of efficacy because I wish to avoid any confusion between Hobbes's system and modern legal positivism. And I wish us to avoid mistaking it for contemporary positivism because of the closeness of his system to the theory of legal positivism. We may assign to legal positivism all theories that do not recognize that there exists natural law alongside positive law. For these theories there is no law other than positive law. As seen, Hobbes establishes the law of nature as the foundation of positive law. Therefore he is not a legal positivist. If a modern positivist retraces his steps to the fundamental norm of the positivist legal order, this law is not a law of nature, but a hypothesis or a conventional premise. If he seeks a principle legitimating the legal order, he does not look for it in a norm which transcends that order, but in the fact, which is empirically verifiable, that the legal order is de facto obeyed. Indeed, in a modern positivistic theory the principle of efficacy replaces Hobbes's general law of nature, and thus clears away even the last trace of natural law theory.

3.   This analysis, which places Hobbes's thought between natural law theory and legal positivism, would be incomplete if we did not remark that Hobbes is far away from drawing all possible consequences from his premises. We should not be

more Hobbesian than Hobbes. Despite his intentions and his statements, which we have just analyzed, Hobbes admits in some cases the right to resist an unjust law. In discussing the slave's obedience toward his master he already noted: "By virtue therefore of this promise, there is an absolute service and obedience due from the vanquished to the vanquisher, as possibly can be, *excepting what repugns the divine laws.*"[35] At the beginning of the third part of *De Cive*, he briefly summarizes his thought and says: "They who have gotten the sovereign command, must be obeyed simply, that is to say, *in all things which repugn not the commandments of God.*"[36] Let us remember that laws of nature and divine commandments are for Hobbes one and the same thing. The difference between them does not regard their content, but only their source. In another passage, he writes: "That which is prohibited by the *divine law,* cannot be permitted by the *civil;* neither can that which is commanded by the *divine law,* be prohibited *by the civil.*"[37] Nonetheless, once he has conceded this principle, Hobbes tries to limit its effects as much as possible, by defining exactly the cases in which disobedience is legitimate, and recognizing the right of resistance only in extreme situations, so that these decisions are not left to the discretion of individuals.

As is well known, and has been illustrated several times, from the fundamental ethical maxim according to which life must be preserved, Hobbes draws the conclusion that the right to life is inalienable. But we do not always remember that Hobbes aims at protecting the right to eternal life, not only to this earthly life. The sovereign may command anything except that which jeopardizes earthly and eternal life. If he issues such a command, the right of resistance arises, or, to quote, "the right of disobedience."[38] Cattaneo has recently analyzed in detail the cases relating to the right to life.[39] But let us be careful. If we wish to draw all consequences from Hobbes's

35. *De Cive*, VIII, 1, pp. 109. Italics are mine.
36. Ibid., XV, 1, p. 204. Italics are mine. See *Leviathan*, XXXI, p. 232.
37. *De Cive*, XIV, 3, p. 185.
38. *Leviathan*, XXI, p. 142.
39. Cattaneo, *Il positivismo giuridico inglese*, pp. 88ff., 103ff.

premises, we should recognize that here too the sovereign gets the upper hand. For we have seen that for Hobbes it is the sovereign who defines theft, homicide, and adultery. It is the sovereign who decides that to kill in self-defense, or to kill an enemy in war is not homicide. In the same way, he can decide that to kill a subject in other circumstances is not homicide, as in the case of capital punishment.

Hobbes makes extremely slender concessions to the freedom to disobey with respect to the right to eternal life. Divine laws are either laws of nature—which the state alone may interpret—or laws regarding worship. In relation to the latter, Hobbes analyzes the duties of human beings in the kingdom of God according to nature, the Old Testament, and the New Testament. The duties in the kingdom of God according to nature concern either conventional or natural ways of worshipping God. In the former case, it is the state which must determine these; in the latter, the state must also intervene to make public worship uniform, and to give one interpretation, valid for all subjects. "It may therefore be concluded, that the *interpretation* of all laws, as well *sacred* as *secular* (God ruling by the way of *nature* only), depends on the authority of the city. . . . Whatsoever God commands, he commands by his voice. And on the other side . . . whatsoever is commanded by them both concerning the manners of honouring God, and concerning secular affairs, is commanded by God himself."[40]

Hobbes admits only two exceptions to the duty of obedience: (1) when the sovereign commands subjects to offend God; (2) when he commands subjects to honor himself as if he were God.[41] In analyzing briefly duties toward God according to the Old Testament in chapter XVI of *De Cive*, Hobbes tries to show that the Hebrews were bound to obey their chiefs in all things unless a superior's command should imply the negation of divine providence or impose idolatry. Hobbes concludes: "In all other things they were to obey. And if a king or priest, having the sovereign authority, had commanded some-

40. *De Cive*, XV, 17, p. 222. See *Leviathan*, XXXI, p. 240.
41. But even this exception is eliminated in *Leviathan*, XLV, p. 427.

what else to be done which was against the laws, that had been his sin, and not his subject's; whose duty it is, not to dispute, but to obey the commands of his superior."[42] And finally, in discussing duties toward God according to the New Testament, Hobbes on the one hand concedes that "the subjects ought to obey their princes and governors, excepting those which are contrary to the commands of God." But on the other hand he immediately takes it away: "The commands of God, in a Christian city, concerning *temporal affairs* . . . are the laws and sentence of the city derived from those who have received authority from the city to make laws and judge of controversies; but concerning spiritual matters . . . are the laws and sentence of the city, that is to say, the Church."[43] In conclusion: "In a Christian commonweal obedience is due to the sovereign in all things, as well as *spiritual* as *temporal*."[44]

As we can see, Hobbes was willing to leave some margin for civil disobedience in order to guarantee the security of earthly life. But he was much less liberal when the security of eternal life was at stake. I look to my own life, for the state looks to my eternal life. Once again, the crucial norm which Hobbes employs to reinforce the principle of obedience is the law of nature that prescribes obedience to civil laws. This law of nature is also, like all laws of nature, a divine commandment; therefore it is a command, which must also be obeyed if one wishes to save one's eternal life. How can we admit that the citizen disobeys the state in order to ensure his own eternal life, when one of the conditions for ensuring it is to obey the divine/ natural law that prescribes obedience to the state? By obeying the state, the citizen thus kills two birds with one stone. He gains peace both on earth and in heaven. The conclusion of Hobbes's system further proves that Hobbes prefers the natural law theory of the third type. Among all the laws of nature, the one prescribing obedience to civil laws takes over. It is the essence of this law that, once it has been recognized and re-

42. *De Cive*, XVI, 18, p. 249. See *Leviathan*, XL.
43. *De Cive*, XVIII, 13, p. 315. See *Leviathan*, XLIII.
44. *De Cive*, XVIII, 13, p. 315.

spected as the precondition for earthly security and eternal salvation, it makes all other laws of nature invalid, by founding the validity of all civil laws. "The law of Christ therefore concerning killing and consequently all manner of hurt done to any man, and what penalties are to be set, commands us to obey the city only."[45]

The starting point of this essay was the acknowledgment that, through various paths, modern natural law theory begins with Hobbes. Its point of arrival is the acknowledgment that Hobbes's natural law theory is such as to pave the way to legal positivism, more than to perfect the edifice of traditional natural law theory. However, it would be mistaken to conclude that natural law theory falls into the arms of legal positivism. Quite the contrary. The truth is that Hobbes invents, elaborates, and refines the most sophisticated ingredients of natural law theory—the state of nature, the laws of nature, individual rights, the social contract. But he ingeniously employs them to build a gigantic obedience machine. We shall have to wait for Locke if we wish to find the method of natural law theory, which Hobbes handles so well, joined to and harmonized with the typical ideology of natural law theory, which establishes limits to the power of the state, and which Hobbes refutes and rejects. Modern natural law theory comes to us through Hobbes, but is affirmed only through Locke.

45. Ibid., XVII, 10, p. 266.

SIX

Hobbes and Partial Societies

1.   In these last thirty years, Hobbes's thought, and in particular his political thought, has become the objects of an enormous number of studies, which are philologically more and more accurate, historically richer and richer, and theoretically more and more sophisticated. But we are still far from having explored in all directions the immense territory of knowledge, which the sage of Malmesbury relentlessly covered in his extremely long life. Scholars have obviously focused on Hobbes's great themes: liberty and necessity, freedom and power, state of nature and civil society, natural law and civil law, the social contract and political obligation, and the relationship between subjects and the sovereign, and between Church and state. But Hobbes's political works, especially *Leviathan*, include countless particular reflections on the organization and the functions of the state. Scholars have not yet studied them sufficiently. These reflections are a mine which is inexhaustible, or at least not yet exhausted, and which is rich in precious materials still to be dug up and brought to light. Among these, I assign a prominent position to chapter XXII of *Leviathan*,[1]

1. I compare Oakeshott's edition of it with the original Latin edition, as edited by W. Molesworth, *Thomae Hobbes Malmesburiensis Opera philsophica quae latine scripsit omnia* (London: John Bohn, 1841), vol. III. I have also checked both

devoted entirely to partial societies. This chapter has not yet been analyzed as it deserves, if I am not mistaken, although it did not escape the attention of the great and still unsurpassed historian of the *Genossenschaftslehre*, Otto von Gierke.[2]

This chapter is interesting because it reveals Hobbes's broad knowledge of all aspects of his society, and the meticulous care with which he illustrated them, especially in his major work. But it is also interesting because it corrects the traditional view of Hobbes as the thinker who eliminated any intermediate sphere between the individual and the state. In doing so, Hobbes is supposed to have anticipated the monistic theory of the state, which many have identified as the essence of the modern state. Among all these, I should like to cite a theorist of

---

the French translation, edited by F. Tricaud, (Paris: Sirey, 1971), and the Spanish one, edited by Manuel Sanchez Sarto, (Mexico: Fondo de cultura economica, 1980).

2. The *Genossenschaftslehre* is the doctrine of corporations. O. von Gierke, *Das Genossenschaftsrecht*, vol. IV: *Die Status- und Korporationslehre der Neuzeit* (1913; reprint, Graz: Akademische Druck- u. Verlagsanstalt, 1959), pp. 355–61. Of Gierke see also *Johannes Althusius und die Entwicklung der naturrechtlichen Staatstheorien*, (1880). Hobbes's analysis of *systemata* is also mentioned by Santi Romano (*L'ordinamento giuridico*, with additions [Firenze: Sansoni, 1945], pp. 26–27, note 29), who probably found them mentioned by Gierke. Regarding the problem of the derivation of Santi Romano's theory of the legal order from Gierke's doctrine of corporations, see M. Fuchs, ("La *Genossenschaftslehre* di O. von Gierke come fonte primaria della teoria generale del diritto di Santi Romano," *Materiali per una storia della cultura giuridica* 9, no. 1 [June 1979]: 65–80), who espouses Tarantino's thesis ("Brevi riflessioni sui precedenti dottrinali dell'istituzionalismo di Santi Romano," *Rivista internazionale di filosofia del diritto*, 64 [1977]: 602–4). By Tarantino, see also *La teoria della necessità dell'ordinamento giuridico: Interpretazione della dottrina di Santi Romano* (Milan: Giuffrè, 1980). Regarding Fuchs's thesis, Tarantino has expressed his position in "Dell'istituzionalismo: Ancora sui precedenti della dottrina di Santi Romano," *Materiali* 11, no. 1. (June 1981): 169–80. Tarantino is less drastic than Fuchs in deriving Romano from Gierke, and takes into consideration other sources, such as Rosmini's *Filosofia del diritto*. G. Sorgi captures the importance of Hobbes's *systemata subordinata* in *Per uno studio della partecipazione: Hobbes, Locke, Tocqueville* (Lecce: Milella, 1981), pp. 83–88. (After this essay had already been published, P. Pasqualucci extensively treated the theme of partial societies in Hobbes in "Thomas Hobbes e Santi Romano ovvero la teoria hobbesiana dei corpi parziali," *Quaderni fiorentini per la storia del pensiero giuridico moderno*, no. 15 [1986]: 167–306; and Sorgi returns to it in *Quale Hobbes* [Milan: Franco Angeli, 1989], 188–217.)

communitarian pluralism, R. A. Nisbet. For him "few writers have had more influence upon the development of the modern centralized State than Hobbes." Therefore one might observe that "the modern State . . . is an inverted pyramid, its apex resting upon the 1651 folio edition of Hobbes's *Leviathan*." And this happens because "neither the family, the church, nor any other system of authority is allowed by Hobbes to intervene in any significant way between the individual and the absolute power of the state." In other words: "For Hobbes there are but two essential elements of civil society: the individual and the sovereign."[3]

Hobbes is certainly considered the fountainhead of a political theory which sees the state as the product of a compact stipulated among individuals. The two main subjects of the political universe are, on the one hand, individuals *uti singuli* [as individuals], and, on the other hand, the sovereign. But where the latter begins, the former end, and there appears to be no room for intermediate bodies. Hobbes's theory is dichotomous: we are either in the state of nature or in civil society; there are either discrete individuals who are constantly struggling with one another, or one sovereign (either person or assembly); power is either divided into as many units as are the individuals who live in the state of nature, or is shared power.

Commentators have often noted the similarity of Hobbes's procedure and that of Rousseau. Nonetheless, Hobbes is not Rousseau, who condemns partial societies as the vice of a well-constructed republic. Hobbes is a realistic thinker, whereas Rousseau is an ideologue. Hobbes is a very complex thinker, despite the apparent simplicity of his theory. He is ambiguous, despite his apparent clarity. He is twisted, despite his apparent linearity. The importance which he assigns to partial societies, their variety and function (whether positive or negative), is a feature of his political realism. This reveals that he is an unprejudiced observer of what actually is, as much as a rationalist

3. R. A. Nisbet, *The Quest for Community* (New York: Oxford University Press, 1953), pp. 129–30.

philosopher who devoted himself to the study of the state with the purpose of applying to it the rigorous method of the demonstrative sciences. The history of the doctrine of partial societies—*universitates* or *collegia* in Roman law, *Genossenschaften* in German law—has taken a different path from that taken by the history of the theories of the state. Both the former and the latter have often been the objects of independent studies. Nonetheless, the introduction of a specific analysis of partial societies in a general treatise on politics was not unprecedented. The most important example was undoubtedly Althusius's *Politica methodice digesta.*

2.   Hobbes devotes the second part of *Leviathan*, which begins with chapter XVII, to the analysis of the state (*Of Commonwealth*). In the five chapters which precede chapter XXII, Hobbes deals with the traditional great themes of political philosophy, or of the general theory of the state. These are the origins of the state (chap. XVIII), the rights of the sovereign and subjects respectively (chaps. XVIII and XXI), the forms of government (chap. XIX), and the other forms of power besides the political one, that is, paternal and despotic power (chap. XX). In chapter XXII, which is devoted to partial societies, Hobbes begins his analysis of themes pertaining to the special[4] theory of the state. The chapter begins as follows: "Having spoken of the generation, form, and power of a commonwealth, I am in order to speak next of the parts thereof."[5] Hobbes aims at analyzing two "parts" of the state: partial societies, to which he devotes chapter XX, and public officials, to whom he devotes the subsequent chapter.

We should remark first that Hobbes resorts to the organicistic metaphor in order to locate both of these parts within his system. He devises new analogies between the organs of the body politic and those of the human body, in addition to the analogies which made the introduction to *Leviathan* famous. Here, Hobbes offers a sketchy description of the state, by elab-

4. As opposed to general. —Trans.
5. *Leviathan*, XXII, p. 146.

orating a detailed analogy between a few features of a natural body, and the corresponding ones which characterize that artificial body which is "the great Leviathan," "a Commonwealth or State," and in Latin *"civitas."* He devotes two references to the organicistic interpretation of partial societies.

    a. At the end of the chapter we can read that these societies are to be compared to muscles, if they are legitimate; to tumors, bilious fluids, and abscesses, which are generated by the unnatural confluence of ill humors, if they are illegitimate.

    b. At the beginning of the subsequent chapter, which is devoted to public officials, we can read: "In the last chapter I have spoken of the similar parts of a commonwealth: in this I shall speak of the parts organical, which are public officials."[6]

In the first description of the state as an artificial body, partial societies are not mentioned. The analogy with muscles appears for the first time in chap. XXII, while magistrates are here compared more specifically to joints (in Latin, *artus*). These are in any case rather imprecise analogies, which cannot be subjected to a highly rigorous analysis. The analogy between partial societies and muscles only confirms how important they are for Hobbes in his view of the body politic as a whole.

A second feature of Hobbes's position becomes immediately apparent. From the very first lines, Hobbes calls the partial societies which he is about to analyze "parts" of the state. This means that he does not take them into consideration by themselves, but in relation to the state, which he conceives as a whole divided into parts which would not exist without the whole. In the history of political thought, two opposite con-

6. Ibid., XXIII, p. 156. The distinction between organic and similar parts is taken from Aristotle, who bases on them alone his description of the various parts in animals both in *De partibus animalium*, 646a, and in *Historia animalium*, 491a. The former, which can either be external, such as eyes and ears, or internal, such as brain and kidneys, are called anomeomerous. The latter, such as blood or muscles, are called omeomerous. According to Aristotle, muscles are to be considered omeomerous.

ceptions alternate with regard to the positioning of partial societies within the state. On the one hand, there is the monistic conception, which begins with Aristotle, according to whom there is only one perfect society, which is political society. This is the polis,[7] within which there exist lesser societies, such as the family, the village, or any society with particular ends.[8] These are imperfect societies, which are parts of a whole. And the whole is prior to the parts in an organicistic conception of the state, such as the ancients mainly held. On the other hand, there is a pluralistic conception. According to Gierke, who has elaborated the contrast between these two views, the pluralistic conception would stem from the German tradition of *Genossenschaften*. In this tradition, collective bodies were represented as original bodies, and they were recognized as having a personality distinct from the personality of individual members.[9]

The opposition between the monistic and pluralistic conceptions regained strength at the beginning of this century when the general theory of law divided into two schools. These

7. Which today we identify with the state, although we have to force the analogy a bit.

8. Aristotle analyzes societies which have particular ends in book VIII of the *Nicomachean Ethics*, which is devoted to friendship. He says that these associations (*koinoniai*) are "parts of the political community," and thus "fall under political association; for this aims not at the advantage of the moment but at that which extends over the whole of life" (J. A. K. Thomson, (trans.) [Harmondsworth: Penguin Books, 1952], 1160a, p. 274).

9. Gierke summarizes the contrast between the Roman and the Germanic conceptions of the relationship between the whole and the parts as follows: "There is a characteristic contrast between the Roman and the Germanic conceptions of corporations. To the Romans, townships and corporations appeared as copies (*Abbild*) of the constitution of the state; whereas to the Germans the state presented itself as the union and growth of elements already present in associations of the corporate and authoritative type (*genossenschaftliche und herrschaftliche Verbanden*)" (*Das Genossenschaftsrecht*, vol. III, p. 69, n. 125). According to Gierke, in the doctrine of Roman jurists corporations are parts of public law. This means that they "derive their particular existence from the only original and sovereign subject of public rights," and are therefore "a part of the state, and as such appear to be made in its likeness in all their aspects" (ibid., p. 69).

were, respectively, the school which maintained that the state is the only source of law, and the school which upheld the pluralism of legal orders.[10] Since Hobbes defines partial societies as "parts" of the state, he must be counted among the monists. And we could not expect a different position from such a coherent and consistent theorist (and ideologue) of the unity of the state as was the author of *Leviathan*.

3.   As we have said already, before coming to the analysis of partial societies, Hobbes devotes a chapter to the paternal government of the family and to despotic government, following a tradition which dates back to Aristotle. As we shall see shortly, the family does belong to the category of partial societies, and is thus included in chapter XXII. But Hobbes follows those who do not make the specific account of paternal and despotic government overlap with the account of the family household within the analysis of partial societies. For starting with Aristotle, the family-household has been taken into consideration in the phenomenology of the different forms of power, to be distinguished from political power, rather than in the phenomenology of forms of societies.

There is a further reason why Hobbes's specific account of partial societies in *Leviathan* is of interest to us. This account represents an innovation with respect to those which he offered in his previous works, when he devoted only a short paragraph to this theme. In *Elements*, it is paragraph nine of chapter XIX; in *De Cive*, it is paragraph ten of chapter V. In both these works, Hobbes arrives at the argument of partial societies, after describing the covenant of union, and after defining the body politic or civil society. His aim is to remark that, alongside the power common to all members of the same

10. This theme has recently been the object of new studies, both in Italy and in Germany. In Italy the doctrine of the pluralism of legal systems has met with great success, especially through Santi Romano's work. In Germany this new interest has been motivated by the worsening of the phenomenon called "pluralism," which at the beginning of the century was responsible for the crisis of the monistic conception of the state.

community, there may be partial associations among a few members of that community. In *Elements*, these are called corporations; in *De Cive, personae civiles* [civil persons in the English version].

Hobbes defines corporations as subordinate associations, which have as their ends "certain common activities for some common benefit or of the whole city." And even more briefly, he defines *personae civiles* as companies of persons who have joined together "for the doing of certain things." Furthermore, common to both works is the example of societies of merchants [*sodalitates mercatorum*], an example which can also be found in the chapter from *Leviathan* which I am analyzing here. In regard to their relationship with the political association, in *Elements* Hobbes writes that partial societies have as much power over the individuals belonging to them as the state of which they are members permits them to have. In *De Cive*, he uses the formula *permittente civitate sua* (by the permission of the city). In both cases we are dealing, as anyone can see, with significant hints, which are however sketchy and superficial.

4. Up to now I have spoken of partial societies, for I wished to use a term which is generic and easily understandable. But Hobbes employs another term, which deserves a few comments. Chapter XXII, which we are analyzing here, is entitled "Of Systems Subject, Political and Private" [in the Latin version *De systematibus civium*]. Let us leave aside for the time being the adjective "subject," which shows that Hobbes is interested in partial societies as subject or subordinated to the sovereign power. Note that the term which Hobbes uses to indicate collective bodies is *systems*, whereas in the usual language of jurists, they are called *universitates, corpora,* and *collegia;* and in medieval Latin, *corporationes.* In this sense, the term *systems* has no precedent in the English language, at least as far as we can tell from the dictionaries. These, under "system," in the sense of assembly, indicate only Hobbes's use, and not even, to my knowledge, that of any previous political

writers.[11] Hobbes himself, by the way, did not use this term in his political works written before *Leviathan*.

Hobbes's definition of "system" is quite clear, although slightly hasty. (It is hasty because it does not allow us to appreciate the variety, latitude, and complexity of the phenomenon which the term comes to designate.) "By *systems*," he writes, "I understand any number of men joined in one interest, or one

11. The word *system* was already used by Grotius, but in the narrower sense of confederation of states. "Thus it may happen that several states establish close ties with one another through a federation, making what we might call a *systema*, as Strabo says in more than one place; yet each of them taken individually does not cease to maintain its condition of perfect state" (*Of the Law of War and Peace*, I, 3, 7). In his French translation of this work, Jean Barbeyrac translates *systema* as *"système ou corps composé,"* and in a footnote he quotes two passages from Strabo in which the term *systema* is used with the meaning accepted by Grotius. Of these two passages, the first regards the Amphictyonic league (Strabonis Rerum Geographicarum Libri XVII, (Book IX, 7, C 420); the second, the Lycian league (Book XIV, 2, C 664). As is well known, Pufendorf, like Grotius, speaks of *systemata civitatum* in various paragraphs of chapter V of Book VII of the *Law of Nature and Nations,* which is devoted to the classical theme of the forms of government. Dr. Fiammetta Palladini, author of the well-informed and well-documented work, *Discussioni seicentesche su Samuel Pufendorf: 1663–1700* (Bologna: Il Mulino, 1978), kindly informed me of passages in previous works, in which Pufendorf dealt with the same theme, and used the same term. One is the *Dissertatio de systematibus civitatum,* written probably between 1664 and 1668, included in *Dissertationes academicae selectiores* (1675), and *De statu Imperii Germanici* (1667). It is well known that Hobbes was one of Pufendorf's main sources. And in the case of the term *systema,* there is a reference to the author of *Leviathan.* Pufendorf defines the *systemata civitatum* following Grotius, as "several states linked to one another by such particular and strong ties that they seem to constitute one body, although each of them retains the supreme authority in itself." He then adds that "it is not appropriate to refer to a state as a system, if the state is composed of several subordinate bodies, as Hobbes does in chapter XXII of *Leviathan,* where he compares the parts of the city to the muscles of the human body" (*Law of Nature and Nations* VII, v, 16). According to Dr. Palladini, here Pufendorf seems to criticize Hobbes's use of the term *systema* to identify states composed of subordinate bodies. For Pufendorf, the term "system" designates associations of true states, although a system is internally articulated. This is confirmed by the interpretation which the French translator, Jean Barbeyrac, assigns to this passage: "Il paroit par cette définition qu'on ne dois pas, comme fait Hobbes, mettre au rang des Etats composés ceux qui renferment simplement plusieurs corps subordonnez." Actually, Hobbes did not call *systema* only the states composed of lesser social and political bodies. He had used the word in a more

business."[12] Hobbes includes in the category of "systems," as well as its synonym *universitates,* public agencies, such as provinces or townships, as much as religious communities, commercial companies, or guilds. We might argue that, with the term "interest," Hobbes wished to refer to the aim of public agencies; and, with the term "business," to that of private associations. But the definition is in any case too scanty to enable Hobbes to describe a complex reality. This becomes apparent when we analyze the typology to which Hobbes devotes most of chapter XXII, which is well constructed and articulated.

Why "system"? We should not forget that Hobbes is learned in classical Greek. He began his career as a scholar with a translation of Thucydides, and ended it with a translation of Homer. In classical Greek, *systema* refers not only to a collection of inanimate parts, but also to a group of people. Consequently, it means meeting, assembly, congress, and so forth, and a group of communities as well, as in our terms confederation or federation. We can find the term *systema* with these connotations in Aristotle, Polybius, and Plutarch, and in juridical language, which employs it as a technical term. In the *Corpus juris civilis,* when texts are reported both in Latin and Greek, *systema* corresponds to *collegium.* We still have to wonder why Hobbes used the term *systema,* which is clearly a Grecism, in the Latin version, when he had at his disposal Latin terms which were widely used in England, and which he himself had used in his

---

general way to designate any political or social body, including the state, either articulated or simple, given the definition of *systema* which he offers at the beginning of chapter XXII. In the Latin version which Pufendorf had available it reads as follows: "By *systems* I understand any number of men joined in one interest." But Pufendorf's restrictive interpretation of the use of *systema* in Hobbes's language seems to be confirmed by an analogous passage from Pufendorf's *Dissertatio* cited above: "And thus it is clear that a true state is not a system, for it is composed of several subordinate bodies, which are called *systemata* by Hobbes, and are compared to the muscles in the human body" (sec. 8). Again following Dr. Palladini, there is at least one context in which Pufendorf uses the term *systema* in the generic sense of *corpus.* In speaking of *entia moralia,* he calls them "moral persons which may be either discrete individuals or human beings united in one system through a moral bond" (*De iure naturae et gentium,* I, i, 12). [Transl. mine—TRANS.].

12. *Leviathan,* XXII, p. 146.

previous works. A student of Hobbes's thought has advanced the hypothesis that the Latin version of *Leviathan* was written before the English version, even though it was published later. But Hobbes's use of the term *systema* might lead us to reject this hypothesis.[13]

5. In chapter XXII, Hobbes analyzes, as we have already said, those systems which are subject to the state (in Latin *subordinata*). Hobbes uses the term "system," as well as the traditional terms corresponding to it, such as the Greek *koinonia*, and the Latin *societas*, in a general sense which includes all kinds of associations. It also includes the political association, Aristotle's *koinonia politike*, and the *societas civilis* of medieval and modern political writers who follow in Aristotle's footsteps, at least until Kant.[14] It is therefore necessary for Hobbes to introduce a first distinction within the general category systems, between "absolute and independent systems," and "dependent systems." Partial societies are dependent systems. Independent systems are those that are subject to no one else but their own representatives. This is a class with only one member. For Hobbes, only states belong to it.[15]

Hobbes qualifies independent systems with two adjectives, absolute and independent, which also reinforce one another. The first of these, absolute, regards the power of the sovereign over his subjects. It means that the sovereign is not bound to the laws through which he regulates the behavior of his subjects. The second, independent, regards the power of the sovereign with respect to other sovereigns. It means that every sovereign enjoys the same status as do individuals in the state of nature, which is a condition of reciprocal independence. Inversely, all others are subordinate systems. For, except for

13. This is F. C. Hood's hypothesis, in *The Divine Politics of Th. Hobbes: An Interpretation of Leviathan* (Oxford: Clarendon Press, 1964), pp. 54ff.

14. On the history of the term *civil society*, I refer to the two entries "Società civile," which I wrote for the *Dizionario di politica* (Turin: Utet, 1976), and for *Enciclopedia Einaudi* (Turin: Einaudi, 1981), vol. XIII.

15. Only for Hobbes, for usually the political theorists criticized by Hobbes consider also the Church to be an independent system.

states, all other systems are "subordinate to some sovereign power, to which every one, as also their representative, is *subject.*"[16] The crucial term in this context is "representative," to which I shall return later. For the time being, it suffices to say that a system is a real system only if the individuals who compose it recognize either a natural person or an assembly as their representative. Hobbes calls these systems "regular," to distinguish them from the irregular ones (see below.) On the basis of this crucial qualification, states are then systems. That is, they are groups of individuals who have only one representative (the sovereign), while partial societies (the regular ones, to be precise) are systems, that is, groups of individuals, whose representative depends on the representative of the general system. In other words, the individual, as a subject of the state, has no other representative than the sovereign. And as a member of a family, he recognizes as his representative the head of the family, who, in his turn, recognizes as his representative the sovereign, who is superior to the head of the family.

This distinction is not new. It faithfully reflects the monistic conception of power, which finds a consistent and tenacious supporter in Hobbes. It is a reformulation of the old distinction, which was well-known to medieval jurists, between *civitas superiorem recognoscens,* and *civitas superiorem non recognoscens.*

6.   After this first general distinction, which allows Hobbes to define the subject matter of chapter XXII,[17] there follows a typology of partial societies. This deserves a few comments.

The typology of partial societies was for centuries a part of the general doctrine of corporations, although it had not been codified so rigidly as the typology of the forms of government. This had been handed down over the centuries in the formulation of Aristotle's *Politics.* The doctrine of corporations was elaborated by jurists with strictly juridical aims. These

16. *Leviathan,* XXII, p. 146.

17. Hobbes himself takes care of warning the reader that he has analyzed the absolute and independent systems in the previous five chapters.

were the regulations of relations between the members of a corporation and the corporation as a whole, and between the corporation and other legal persons which might establish relationships with the corporation. The criteria of classification had therefore always been exclusively juridical. They concerned the corporation as a subject of law. That is, they established in what sense and within what limits the corporation could be considered a subject of rights, and of what rights. This warning is necessary because the typologies of social systems that are familiar to us have been elaborated by sociologists and anthropologists, who employ completely different criteria. These regard either the various structures or the different functions of various kinds of social groups. As clarifying examples, let us think of Tönnies and Durckheim's two great dichotomies: society and community, mechanical and organic solidarity; or of Weber's more articulated classification in the first paragraphs of *Economy and Society.*

In the juridical tradition, the classification of partial societies distinguishes between private and public agencies, between agencies which have legal personality and those which do not, between agencies for which the principle of unity springs from within (*Körperschaften*), and those for which the principle of unity is imposed from without (*Anstalten*), according to Gierke's terminology. Let us consider the classification which Althusius proposes in his great political work, which can be considered a general theory of social systems (*consociationes*). He starts from the great dichotomy of the juridical world, distinguishing between private and public. From this, successive lesser dichotomies branch out, which in the end provide a complete and exhaustive map of all agencies which we can comprise under the universal category of *consociationes.*

From this point of view, Hobbes's typology is not at all innovative, for he elaborates it by relying exclusively on juridical criteria. It has been noted several times that Hobbes is quite expert in juridical thinking, although the study of Hobbes's juridical sources until now has been far from satisfactory.

All the subdistinctions which Hobbes employs to build his typology of subordinate systems are clearly juridical. The first subdistinction is the classical one, between private and public systems. (Hobbes calls the latter "political.") The second subdistinction, which only concerns private systems, is also the classical one: private systems may be legitimate or illegitimate. Public systems are by their own nature always legitimate. They are instituted by the sovereign power, and they owe their existence only to the sovereign's authority. Private systems may be legitimate or illegitimate, because they are constituted by the subjects themselves, or by a foreign sovereign, who is a public authority at home but a private individual in someone else's home. Legitimate private systems are those that the sovereign permits; illegitimate, those that he prohibits. Hobbes does not tell us whether those instituted by a foreign power are always illegitimate. However, he provides examples of legitimate private systems, which are instituted by the subjects among one another, such as the family; and examples of illegitimate ones, such as corporations of beggars, thieves, and gypsies. But in the instance of private systems instituted by a foreign power, he only adduces examples of illegitimate ones. An example is a party constituted by a state within the territory of another state, with the aim of destroying the legitimate power of the latter. (A contemporary reader immediately thinks of the official reasons given by some states to prohibit the constitution of communist parties formally aligned with the Soviet Union.) We could cite legations as examples of a system instituted by a state within the territory of another state, which are recognized by the latter and are therefore legitimate. But legations are public systems.

The distinction between legitimate and illegitimate private systems also allows us to clarify the difference between public, or political systems, which are by nature legitimate, and private legitimate systems. Public systems are instituted by the sovereign power; legitimate private systems are instituted by the members themselves of that particular system. The sovereign power merely allows them or tolerates them, that is, more simply, it does not prohibit them. At the beginning of chapter XXII, Hobbes laconically says that these private systems are "allowed" by the sovereign power. Later, he specifies

that "private bodies regular, and lawful, are those that are constituted without letters, or other written authority, saving the
laws common to all other subjects."[18] This definition would be
clear, if it were not for the fact that Hobbes defines illegitimate
private systems as those in which individuals unite "without
any public authority at all," thus employing a formula which
does not differ from that used to define legitimate private systems ("without letters, or other written authority"). The difference would thus consist only in that legitimate systems are
regulated by the same laws that regulate all other persons,
whereas illegitimate systems either escape or violate those
laws. Hobbes's remarks are in any case too sketchy to allow us
to analyze this theme in greater depth. Examples clarify his
distinction better than definitions.

7.   The most interesting of the three distinctions is that between regular and irregular systems. Regular systems are
those which have a representative, and which therefore constitute a moral or artificial person; the others are irregular. This
distinction does not coincide with that between dependent
and independent systems, even if the latter can only be regular. Neither does it coincide with the distinction between public and private systems, even if the examples which Hobbes
provides of irregular systems are all private systems. It also
does not coincide with the distinction between legitimate and
illegitimate systems, for both regular and irregular systems
may be legitimate or illegitimate. The criterion of distinction
between regular and irregular systems is representation. The
criterion to distinguish between legitimate and illegitimate
systems is authorization. There may therefore be authorized or
unauthorized systems with or without representatives. In
other words, there are authorized systems with or without representatives, and unauthorized systems with or without representatives.
    The first reason why the distinction between regular and ir-
regular systems is of interest is that it is based on the principle

18. *Leviathan*, XXII, p. 153.

of representation. To this Hobbes devoted chapter XVI of *Leviathan*, which is very dense and not always easy to interpret. The central theme of this chapter is the distinction between two kinds of persons, the natural and the artificial. A natural person is one whose words and actions are considered his own. An artificial person is one whose words and actions are considered to represent words or actions of another man (or another thing). What characterizes an artificial person is that there is no identity between the actor and the author. The actor is the one who acts in the name and on behalf of others. The author is the one who gives the actor the authority to act in his name and on his behalf. Things too, such as a church, a hospital, or a bridge, may constitute artificial persons. In this case the author, who grants the authority to act, cannot be the thing, but is the owner or a public official who assigns to an individual or a council the management of the thing. Things, unlike human beings, can only be personified after civil power has been instituted. Besides individuals and some things, human beings can have representatives without any authors. This is the case with persons deprived of reason, such as children and madmen, and with idols and false gods, who among the Romans were represented by priests, and even with the true God, whose representatives were Moses, who governed the Hebrews not in his own name, but in the name of God, and then Jesus, who preached not for himself but as the messenger of his Father.

The theme of representation is central to Hobbes's political philosophy, for the state is the moral person by definition. Chapter XVI, which I am here summarizing, precedes the central chapter of *Leviathan*, which ends with the definition of the state. This definition is, so to speak, foretold in chapter XVI: "A multitude of men, are made *one* person, when they are by one man, or one person, represented; so that it be done with the consent of every one of the multitude in particular. For it is the *unity* of the representer, not the *unity* of the represented, that maketh the person *one*. And it is the representer that beareth the person, and but one person: and *unity*, cannot otherwise be understood in multitude." Then Hobbes defines the state: "*One person, of whose acts a great multitude, by mutual covenants one with another, have made themselves every one the author, to the end he may use the strength and means of them all, as he shall think expedient, for their peace and common defence.*"[19] This definition emphasizes the distinction between the two figures of the actor and the author which characterizes the relation of representation. The representative is the actor: he has the authority to act also in the name of the represented. The author is the represented who confers to the representative the authority to act.

An artificial person is a unified entity because it has a representative. But this does not mean that the representative is to be a natural person. It can also be an assembly. In this case resort must be had to majority rule. Hobbes is explicit on this point. But he offers a curious explanation for it: he says that positive and negative voices neutralize one another. That party wins in which the affirmative voices exceed negative ones, or vice versa. "For if the lesser number pronounce, for example, in the affirmative, and the greater in the negative, there will be negatives more than enough to destroy the affirmatives; and thereby the excess of negatives, standing uncontradicted, are the only voice the representative hath."[20]

8.   With respect to regular systems we must first of all distinguish between regular political (or public) systems and private ones. Hobbes devotes most of chapter XXII to analyzing the former, which he calls "political bodies." According to Hobbes, there is a nearly infinite variety of them, both because of the various ends which justify their institution, and because of the different situations in which they are born. In particular, Hobbes considers provinces, defined as the regions where the sovereign does not dwell but governs by commission, and commercial companies. These are the associations to which the sovereign has granted the monopoly of a specific trade both within and without the country. Since these political

19. Ibid., XVI, p. 107, and XVII, p. 112.
20. Ibid., XVI, p. 107.

bodies are public, but depend on the sovereign,[21] their power, that is the power of their representative, is limited. It is the sovereign who established the limits of that power. Hobbes draws upon this relationship of subordination or subjection of the body politic to the sovereign so as to repeat once more his fundamental thesis that "the sovereign in every commonwealth, is the absolute representative of all the subjects; and therefore no other can be representative of any part of them, but so far forth, as he shall give leave."[22] If the sovereign gave permission to a political body to have a representative with absolute power over all aims of the members, this would mean that the sovereign had given up the government and divided power. We can make a further distinction within the category of regular and legitimate political bodies by considering their duration. There are permanent and temporary political bodies. As examples of the latter, Hobbes indicates political bodies that have consultative functions. The sovereign appoints them in order to obtain information about the state and the needs of his subjects in a specific area of the nation. He then dismisses them, once they have performed their task.

Hobbes considers private those regular and legitimate bodies that are instituted without letters patent or special written authorization, because they are regulated by the common law. Hobbes gives only one example of this kind of regular system: the family, which is represented as a body by the father. And the family belongs to the category of regular systems, because it is a body which has a representative.

As already noted, there are also bodies which are regular but illegitimate. These are criminal associations (or companies of gypsies), or corporations which are formed in a nation by the authority of a foreign person. Individuals unite in the latter in order to propagate their doctrines more easily, or in order to form a party against the legitimate power of the sovereign. These two examples are interesting, for they show clearly, better than any analysis, that regularity and legitimacy do not

---

21. They are not independent or sovereign.
22. *Leviathan*, XXII, pp. 146–47.

have to coincide. Both criminal associations and foreign political parties which act in someone else's nation are endowed with representatives, that is, of persons who act in the name and on behalf of their members. But these associations are illegitimate, because they are neither recognized nor authorized by the sovereign.

The typology of irregular systems is more interesting, because it is less common. Irregular systems are also divided into legitimate and illegitimate. But while Hobbes devoted his account of regular systems mostly to the legitimate ones, he emphasizes especially illegitimate cases of irregular systems. We can distinguish two species: leagues and gatherings of the people. Hobbes means by "league" an association of individuals who have stipulated an agreement in order to attain a common aim, such as defense. But defense against whom? If it is defense against the power of the state, Hobbes has no hesitation in saying that such leagues are usually not necessary, and it is therefore better to avoid forming them at all. Besides, they are often illegitimate, when their purpose is criminal. Only leagues among states are necessary and legitimate. Since there is no power above individual states which can demand obedience from them, a union among states is the only means that nations have to provide for their mutual defense. But this is not so for the subjects of a state, whose protection has been entrusted to the power of the state itself.

Such a convinced and consistent theorist of the unity of the state as Hobbes does not look with favor upon the formation of parties or factions. (Hobbes usually calls them factions or conspiracies.) He had already emphasized the harm which the formation of parties does to the state in two passages from *De Cive*. One is in chapter XII, where Hobbes analyzes the causes of disintegration of the state. Among these causes, besides the propagation of seditious doctrines, Hobbes considers the formation of groups aiming to act on the basis of those doctrines. He compares these groups with Medea's sisters, who cut their old father into pieces and cooked him in order to revive him. (And on the contrary they killed him.) The other passage, in the following chapter, explores the duties of sovereigns.

Among these, Hobbes lists the duty to dissolve parties, which are considered a state within a state. He defines the party or faction as "a multitude of subjects gathered together either by mutual *contracts* among themselves, or by the power of some one, without his or her authority who bear the supreme rule."[23]

Hobbes lists other groups among the irregular and illegitimate systems of the genus "factions."[24] These are groups which are formed within an assembly with the aim of taking it over, which he calls "secret cabals"; the armed escort which a private lord organizes for his own defense;[25] and parties in the strict sense of the term, which are formed to seize power, both in the religious domain, such as sects of the papists, and in the political domain, such as patricians and plebeians in Rome. All these three kinds of associations are illegal: "cabals," because they cause the interests of a group to prevail over the general interest; armed sects, because defense pertains only to the state, and is indeed the main reason for the rise of the state; and parties, because they are "contrary to the peace and safety of the people, and a taking of the sword out of the hand of the sovereign."[26]

9.   In contrast with the traditional image of Hobbes as a rationalist, who builds a theory of the state by deducing it from first principles, the author of *Leviathan* is in fact an acute observer of reality. We can find a few interesting remarks in the pages devoted to the second species of irregular systems, that is, the "concourse of people." As we should now say, the pages which Hobbes devotes to leagues and their various species regard what today, in works of public law, pertains to the right of association; while his pages on the concourse of people cover the part of public law which refers to the right of assembly. Hobbes is as severe in his account of the right of assembly, as he is with regard to the right of association. In modern pub-

23. *De Cive*, XIII, p. 175.
24. Distinct from "concourse of people."
25. Like the *bravi* in Manzoni's *The Betrothed*.
26. *Leviathan*, XXII, p. 155.

lic law the right of association and the right of assembly are the rule, while the prohibition to associate or gather is the exception. Hobbes discusses this theme in analyzing irregular systems, among which he includes both associations and assemblies, which may be legitimate or illegitimate. And he turns the relationship between rule and exception upside down. There is very little room for legitimate associations and assemblies in Hobbes's system.

For Hobbes, whether a concourse of people is legitimate or not depends both on the reason why the gathering occurs and on the number of people participating in it. The gathering of human beings in church to participate in a religious function, or in the theater to watch a performance is legitimate. But it becomes suspicious, and therefore illegitimate, if "the numbers are extraordinarily great,"[27] and if the reason for this enormous participation is not apparent, that is, not justifiable. Since the gathering is declared illegitimate, the sovereign has the right to dissolve it, and, in that case, to punish at least the promoters of the meeting, if not all participants. There is an example which, better than any other, shows the contrast between the latitude of the right of assembly in modern democratic states, in which that right is protected by the constitution, and the limits within which Hobbes circumscribes it. The example is the following. It is permissible for one thousand persons to gather together to present a petition to a magistrate. But it is not permissible that this petition be presented by all those who have approved of it, for a few persons suffice for performing that task. Hobbes offers the following argument to justify this restriction. It is an argument which today we should call on ground of public order: "It is not a set number that makes the assembly unlawful, but such a number, as the present officers are not able to suppress, and bring to justice."[28] A gathering becomes a riot when there are more participants than necessary. To support his position, Hobbes quotes a passage from the Acts of the Apostles. When a multitude of people made an accusation against two of Paul's com-

27. Ibid.
28. Ibid.

panions, the magistrate spoke of "sedition," because there was
no good reason to justify such a great concourse of people.[29]

10.   This summary shows how articulate, complex, and accurate is Hobbes's typology of partial societies. I shall try to
give some order to Hobbes's range of distinctions and subdistinctions, which succeed one another without overlapping. To
this end, it may be useful to establish the following points:

   a. The category of partial societies, which Hobbes calls
      "subordinate," derives from the first and more gener-
      al distinction between independent and dependent
      systems. (The only example which Hobbes gives of
      an independent system is the state.)
   b. The first distinction within the class "dependent
      systems" is that between public and private systems.
   c. Private dependent systems may be regular or
      irregular.
   d. Both regular and irregular systems may be legitimate
      or illegitimate.

It follows from this that both independent and public dependent systems are always both regular and legitimate, while
there are four subspecies within the species "private systems":
(a) legitimate regular systems; (b) illegitimate regular systems;
(c) legitimate irregular systems; (d) illegitimate irregular
systems. In other words, publicness, and even more independence, are always coterminous with regularity and legitimacy,
whereas irregularity and illegitimacy help us to distinguish
among private systems.

In *De Cive*, Hobbes only mentions *personae civiles* [civil per-
sons] as subordinate bodies. By contrast, the text of *Leviathan* is
more complex and innovative. For here Hobbes introduces
the species "irregular systems." These do not have a representative, and therefore cannot technically be called *personae
civiles*. It is worthwhile to look at the species "irregular systems," which do not have a representative and thus are not
civil persons, from the point of view of Hobbes's general the-

29. Acts, XIX, 40.

ory of the state. For this class of associations allows us to identify in Hobbes's system a private sphere, which is regulated by
the common law, and which escapes the direct power of the
state. This shows once more, if need be, the difference between the Hobbesian state, as authoritarian as it is, and modern totalitarian states. This should not lead us to mistake the
Hobbesian state for the liberal state, however, in which the private sphere is legally protected through the recognition of the
rights of liberty. The liberal state is a state based on the rule of
law, whereas the Hobbesian state is not. It is not, because freedom from the state is in Hobbes's state a freedom de facto. The
faculty to associate and assembly is not a right recognized by
the state, as occurs with liberal written constitutions. It is
merely the effect of a discretionary authorization on the part of
the sovereign.

In similar fashion, Hobbes's acceptance of public and private
political bodies within the state has nothing to do with the doctrine of intermediate bodies, which is put forward by supporters of temperate, or limited, or moderate monarchy; or, to
employ the phrase of Claude de Seyssel's, *monarchie reglée*. It
goes without saying that Hobbes's state is not a limited state,
because the sovereign power is either absolute or is not sovereign. All political bodies, both public and private, belong to
the very large category of "subordinate systems." That is, they
are subordinate to the state, which is the only independent
body politic. This subordination becomes apparent when we
consider that they have a legal personality only because they
are either instituted or authorized or permitted (or tolerated insofar as is convenient) by the state. No one of them can constitute a limit to the power of the state. And no one of them can
perform the function of providing a counterweight to the
power of the sovereign, which is the function proper to intermediate bodies in the doctrine of the limited state.

11.   Hobbes's typology of partial societies is well articulated
and well built. However, it does not deserve to be taken into
consideration because it represents by itself a new chapter in
the doctrine of corporations. Rather, it is worth analyzing be-

cause it prompts us to recognize that Hobbes's doctrine of the state is more complex than commentators have usually maintained, as I remarked at the beginning of this essay.

The historical importance of Hobbes's doctrine of corporations was already stressed by Gierke, with his remarkable acumen and his exceptional knowledge of the history of corporations. According to Gierke, Hobbes was the first natural law theorist who abandoned the traditional organic conception of collective bodies. He was therefore the first who considered not only the state, but also the partial societies which are formed within the state as being instituted through an agreement of the individuals who give life to them. He was, finally, the first who represented them as artificial persons (as artificial as are machines).[30] The best proof of this individualistic construction of collective bodies is Hobbes's doctrine of representation. We have seen that the representative of a multitude which has become a political or private body may be either an individual or an assembly. (In the doctrine of the forms of government, to this distinction corresponds the distinction between monarchy, and aristocracy or democracy.) The actions of both the individual and the assembly are to be imputed to the group of individuals who compose the collective body only if those actions are performed within the limits of the commission which the representative has received. The individual who represents another or other human beings "whatsoever he does in the person of the body, which is not warranted in his letters, nor by the laws, is his own act, and not the act of the body, nor of any other member thereof besides himself."[31] If a representative assembly makes a decision that is not authorized by letters patent or by laws, its decision is only binding for those who have made it. But it is not binding for those who have voted against it, or were absent, and therefore did not vote. "The assembly cannot represent any man in things unwarranted by their letters, and consequently are not involved in their votes."[32] The relation of representation is, as already

30. Gierke, *Das Genossenschaftsrecht*, vol. IV, p. 360.
31. *Leviathan*, XXII, p. 147.
32. Ibid., XXII, p. 148.

stated, a relation between author and actor. There cannot be representation if the actor acts beyond the limits of the authority which the author has given or transferred to him. It is less well known that, in Hobbes, there is no trace of the organic conception of representation. We can confirm this by analyzing Hobbes's account of partial societies, in particular of regular societies, which are mostly artificial persons, like the state, even though they are subordinate to the state.

Hobbes has been considered, not without ground, the theorist of the absolute state by definition. It may thus appear paradoxical that it was not out of the organic conception of representation, but rather out of the individualistic and atomistic conception, that modern democracy was born.

seven

By Way of Conclusion

The fifth of April [1988] was the four hundredth anniversary of the birth of Thomas Hobbes. Conferences devoted to him are taking place in many nations, including Italy. One of these is in Milan, another in Naples, a third and a fourth in Siena, and then in Naples again, after the summer. To be sure, we cannot judge the importance of a philosopher on the basis of the number of conferences concerning him. More and more often conferences are organized to promote tourism and to offer a source of enjoyment to participants. But all are agreed about the vitality of Hobbes's philosophy. His works are an inexhaustible source, even today, of reflections on themes that are still of great relevance. It suffices to remark that Hobbes's fundamental problem is the problem of war and peace, to which he returned continually in his mature years.

Hobbes's political system is based on a great dichotomy, which is extremely simple and clear. There is a *state of nature*, in which human beings live without positive laws to force them to reciprocal respect. And there is *civil society*, in which there exists a common power which forces them, against their will, to comply with the laws necessary to ensure peaceful cohabitation. The former is a state of constant and universal war. The latter is a state of permanent peace. The starting point of the entire construction is the idea that human beings generally prefer peace to war. They therefore prefer to live in civil society rather than in the state of nature.

The passage from one condition to the other may occur in either of two ways: through conquest, where the stronger imposes himself on others; or through a compact, by means of which all those interested agree to give up the individual use of force and to institute a common power. The former solution is typical of the realistic conception of politics, which considers society from the point of view of the passions at work in it, which need to be leashed by an external power. The latter solution is proper to the rationalistic conception of politics, according to which politics is the domain in which opposite interests clash. But those interests can be harmonized through procedures which leave considerable room to rational calculation. Examples of these two conceptions are the theories of Machiavelli and Locke.

Hobbes's philosophy lends itself to both interpretations, of which now one prevails, now the other. In these last years both have been advanced at the same time. This explains the strong presence of the author of *Leviathan* in today's debate. The realistic conception of politics has been influenced, at least in Italy, by the widespread diffusion of the thought of Carl Schmitt. The rationalistic conception has regained ground thanks to the reevaluation of contractual doctrines, and the ensuing debate on the role of calculating reason in practical matters, including politics. (For Hobbes, reasoning is precisely calculation.)

For Hobbes peace had become the fundamental problem. He lived in an age of ferocious and prolonged civil war. This is the kind of war which gives, more than any other, a good idea of the "war of all against all." (We have only to think of what has been happening in Lebanon for years.) For us, too, peace has become one of the fundamental problems of our times. This is because of the increased might of weapons which puts humankind as a whole, rather than single nations, in danger of unprecedented destruction. But our problem is that of the war among states, rather than the problem of the war among individuals or groups within a state. The solution, however, does not change. The Hobbesian model remains intact. International peace, too, can only be attained if a power endowed with superior force imposes itself on all others, through an agreement among states with the aim of giving life to a common power. To employ classical terms: we can choose between empire and league.

Contractual theories offer the model of the league, not of the empire. But Hobbes knew all too well that a mere association of persons, groups, or nations with a common end is not enough to establish a lasting peace among the associates. Beside a common end, we also need a common power. A common power does not take shape through a simple pact of association or mutual help, as is an alliance in the international system. That power is only formed by a covenant of union, through which all voluntarily subject themselves to the power of one person, which may be a natural person in a monarchic state, or an assembly in a democratic state.

In his project for perpetual peace, Kant only talked about a pact of association—we should say today a confederation—although he knew that for the first time a federal state had been constituted in the New World, a few years before he wrote his little treatise. Hobbes had not even gone so far as Kant, in relation to the issue of international peace. He was convinced that the international system was destined to remain in a state of nature, and therefore of permanent war. Hobbes never asked himself how to transfer the covenant of union from the domestic to the international arena. Why?

First of all, as already noted, the problem that haunted him all his life, and from which his political work was born, was that of civil war. Second, the only alternative to the covenant of union is the system of balance among states. This is possible in the international system, where the actors are few, as they were in Hobbes's time. But it is impossible when the actors are thousands, or tens of thousands, or even millions, as individuals are in the state of nature. Third, in the international system, states have a better chance to defend themselves from other states, and to survive, than do individuals in the state of nature.

Can these arguments be valid today as they could be in Hobbes's time? Today the power of weapons has increased, as has enormously the number of states. The increased number of states makes the balance more precarious. The increased power of weapons makes the possible break of that balance more terrifying.

We confront today with regard to international peace the same dramatic problem that Hobbes confronted three centuries ago with regard to internal peace. The ideal solution is also the same. The League of Nations was a first attempt, which miserably failed. The United Nations Organization has attempted to make a step forward toward the constitution of a common power through the institution of international armed forces. But the step forward has not gone beyond the stage of good intentions. What we have witnessed in these recent years is a return to the system of balance. But this development is actually a step backward. We should never forget that the system of balance has always been a truce between two wars. I see no reason why things should be different today. It may well be that the balance based on terror is more stable than the balance based on fear, to which Hobbes's contemporaries and Hobbes himself entrusted their hopes for peace.

The covenant of union is an ideal and unrealistic model. Nonetheless, it has not lost its heuristic strength. That is, it can still make us understand the reasons why domestic and international systems differ even today. And it makes us understand what direction our efforts should take if we believe that peace is today, more than ever, a common good.

Appendix

Considerations upon the Reputation, Loyalty, Manners and Religion of Thomas Hobbes of Malmesbury, written by himself by way of letter to a learned person

This year we celebrate the third centennial of the publication of Hobbes's fundamental work, *Leviathan* (London, 1651). Since its first appearance, *Leviathan* has been the cause of harsh disagreements, passionate discussions, and resentful reactions. Many picked up their pens to denounce the scandal and to declare that Hobbes's political edifice was monstruous morally (charging it with materialism and utilitarianism) and religiously (charging it with atheism). Among these vehement critics was the mathematician John Wallis, Savilian Professor at Oxford. He began a harsh scientific polemic with Hobbes when *De Corpore* appeared (1655). He had fired at him a merciless *Elenchus Geometriae Hobbianae*, which denounced Hobbes's mistakes and silly boastings. Wallis then continued his polemic by commenting with greater and greater severity on every new response that Hobbes offered.[1] Wallis had been

1. Hobbes answered the *Elenchus* with the ponderous work *Six Lessons to the Professors of the Mathematics,* one of the Geometry [Wallis], the other of Astronomy [Ward], in the chairs set up by the noble and learned sir Henry

stung to the quick by an allusion which Hobbes had made in the course of their polemics,[2] to certain secret papers belonging to Charles I. John Wallis deciphered these for the Parliamentarians, and then boasted about this in his inaugural address at Oxford in 1649. Since the dispute between Hobbes and Wallis had degenerated to the level of personal attacks, Wallis threw a new and peculiar accusation against Hobbes, and especially against *Leviathan*, that *Leviathan* had been written by the monarchist Hobbes, when the destiny of the English monarchy had already been decided, so that he could enter into Cromwell's good graces and obtain permission to return to his country after eleven years of exile. Wallis's pamphlet, in which he formulated this charge, was entitled *Hobbius Heautontimoroumenos*, and was published in 1662.[3] In it Wallis returned Hobbes's accusation of having betrayed the King in favor of

---

Savile in the University of Oxford, 1656, (in *EW*, VII, pp. 181–356). Wallis answered with *Due Correction for Mr Hobbes or School-Discipline for not saying his Lessons right*. This was followed by Hobbes's violent pamphlet: *Stigmai, Ageometrias, Agroichias, Antipoliteias, Amatheias, or Marks of the absurd Geometry, rural Language, scottish-church Politics and Barbarism of John Wallis*, 1657 (in *EW*, VII, pp. 357–428). The adversary replied again with *Hobbiani Puncti Dispunctio*. In 1657 Wallis's fundamental work, *Mathesis Universalis*, was published. In 1660 Hobbes criticized it thoroughly: *Examinatio et Emendatio Mathematicae hodiernae, qualis explicatur in libris Johannis Wallisii* (*EW*, IV, pp. 1–232). In this period Hobbes started his polemic with Robert Boyle with the piece *Dialogus Physicus sive de Natura Aeris*, 1662, (*Opera Latina*, IV, pp. 233–96). Boyle answered it with the *Examen of Mr. Hobbes his Dialogus*, and took up the same argument twelve years later in *Dissertation on Vacuum against Mr. Hobbes*. As noted in the text of this essay, Wallis answered Hobbes's polemical allusion, made in *Dialogus*, to Wallis's deciphering of the king's secrete papers, by writing the small treatise to which Hobbes answered with the *Considerations* which I present here.

2. In the *Dialogus Physicus sive de Natura Aeris*, which Hobbes wrote against the great chemist Roberte Boyle in 1662.

3. The complete title of this work, which has been given me by Professor Ernesto De Marchi, who is now in England, is the following: *Hobbius Heautontimoroumenos or A Consideration of Mr. Hobbes his Dialogues in an Epistolary Discouse addressed to the Honourable Robert Boyle*, by John Wallis D.D. Professor of Geometry in Oxford, Oxford, Printed by A. & L. Lichfield for Samuel Thomson, at the Bishopshead in S. Pauls Church-yard, 1662. I also owe to Professor De Marchi an accurate revision of the translation published here. [That is, in the Italian version.—Trans.]

Parliament by charging his adversary with having betrayed the King for Cromwell. It was hard to say which of the two accusations was the nastier, in that age of the restored monarchy (the year of grace 1662). Things were made worse by the fact that both protagonists were illustrious citizens, who by now enjoyed the favors of the monarch.

Confronted with such a swift and bold counterstrike, Hobbes could not keep silent. He answered in the same year, 1662, with the pamphlet which is here presented to Italian readers in translation for the first time: *Considerations upon the Reputation, Loyalty, Manners and Religion of Thomas Hobbes of Malmesbury, written by himself by way of letter to a learned person.* Given the type of charge made against him, Hobbes was forced to go back to his political interests, his years in exile, and his return to England. He had to tell, albeit succinctly, the story of his life, which explains why the essay is of biographical interest. Moreover, since he had to respond (though with arguments which were not new) to the accusation of impiety and atheism, he was forced to entertain questions of a doctrinal nature. Therefore the pamphlet, which we have chosen to publish because it is not easily accessible to readers, even if it is very well known and often cited, is also interesting from a philosophical point of view. Accused of having justified Cromwell's power with his work, Hobbes answered in peremptory terms and with his typically unassailable arguments, by presenting once again his theory of obedience. He thus uncovered the most secret reasons for his conception of sovereignty.

Whether Wallis's accusation was well-founded or not and thus whether Hobbes's defense can be considered legitimate, is a question which we cannot discuss exhaustively in this context. There is no doubt that the problem which moves Hobbes's thought is that of reestablishing peace rather than of restoring monarchy. His aim was thus to ensure obedience to any person who would assume power in a stable fashion and thus guarantee the preservation of peace. It is well known that during his exile in France, Hobbes was tutor to the Prince of Wales (October 1646). Nonetheless, he never engaged in actions that might have definitely compromised his chances to return to his country when peace was reestablished, even if the other party should win. It is also a fact that in his first polemical answer to his mathematical adversaries,[4] Hobbes allowed himself a boast, which a few years later he would gladly have retracted: "I believed it [*Leviathan*] framed the minds of a thousand gentlemen to a conscientious obedience to present government, which otherwise would have wavered in that point."[5] It is also true that in the last pages of *Leviathan*, which contain a few general conclusions, Hobbes tried to justify and legitimize obedience to Cromwell, as he openly recognizes in the pages of this pamphlet. There he considers subjects who have remained faithful to the monarchy as released from their compact, once conquest by another sovereign has occurred.

No one of these arguments appears decisive. *Leviathan* remains for us what Hobbes wanted it to be: a solid, unshakable monument to the doctrine of obedience. When Hobbes wrote it, the doctrine of obedience may have seemed more advantageous to the conqueror than to the deposed monarch, to whom Hobbes had undoubtedly addressed his previous work, *De Cive* (1642). Nonetheless, Hobbes did not modify (and did not even soften) his doctrines in order to adapt them to a new situation. Neither, throughout the book, did he make any concession[6] to the new power which was establishing itself. And, what matters most, he never ceased to respect the English monarchy or to admire the monarchic form of government, to which he remained faithful throughout his entire life. All this despite the fact that it would have been easy for him to disguise his sentiments had he really wished to write a book with the aim of attracting the favor of a republican government. Whoever has read *Leviathan* knows well that one cannot find a single adulatory sentence toward the future Lord Protector; yet Hobbes does not miss a chance to express deference toward monarchic institutions and their representatives.

4. *Six Lessons to the Professors of the Mathematics*, etc., which was written when Cromwell was in power.

5. *EW*, VII, p. 336.

6. Not even indirect ones.

A Brief History of Hobbesian Historiography[1]

1. Origin and First Developments of Hobbesian Critical Studies

Hobbes was considered a "cursed" writer for nearly two centuries, and, as a philosopher, a minor thinker of the British empiricist school: nothing more and nothing less than a disciple of the great Francis Bacon. Tenneman devoted a few dull pages to him, between Grotius and Herbert of Cherbury. Hegel is fascinated by Hobbes's robust political realism; but he quickly drops him, for he does not find in his works "anything speculative, or properly philosophical" (*Lectures on the History of Philosophy*, Cambridge, Cambridge University Press, 1989, III, 1, B, 3). Kuno Fischer ratifies the image of Hobbes as a Baconian without qualities, in his work on the Baron of Verulam (1856). In the meantime, between 1829 and 1845, Hobbes's English and Latin works were published, in an edition which is still standard today, by the radical writer Sir William Molesworth, who was a friend of James Mill and George Grote, and in whose circle were Hobbes's first admirers (*The English Works of Thomas Hobbes*, 11 vols. [London: John Bohn, 1829–45]; *T. Hobbes Malmesburiensis Opera philosophica quae latine scripsit omnia*, 5 vols. [Londini apud Joannem Bohn, 1839–45]).

The first complete monograph to do away with Hobbes's "Baconianism" was written in 1866 by George Croom Robertson for the series "Philosophical Classics for English Readers," published by J. B. Lippincott of Philadelphia. A few years later Georges Lyon's book appeared in the series "Bibliothèque de philosophie contemporaine," published by Alcan (1893). From the very first pages, Lyon emphasizes the differences between Hobbes and Bacon, rather than their affinities. In the same years, Ferdinand Tönnies "patiently" studied Hobbes's works, admiring "the energy and consistency of his construction of the state" (*Gemeinschaft und Gesellschaft*, p. 21). As Tönnies himself acknowledged, he relied on Hobbes in order to bring the

---

1. This book review includes only texts published up until 1974, when this review was first published.

great Hobbesian dichotomy between natural society (*Gemein-schaft*) and artificial society (*Gesellschaft*) down from the heaven of abstractions to the earthly test of history and sociology. Tönnies's monograph (*Hobbes Leben und Lehre*) was published for the first time in 1896, (Stuttgart, Friedrich Frommann) and for the third and last time in 1925. It may be considered the beginning of critical historiography on the philosopher of Malmesbury. With this work the twofold image of Hobbes as a minor thinker and empiricist philosopher is definitively left behind. Since then, the author of the trilogy *De Corpore, De Homine,* and *De Cive* emerges more and more as one of the major thinkers of the modern age. The thinkers with whom he is to be compared, and who allow us to understand his historical role more adequately, are Descartes, whom Hobbes greatly admires while seeing him as his antagonist, and Galileo, to whom Hobbes gives unparalleled praise in the dedicatory letter of *De Corpore.*

In subsequent years, Hobbesian historiography has been discovering tighter and tighter links between Hobbes's materialistic and mechanistic conception of the world, and the birth, growth, and triumph of modern science. I wish merely to cite a few of the main steps in the philosophical, not just political, interpretation of Hobbes's system: W. Dilthey "Der Entwicklungsgeschichte des Pantheismus," *Archiv für Geschichte der Philosophie* 13 (1900): 307–60, 445–82; E. Cassirer, *Das Erkenntnisproblem in der Philosophie und Wissenschaft der neuern Zeit* (Berlin: B. Cassirer, 1907), English tr. *The Problem of Knowledge: Philosophy, Science, and History since Hegel* (New Haven, Yale University Press, 1950); F. Brandt, *Thomas Hobbes's Mechanical Conception of Nature* (London, 1928, but the first edition is Danish, 1921); J. W. N. Watkins, *Hobbes's System of Ideas* (London: Hutchinson University Library, 1965). This literature has been enriched by several comprehensive studies, which are the most revealing sign of the growing interest which contemporary philosophy has in the creator of *Leviathan:* L. Stephen (1904), A. E. Taylor (1908), G. E. Catlin (1922), Adolfo Levi (1929), B. Landry (1930), J. Laird (1934), and G. B. Gouch (1939).

Appendix

Hobbesian studies have flourished exceptionally in the last fifteen years. These recent works, which have engaged in a more and more analytically rigorous and subtle inquiry, have been appearing one after the other, especially after the change in direction produced by Warrender's book (about which I shall say more below). Besides that of Watkins, already cited, they are R. Polin, *Politique et Philosophie chez Thomas Hobbes* (Paris: Puf, 1953); R. Peters, *Hobbes* (London, Pelican Books, 1956); F. C. Hood, *The Divine Politics of Thomas Hobbes* (Oxford: Clarendon Press, 1964); N. M. Goldsmith, *Hobbes's Science of Politics* (New York and London: Columbia University Press, 1966); F. S. McNeilly, *The Anatomy of Leviathan* (London: Macmillan, 1968); D. P. Gautheir, *The Logic of Leviathan* (Oxford: Clarendon Press, 1965), and the miscellaneous volume *Hobbes-Forschungen* (Berlin: Duncker & Humboldt, 1969), which collects the results of a conference on Hobbes held in Bochum in 1967. Recently, nearly a century after Tönnies's edition, scholars have again started to explore and sometimes to publish Hobbes's unpublished or rare writings: "Tractatus opticus," edited by F. Alessio, in *Rivista critica di storia della filosofia* 18 (1963): 147–228; and *Essays* (which appeared anonymously in 1620 with the title *Horae subsecivae*), edited by F. O. Wolf (Stuttgart: Frommann, 1969).

In Italy, the tradition of Hobbesian studies never ceased to be active—from Rodolfo Mondolfo's study, *Saggi per la storia della moral utilitaria: I. La morale di T. Hobbes* (Verona: Drucker, 1903) to the monograph by Adolfo Levi already cited. But renewed interest in Hobbes's political philosophy has characterized the work of young scholars. Besides M. A. Cattaneo's studies, cited below, and the edition of "Tractatus Opticus," already mentioned, it is worth mentioning A. Pacchi's study, *Convenzione e ipotesi nella formazione della filosofia naturale di T. Hobbes* (Firenze: La Nuova Italia, 1965). We also owe to Pacchi the review essay "Cinquant'anni di studi hobbesiani" (*Rivista di filosofia* 57 [1966]: 306–35), which is a good complement to this introduction, and *Introduzione a Hobbes*, with a detailed bibliography, in the series "I filosofi" published by Laterza, (Bari, 1971). In 1962 the *Rivista critica di storia della filosofia* devoted a whole issue to Hobbes. The contributors were, besides well-known foreign scholars such as Warrender and Polin, F. Alessio, N. Bobbio, M. A. Cattaneo, M. Dal Pra, E. Garin, and C. A. Viano. In 1971 A. G. Gargani's work *Hobbes e la scienza* (Turin, Einaudi) appeared. He considers Hobbes to be one of the most conscious and coherent interpreters of the new materialistic and mechanistic conception of the world that was the product of the scientific revolution. This interpretation offers the best evidence for the importance of Hobbes's thought for the history of philosophy in this century.

2. Themes of the Hobbesian Debate in the Last Thirty Years

The main objective of the scholars who were the protagonists in the first decades of renewal of Hobbesian historiography—from Tönnies's book (1896) to the one by Laird (1934)—was twofold. Their first task was to identify the threads that would allow them to connect Hobbes's thought to the philosophical and scientific thought of his time. The second was to provide a unitary reconstruction of his thought. In particular, they hoped to explain his political ideas by setting them in the context of his general philosophical system. Some of them stressed the unity of method,[2] and others isolated a few characteristic features of Hobbes's conception of the world and of knowledge. These are mechanism, materialism, and nominalism, which provide a link among the three parts into which his system is divided: that is, physics, anthropology, and politics. In 1938 Carl Schmitt's book, *Der Leviathan in der Staatslehre des Thomas Hobbes* was published (Hamburg: Hanseatische Verlagsanstalt, 1938), which pushes this line of interpretation to its extreme consequences. The Leviathan is a great machine, a *machina machinarum*. As such, it is nothing other than the interpretation of the state in mechanistic terms. Hobbes's approach merely reflects the progressive technicization of the apparatus

---

2. For Hobbes the method by definition is the geometric method. Hence derives his attempt, which he thinks is unprecedented, to apply it to the study of politics.

of the state, which is characteristic of the modern bureaucratic state.

In the same years, L. Strauss, *The Political Philosophy of Hobbes: Its Basis and Genesis*, (Oxford: Clarendon Press, 1936; 2d ed., Chicago: The University of Chicago Press, 1952), and A. E. Taylor, "The Ethical Doctrine of Hobbes," *Philosophy* 13 (1938): 406–24, suddenly stopped and inverted this interpretative trend. For both, Hobbes's ethics (and politics) are completely independent of his philosophy, and of the so-called scientific method which he attempted to apply to them. Strauss contends that Hobbes's political thought took shape in his youth through his acquaintance with the classics,[3] before his infatuation with Euclid, and, in general, with Galileo's scientific revolution. Hobbes is not, as he claims to be, a political scientist. He is a moralist who places his anthropological pessimism and his reflections on human nature within a rationalistic frame. Taylor considers Hobbes's egoistic psychology, which is usually accepted as the foundation of a scientific theory of politics, to be completely separate from the ethics which inspires it, and from the deontology which derives from it. According to Taylor, Hobbes's politics is not founded on the observation of human nature, but on deriving the duties of the citizen both from the sovereign and the divine will. As a consequence, the law of nature is binding not because it is a prudential piece of advice based on a rational calculation, but because it is a command, ultimately springing from the divine will. While Strauss uncovers the humanist under the scientist, Taylor uncovers the theist, and a religious spirit, under the rational atheist. But in 1939 Gooch still reasserted the standard assessment, according to which Hobbes "although professing himself an orthodox Christian, was wholly devoid of religious spirit" (p. 20).

Since then the debate has been revolving around these two themes: (a) whether Hobbes's political philosophy is dependent on or independent of his philosophical system; and (b) whether Hobbes's ethics is a rationalistic ethics, or, in the last analysis, a theological one. The first theme has called into

---

3. Hobbes's first work was, as known, a translation of Thucydides.

question the claim that Hobbes's politics is scientific and demonstrative. The second theme has raised the question of the ultimate foundation of political obligation in Hobbes. At the center of all most recent analyses and polemics is H. Warrender's book, *The Political Philosophy of Hobbes: His Theory of Obligation* (Oxford: Clarendon Press, 1957). According to Warrender, Hobbes is not the precursor of legal positivism, as a long-standing and unquestioned tradition has defined him. We should seek the foundation of obligations, including political obligations, not in the command of the sovereign, but rather in the laws of nature which arise in the state of nature. (The state of nature is therefore not a condition without duties.) These laws ultimately derive from divine commands, which are sanctioned through the threat of eternal damnation or the promise of eternal salvation. W. B. Glover, in his book *God and Thomas Hobbes* (1960, now in *Hobbes Studies* [cit. p. 207], pp. 141–68), then confirmed the thesis that Hobbes is a Christian and religious writer. F. C. Hood, in *The Divine Politics of Thomas Hobbes*, cited in section 1 above, has pushed this thesis to its extreme consequences, so extreme that, if the portrait of Hobbes which emerges from them were correct, Hobbes would be a totally unoriginal thinker, and we could not understand why for centuries his theories have caused so much fuss.

The line of interpretation that goes from Taylor to Warrender has inevitably caused strong and reasonable reactions. Plamenatz's "Mr. Warrender's Hobbes" (1957), and S. M. Brown, Jr.'s "The Taylor Thesis: Some Objections" (1959), now both in *Hobbes Studies*, pp. 73–87, and 57–71, respectively, deserve to be mentioned. With his monographic work, *Hobbes's System of Ideas*, cited in section 1 above, J. W. N. Watkins has returned to a more balanced and altogether more commendable interpretation of Hobbes's work. Watkins reasserts the thesis of the tight link between Hobbes's political philosophy and his overall philosophic system: "Hobbes's ideas on nature, man, and civil society are tightly linked to one another, and form a system. Within this system, the key positions are occupied by a number of purely philosophical notions. Besides . . . these philosophical notions contain by implication such a great part of his *political* theory as to provide a drastic solution to the political problems which the Puritan revolution posed for him" (p. 14). Against Taylor and Warrender, Watkins reasserts that Hobbes's laws of nature are prudential rules, not ethical imperatives. With a Solominic judgment, M. Oakeshott, author of an important introduction to *Leviathan*, maintains, in an essay published in 1960, "Moral Life in the Writings of Thomas Hobbes" (in *Rationalism in Politics*, [London: Methuen, 1962], pp. 248–300), that there is an explanation for the double interpretation of Hobbes as either an atheist or a theist. According to Oakeshott, Hobbes's political works contain both an esoteric doctrine for the initiated, and an exoteric doctrine for the common people. The former is consistent with Hobbes's philosophical system, while the latter relies on the ideas which have been implanted in us and teach us that the laws of nature are divine commands.

There are at least two more themes that generate interpretations which diverge as radically as possible from one another. This debate is far from over. On the one side, Hobbes has been vituperated for centuries as a counselor to tyrants, and, in the 1930s, as the harbinger of the totalitarian state. Besides C. Schmitt's book, already cited, and Gooch's judgment, see the work by J. Vialatoux, *La cité totalitaire de Hobbes*, (Lyon: Chronique Sociale, 1936, 1952 (2), and, more recently, H. R. Trevor Roper's sharp portrait, which summarizes the meaning of Hobbes's work with these words: "The axiom, fear; the method, logic; the conclusion, despotism" ("Thomas Hobbes," in *Historical Essays* [London: Macmillan, 1957], p. 234.)

But there are also the more cautious reservations advanced by Watkins in his concluding pages. According to him, Hobbes experienced only one calamity, civil war, whereas we have experienced two, civil war and totalitarianism (p. 172). And yet there has been a growing tendency recently to bring to the fore the liberal spirit which inspired some aspects of Hobbes's conception of the state: (a) he values the principle of legality, especially in criminal law. (M. A. Cattaneo, "La teoria della pena in Hobbes," *Jus* 11 (1960): 478–98; and also "Hobbes e il pensiero democratico della rivoluzione inglese e francese," *Rivista critica di storia della filosofia* [1962]: 487–514.) (b) He does not at all deny the right of resistance. (P. C. Mayer-Tasch, *Thomas Hobbes und das Widerstandsrecht* [Tübingen: Mohr, 1965].) And a different image has recently been opposed to the conventional one, which sees Hobbes as a traditionalist and a conservative, supporter of an aristocratic conception of life, and tied to the old feudal class in decline. This different image has been offered by L. Strauss, *The Political Philosophy of Hobbes*, cited above, pp. 114ff., and, lately, by C. B. Macpherson, in *The Political Theory of Possessive Individualism*, (see chap. 1, n. 7). Here Hobbes is presented as the advocate of the rights of the rising bourgeoisie and as the first ideologue of capitalism. But K. Thomas has done summary justice to this thesis in "The Social Origins of Hobbes's Political Thought," in *Hobbes Studies*, pp. 185–236.

Three Books on Hobbes

Carl Schmitt, *Der Leviathan in der Staatslehre des Thomas Hobbes* (Hamburg: Hanseatische Verlagsanstalt, 1938), 132 pp.

The Leviathan, like the Prince of Machiavelli, is not only the label of a renowned political theory, but is also, considered in itself, a war cry. Thus, over the course of its history, it has become more an object of enthusiasm and resentment than of critical inquiry. As has happened to Machiavelli in recent years, a calm historical critique, free of prejudice and far removed from love and hatred, now aims at restoring the essential historical value of Hobbes's work to our own time. We may consider this new essay on Hobbes as an intelligent attempt, made by one of the most learned and original jurists now living in Germany, to approach the old and mysterious myth of Leviathan in order to draw a general assessment of that myth by indicating the themes that have been at work in the formation of the modern state.

The novelty of Schmitt's effort lies in his attempt to discover, through a study of Christian and Jewish symbology in conjunction with a textual analysis of Hobbes's work, the meaning of the symbol of Leviathan in the conception of the state held by the man who has gone into history as "the prophet of Leviathan." First of all, Leviathan is the "mortal God." And this first connotation has an essentially polemical value for the man who defends the state against the God-grounded claims of the Pope, the Presbyterians, and the Puritans. But the state is also the representative "person," which has come into being through an artificial building process, contractual in nature. Finally, out of this conception of the state as a human product, as the product of human intelligence and industry, a third meaning emerges of the state as "mechanism." Historically, this last concept would become the most important one. The concept of person gives way to that of machine: the state can thus be portrayed as the first artificial product of the modern age, which will in fact come to be called the Age of Technology. It is undoubtedly from this image of the state as machine that that process of technicization begins, by which the state, having achieved independence from any political content and from any religious belief, becomes the neutral state, a mechanism of command.

Here for the first time we confront the modern state. This is the state of legal positivism; a state thousands of miles from the medieval state, in both the domestic and the international systems. Leviathan fully realizes itself in the state of the absolute prince, but here its destiny is fulfilled. What is deadly for it is the distinction between private belief and public confession, a distinction which Hobbes himself already allows us to surmise, and which will then become the historical premise of the liberal state. Once the internal domain of conscience has been accepted and recognized, the myth of Leviathan as the "mortal God" crumbles. Thus, in another sense, Leviathan is the precursor of the state founded on *jus*, which is nothing other than the rule of law. But in this formulation as well the state will encounter the principle of its own decay in that the indirect powers, which have been left outside the political domain, will organize within the state as parties, and will start to bring about its disintegration.

If Hobbes's political edifice still carries a valid meaning today, it is that it has led the struggle against all indirect powers. This deeper meaning has not always been recognized in the course of modern political history. It is a remarkable fact that the nation in which the Hobbesian conception saw neither actualization nor further development was the very nation where it was elaborated, that is, England. We may say that the work of Hobbes has been obfuscated and nearly distorted by the symbol which he chose as its representation. Once the immediate efficacy of the work disappeared, only the symbol remained with all the terror which it evokes. Later, this symbol lost all its strength and with it any chance of prevailing. And yet, concludes Schmitt, we cannot say that all has been lost of Hobbes's extraordinary speculation: Hobbes remains an unparalleled master or politics, the most authentic master of a great political experience.

John Bowle, *Hobbes and His Critics: A Study in Seventeenth Century Constitutionalism* (London: Jonathan Cape, 1951), 215 pp.

We recommend this book—which is far from ponderous, but rich in first-hand information about writers who would otherwise be inaccessible in Italy—to those who wish to acquire some knowledge about the richness and maturity of the political and constitutionalist discussions which occurred in England from 1640 to Locke. A better-informed interest in this subject is growing among us, too, as is shown by the essay on the Levellers by V. Gabrieli (*Rivista storica italiana* [1949]: 162–235), and that on Twysden by E. De Marchi (*Occidente* [1952]: 326–43). The writers of this period are important if considered together, rather than one by one, as representatives of the ideas and movements and of the multiplicity of perspectives, tastes, and styles that pervaded seventeenth-century England. In their attack on Hobbes, considered an unwelcome guest by the English cultural and political tradition, these writers offer us a lively and compelling picture of some characteristic features of public opinion in that nation.

Robert Filmer, the well-known author of *Patriarcha*, and Alexander Rosse are two fiery traditionalists. The latter, in particular, insists on accusing Hobbes of heresy (of Manichaeism). Seth Ward, Bishop of Exeter and Salisbury, refutes the Hobbesian charges against the universities in the name of freedom of thought. William Lucy, Bishop of St David, another traditionalist, is noteworthy for his mean, moralistic tone. George Lawson, author of a *Politica Sacra et Civilis,* represents the opposite side: he is a Puritan, a liberal, and a precursor of Locke. We have a vehement, wide-ranging, and compelling critique, touching upon Hobbes's political as well as religious thought, by John Bramhall, Bishop of Derry. Bramhall had already argued with Hobbes about the problem of the freedom of the will. (And he is the only one to whom Hobbes responds, although only about the charge of atheism.) John Eachard, professor at Cambridge, with his two dialogues between Philantus and Timothy, is the most brilliant and most powerful critic of all, who does not refrain from sarcasm and caricature. The ranks are completed by Edward of Gyde, Prince of Clarendon, and John Whitehall, both men of the law, experts in public affairs, ideologically conservative, whose critiques of Hobbes are informed by a civilized wisdom and a sound sense for public administration. The first pamphlet appeared in 1652, the last in 1679.

It is to be remarked that conservatives and liberals, traditionalists and innovators, strictly observant Anglicans and Puritans, all agree on a few fundamental points: first, in their condemnation of Hobbesian materialism and atheism, in defense of the religious value of natural law, and therefore of a divine sanction of the rulers' actions; and, second, in their rejection of absolutism, to which Hobbes's political theory leads, in defense of a constitutionalist conception, in which political power is limited either by natural, or by common law. Hobbes is a writer who is completely alien to the English tradition. These critics of his, on the contrary, resort (with more or less conviction) to the force of tradition. Hobbes is a doctrinaire, a builder of abstract theories, an architect of politics; his critics, in particular Bramhall, Clarendon, and Whitehall, accuse his excogitations of being "unpractical." Hobbes is a rationalist who has tried as much as possible to avoid resorting to the Holy Scriptures; his critics' books are replete with Biblical references. Common sense and a taste for tradition combine against the scandal of Hobbes's rigorous reasoning, which reaches nonsensical and dangerously innovative conclusions. A quiet fear of God, and a cautious optimism about human nature attempt to countervail the brazen cynicism with which Hobbes subordinates the ecclesiastical authority to the civil, and to oppose that terrifying pessimism which makes evil man arise, and creates the state out of fear. Even private property has been denied by this desecrator, where he asserts that the sole proprietor of the territory of the state is the sovereign, and dares to call it a seditious theory to maintain that private property is an absolute right of citizens.

At times it is vested interests which fight against this disinterested weaver of syllogisms, who uproots the privileges of the powerful, together with the natural rights of citizens. (Although some contest this disinterested spirit, and rebuke him for having aimed, by writing *Leviathan*, at obtaining Cromwell's favor.) At other times it is ideal motives, love of freedom, respect for private life, tolerance of opinions, which refuse to be overwhelmed by the inhuman, iron logic of the sovereign power, founded on an onerous contract, stipulated in a condition of violence and terror. Hobbes is too engaged in the construction of a coherent theory to be concerned with the practical interests of both traditionalists and liberals. But he is also too clairvoyant an investigator of human nature to allow himself to be moved by those who dream about ideal states. On the one hand, the reactionaries, such as Filmer, and the conservatives, such as Clarendon, protest against the contractual foundation of the state, because power does not spring from popular consensus, but rather comes directly or indirectly from God. On the other hand, even the liberal Puritan Lawson does not accept the social contract, but rather labels it a utopian fantasy, because, in his opinion, the state does not come about all at once, but instead gradually, through the successive refinement of human society. And in all fairness things could not have been otherwise: those who, like Hobbes, do not recognize any authority other than that of reason, are doomed to clash with the defenders of authority, be it the authority of traditional religion or that of history.

The problem facing the historian of political thought when confronted with these critics of Hobbes is the following: the criticisms, taken one by one, appear valid and effective; and yet, the Hobbesian monument stands securely on its feet even today. Hobbes's critics, some more, some less, say things which are right and sacrosanct. But it is Hobbes who is a great political writer, and who has left deep traces. His critics, with the possible exception of Bramhall and Lawson, are writers of the second rank, who can only be exhumed if we sweep off the dust which has accumulated in the libraries on the pages of their books. If Hobbes was indeed more a philosopher than a political thinker, as Bowle (following some of these critics) appears inclined to believe; that is, if he was a clairvoyant theoretician and a prince of the heretics, instead of a "statesmanlike writer" (p. 46), then we should not understand how his doctrine has been, and is still considered today, one of the pillars (and will these pillars amount altogether to more than a dozen?) of the history of political thought. It is in two points which Hobbes makes that we must look for an explanation of the relevance of his work, and of the reason why his reasonable critics, seemingly so up-to-date and so alive, are indeed dead; while he, who has been declared dead, is still alive. These two points are very important for the development of political science: (1) Hobbes's political theory is the first rationalistic systematization of the problems of the state and those of the citizen; it is therefore, from a methodological point of view, the first modern theory of the state. (2) Hobbes's political system is the first and fully conscious representation of the fundamental phenomenon of his time, as Maine remarked, cited by Bowle himself (p. 56); that is, the rise of the centralized state, or, as I should prefer to say, of the monopolization of the law by the state, according to the principle: there exists no source of the legal order other than the state, and there exists no source of *jus* other than the law. In relation to the first point his critics are anachronistic, for, in the age of the rise of modern science, they remain attached to vaguely religious themes, and to traditional but scientifically gratuitous conceptions of the divine origin of laws and authority. In relation to the second point, the critics correctly see the danger that inevitably proceeds from Hobbes's theory, namely the totalitarian state of today; but the remedies which they propose are insufficient, or, at least, they are already superseded by the secular vision of the world of which Hobbes's philosophy was a powerful anticipation.

Samuel I. Mintz, *The Hunting of Leviathan* (Cambridge, Cambridge University Press, 1962), 189 pp.

In his time, Hobbes had many enemies: at least in public, he had only enemies. The Hobbesian literature, in the second half of the seventeenth century in England, is quite large and nearly all polemical. Those who were influenced by his thought, or found cues in it for their own work, preferred not to mention him (as Locke did not in his early essays just discovered). If people mentioned him, they did it to discuss him, refute him, reject him, and loathe him.

A few years ago John Bowles's book was published about the political adversaries of the author of *Leviathan: Hobbes and His Critics* (London: Jonathan Cape, 1951). The new book which we announce here completes its predecessor. It refers in particular to the critics of Hobbes's metaphysics and ethics, even if some authors, such as Bishop Bramhall, remain the same.

Hobbes, this *pontifex maximus* of incredulity, was the *bête noire* of his time. The main charge was that of atheism, with which some of his critics—a few venerable theologians of the official church, Cambridge spiritualists, academic philosophers and official jurists—attempted to demolish and isolate him. (Our author, however, thinks that Hobbes was a theist, and in good faith.) Atheism was the logical consequence of the materialist conception which Hobbes held in metaphysics, to which were connected a deterministic conception of ethics and a radical denial of free will. Atheism, materialism, and determinism are the themes to which Mintz devotes particular attention, by collecting, with great care and without entering into unnecessary detail, some of the most interesting texts of the Hobbesian critical literature in the second half of the seventeenth century.

The most conspicuous part of these texts is constituted by the Cambridge Platonists, Henry More and Ralph Cudworth. But Mintz does not neglect minor writers such as Edward Stillingfleet (whose work is also connected with the formation of Locke's thought), Thomas Tenison, author of *The Creed of Mr. Hobbes Examined* (1670), and that Joseph Glanvill who, against Hobbes's daring critique of magical and superstitious practices, sided with the witches (*A Philosophical Endeavour towards the Defence of the Being of Witches and Apparitions*, 1666). In a chapter devoted to the controversy between Hobbes and Bishop Bramhall over the freedom of the will, we also find mentioned an intriguing correspondent of Hobbes, Philip Tanny, who in a letter had expressed some doubts about the solution offered to the problem of freedom, and the bishop, Benjamin Laney, who wrote a comment on the occasion of the reprint of Hobbes's work *Of Liberty and Necessity.*

After the Restoration, the hunt for Hobbes assumed another form, at once more popular and slanderous: Hobbesianism became a synonym of libertinism, that is, of immoralism and impiety. In dramatic poems, in plays, in satires of mores, the Hobbesian man is presented as the tyrant, the Machiavellian, the selfish man of the state of nature, without moral scruples, aiming only at his own advantage.

The singular fate of Hobbes was to be isolated in his time, to be without disciples, but—as the author correctly notes—to have exercised a subterranean influence on his adversaries. These took over his way of reasoning and his method of arguing, which abandons the controversies based on holy texts; and, in order to respond to his challenge, they learned to fight using facts and rational arguments. The breadth, continuity, and acrimonious insistence of the criticisms are the best proof that the challenge has been heard. Machiavellianism's fate was no different: this might have suggested some useful comparisons to the author.

After the storm of those years, Hobbes's work was mostly forgotten. After a century and a half it was unearthed by Bentham's utilitarianism and Austin's legal positivism. In the first half of the nineteenth century, Sir William Molesworth prepared the first edition of Hobbes's complete works, which is still standard today. Never so much as in the last years has Hobbes's thought been the object of so many analytical studies, and of a reevaluation, which has gone so far as to downplay his political conservatism (a liberal Hobbes, or a precursor of liberalism?), or to extrapolate from his work a thread of natural law theory. (The latter is Warrender's thesis, which Mintz, in my opinion, correctly rejects.) Even today there occurs from time to time an outburst of fury, in remembrance of the old rage. Mintz recalls, among others, our own Papini, whose assessment in the *Diavolo* evokes the epithet of devil incarnate, which Samuel Strimesius applied, in 1666, to the sage of Malmesbury.

Index

Absolutism, 56–56, 75, 117, 123–24, 161
Alternative model of natural law theory (Aristotelian model; classical model), 5–10; elements of, 8–10; Hegel on, 24–25; in reactionary thinkers, 20–22
Althusius, Johannes, 7–8, 175, 184
Amour-propre, 98
Analysis, 88
Anarchy, 29
Anglican Church, 64, 78
Arbiters, 125, 128
Aristotelian model. *See* Alternative model of natural law theory
Aristotle: on domestic society, 13; Hobbes on, 34; monistic conception of the state in, 177; on organic and similar parts, 176n; theory of the state, 5–6, 178
Armed sects, 191
Arrogance, 124
Artifice: and nature, 36
Artificial man, 35–38; justification of, 38–39; the state as, 47
Artificial person, 187, 188, 195
Assembly, right of, 191–92
Association, right of, 191–92

Bacon, Sir Francis, 111–12, 205
Balance of power, 200
Barbeyrac, Jean, 180n
Beccaria, Cesare, 140
Bodin, Jean, 6–7, 83, 85, 86, 95
Bourgeois society: and conceptual model, 10–15; the family in, 18–20; Hegel on, 25; and Hobbes, 71–72; market society, 10
Bowle, John, 214–18
Bramhall, John, 215, 219

Cabals, 191
Calculation, 44, 91, 118, 153
Cattaneo, Mario, 70
Charles I, 82
Charles II, 28, 104
Christianity: Hobbes on, 63–65, 79–81
Church and state: Hobbes on, 63–66, 76–78, 80–81; and unity of the state, 29, 74
City: in Aristotelian theory of the state, 5–6, 7
Civil disobedience. *See* Right of resistance
Civil history, 37

Index

Civil law, 56–60; and divine law, 93, 162, 168; as imposing natural law, 129–30; and natural law in Hobbes, 114–48, 159–67; and natural law in natural law theories, 156–58; and religious precepts, 63; and sovereignty, 56, 57, 137

Civil philosophy, 37, 88, 90–91

Civil society (political society): contract founding, 3–4; in conceptual model of natural law theory, 1–2; creating to attain supreme good, 46; and domestic society, 13–15, 15–16, 21; essential elements of, 174; Hegel on, 23, 24–25; Hobbes on, 197; justice in, 116; natural laws' validity outside of, 125; as *pactum societatis*, 47; reasonableness of, 90

Civil war: Hobbes on, 30–31, 42–43; and religious war, 63; as war of all against all, 198

Clarendon, Edward of Gyde, Prince of, 215, 216

Classical model. *See* Alternative model of natural law theory

Coke, Sir Edward, 56, 84, 108n.32, 109n.34, 110–12

Collegium, 181

Common law: Coke and Hobbes on, 110–12; and the private sphere, 194; and sovereignty, 56, 112; and statute law, 84

Conceptual model of natural law theory, 1–25; and bourgeois society, 10–15; elements of, 1–3; the family in, 15–18; variations on, 3–5; reactionary criticisms of, 20–22

Concourse of people, 191–92

Conflict, 40, 71

Conscience, 70, 78, 125–26

Consent: in Aristotelian model, 9; and bourgeois society, 12; in conceptual model, 2–3, 17

Considerations upon the Reputation, Loyalty, Manners and Religion of

Thomas Hobbes of Malmesbury, written by himself by way of letter to a learned person (Hobbes), 203

Constitutionalism, 53, 66, 67

Contract: as basis of the state, 91, 94–95; in conceptual model, 3–4; Filmer and Haller on, 21–22; Lawson on, 216; and private property, 19; as source of sovereign's authority, 142. *See also* Covenant of union

Convention: in Aristotelian model, 9; in conceptual model, 2, 17; irrevocability of, 94

Conventionalism, 95–97, 143

Corporations, 179, 183–84, 194–95

Covenant of union, 46–49; and characteristics of sovereignty, 49–56; international, 199, 200; and obedience to the sovereign, 93

Crown and Parliament, 81–82

Cudworth, Ralph, 219

Death, fear of, 98

Death penalty, 140–41

De Cive (Hobbes), 102–7; on artificial man, 39; on church and state, 64, 65, 80; on covenant of union, 51; deductive legal system in, 151; definition of the state in, 49; on justice of the law, 161; methodological clarity of, 95; and natural law, 129, 130–31, 132; on partial societies, 178–79; on parties, 190; on rights, 155; on source of sovereign's authority, 142; on subordinate bodies, 193; in works of Hobbes, 26, 27

De Corpore (Hobbes): on philosophy, 31; in works of Hobbes, 26, 27, 28, 102

Defensor Pacis (Marsilius), 6

De Homine (Hobbes), 26, 28, 102

Dependent systems, 182, 186, 193

Descartes, René, 206

Dialogue between a Philosopher and a Student of the Common Law of En-

222

gland, A (Hobbes), 27, 56, 84, 107–13
Dignity, 98
Divine law, 93, 162, 168
Divine right of kings, 85–86, 93, 94, 126
Domestic society: Althusius on, 7; and civil society, 13–16, 21; foundation of power in, 15–16; Rousseau on, 17–18
Duty. *See* Obligation

Eachard, John, 215
Economic relations: and domestic society, 14; and the family, 18; Hegel on, 23, 25; and political society, 11; and state of nature, 11, 19
Economics, 13, 25
Efficacy, principle of, 167
Elements of Law Natural and Politic (Hobbes): on artificial man, 38–39; on church and state, 64; on civil war, 30; on mixed government, 61; on partial societies, 178–79; state defined in, 49; in works of Hobbes, 26, 27, 28, 101–2
Empire, 199
Equality: in Aristotelian model, 8; and bourgeois society, 12; in conceptual model, 2; Hobbes on, 72; as objective human condition, 39
Ethical legalism, 57–58, 165
Ethics. *See* Moral philosophy
Executive power, 62

Factions, 190–91
Family: in Aristotelian theory of the state, 5–6, 6–7, 8; in bourgeois society, 18–20; in conceptual model of natural law theory, 15–18; Hegel on, 24–25; as legitimate private system, 185, 189; and monarchy, 21; as partial society, 178; and the state of nature, 13–15

Fear of death, 98
Filmer, Robert, 16, 21, 123, 215, 216
Fischer, Kuno, 205
Freedom (liberty): in Aristotelian model, 8; and bourgeois society, 12; in conceptual model, 2; Hobbes on, 29, 40, 55, 70–71, 98, 100; and law, 155; natural, 21; in state of nature, 100

Galileo, 206
Gaps in a legal order, 132–33, 160
Gargani, A. G., 208
Gemeinschaft, 14, 206
Generosity, 124
Genossenschaften, 175, 177
Geometry, 32, 33, 90–91
Gesellschaft, 14, 206
Gierke, Otto von, 173, 177, 184, 195
Glanvill, Joseph, 219
Government: mixed, 61–62, 82; pure and corrupt forms of, 59. *See also* Political power; Sovereignty; State
Gratitude, 124
Grotius, Hugo: Hobbes compared to, 150–54; as natural law theorist, 114, 115, 149; on systems, 180n

Haller, Ludwig von, 22
Hegel, Georg Wilhelm Friedrich: on bourgeois society, 25; on Hobbes, 205; on natural law theory, 23–25; realism of, 43, 67; totalitarianism in, 69
Henry IV, 76
Heresy, 110, 111
History: Hobbes's use of, 87; natural and civil, 37
Hobbes, Thomas: anticlericalism of, 78; on Aristotle, 34; and the bourgeoisie, 71–72; and Charles II, 28, 104; on Christianity, 63–65, 79–81; on church and state, 63–66, 76–78, 80–81; on civil law, 56–60, 114–48, 159–67; on civil

Hobbes, Thomas (*continued*)
society, 197; on civil war, 30–31,
42–43; on conflict, 40, 71; conser-
vativism of, 69–70, 72; on
corporations, 194–95; on covenant of union, 46–49; critical
studies of, 205–12; and his critics,
66–73; cynicism of, 99; deductive
legal system of, 151; on distinction between law and right, 155;
on equality, 72; ethical conventionalism of, 95–97; exile of, 28,
76, 103; on the family and the
state, 16; on freedom, 29, 40, 55,
70–71, 98, 100; Grotius compared
to, 150–54; historiography of, 27,
72–73; and history, 87; on international peace, 199–200; on
justice, 95–96; and liberalism, 70;
monarchy preferred by, 69, 112,
204; on natural law, 114–48, 159–
67; natural law defined by, 118–
19; as natural law theorist and
positivist, 114–18, 132–33, 142–
48, 155, 165–67, 171, 210; and
natural law theory, 149–71; on
natural rights, 154; nominalism
of, 35, 96, 143; on obedience, 93–
95, 97, 98–99, 126, 140, 158–59,
163–64, 169–70; on obligation,
126, 210; on partial societies,
172–96; peace as fundamental
problem for, 198–99, 203; on
philosophical method, 32–35, 86–
87; on philosophy, 31–32, 37; on
political power, 40–41; political
theory of, 26–73, 86, 114–48,
209–11, 217; on private property,
71–72, 216; realism of, 43, 67; on
reason, 44–46; on religion, 79,
100–101; on representatives, 186–
88, 195–96; on rights of assembly
and association, 191–92; Rousseau compared to, 174; on
sovereignty, 49–56, 60–62, 83; on
the state, 36, 37–38, 74–75, 85–
86, 91–92, 94–95, 99–100, 117,
144, 161, 173–78, 194, 195, 213;
on state of nature, 10, 38–41,
100, 197; on systems, 179–83; on
truth, 96; on types of power, 17;
on unity of the state, 29–32, 60,
83, 190; voluntaristic conception
of law of, 97; and Wallis, 201–3;
on war of all against all, 41–44,
198; works of, 26–27
Homo homini lupus, 89
Honor, 71
Household, 13–15, 178

Ignorance of the law, 134
Illegitimate systems, 185–86, 189–
93
Impartiality, 124, 125, 128
Independent systems, 182, 186, 193
Individualism, 12
Insecurity, 29, 47
Inspiration, 35
Institutes (Coke), 110–11
International society, 42, 138, 146,
199–200
Irregular systems, 186, 190–92, 193
Ius in omnia, 39

Judicial power, 62, 85
Justice: Hobbes on, 95–96; of the
law because it is the law, 161–62,
164; legal, 115–16

Kant, Immanuel, 199
Kelsen, Hans, 132, 142, 145, 167
Knowledge, 33, 35

Laney, Benjamin, 219
Law: divine, 93, 162, 168; gaps in a
legal order, 132–33, 160; ignorance
of, 134; justice of because it is the
law, 161–62, 164; legal justice,
115–16; and rights, 155; two orders of, 129; voluntaristic
conception of, 97. *See also* Civil
law; Common law; Legal positivism; Natural law
Laws of nature. *See* Natural law

Lawson, George, 215, 216

Leagues, 190, 191, 199

Legal positivism, 114–18, 132–33, 142–48, 155, 165–67, 171, 210

Legislative power, 62

Legitimate systems, 185–86, 189, 190–93

Lèse majesté, 146–47

Leviathan, 100, 101, 176, 208, 212–13

Leviathan (Hobbes): on artificial man, 39; attacks on, 29, 110; on church and state, 64, 80; on civil war, 30, 82; on covenant of union, 51–52; *De Cive* compared to, 105; deductive legal system in, 151; definition of the state in, 49; editions of, 27; and *Elements,* 26; on irregular systems, 193; on liberty, 55; on mixed government, 61; on natural law, 132, 133; on natural and civil law, 129; on natural law, 45; on obedience, 204; on partial societies, 172, 175, 178; on political power, 40; publication of, 28; reactions to, 201, 202; on representation, 187; on rights, 155; in works of Hobbes, 102

Liberalism, 70, 152, 194, 220

Liberty. *See* Freedom

Life: earthly and eternal, 168–70; as fundamental value, 98, 140

Locke, John: on the family and the state, 16; and natural law theory, 171; on private property and the family, 18–20, 71; on the state, 128; on state of nature, 4, 10, 43; on theory of trust, 53; on types of power, 17

Logic, 37

Luch, William, 215

Lyon, Georges, 205

Machiavelli, 86

Macpherson, C. B., 10, 71, 212

Majority rule, 188

Market society, 10. *See also* Bourgeois society

Marsilius of Padua, 6

Marx, Karl, 10

Mediators of the peace, 125

Mercy, 124

Method, 32–35, 86–88, 95

Mintz, Samuel I., 218–20

Mixed government, 61–62, 82

Moderation, 124

Molesworth, Sir William, 205, 220

Monarchy: divine right of kings, 85–86, 93, 94, 126; Filmer on, 21; Hobbes's preference for, 69, 112, 204; irrevocability of, 52; Locke on, 16

Moral philosophy: as demonstrable science, 35–36; ethical conventionalism, 95–97; ethical legalism, 57–58, 165; method for, 33

More, Henry, 219

Natural history, 37

Natural law: and civil law in Hobbes, 114–48, 159–67; and civil law in natural law theories, 156–58; content of, 127–28; as defined by Hobbes, 118–19; as destined never to be in force, 122–23; as foundation of civil power, 158–59, 167; ignorance of, 134; imposed by civil law, 129–30; indeterminacy of, 131; prudential rules as, 44–46; as related to an end, 121, 127; and sovereignty, 56–57, 58–59, 65, 117–18, 130–31, 136–39, 141–44; and the state, 135, 147, 165; and state of nature, 133, 159; substantive and procedural laws, 124–25; validity outside civil society, 125

Natural law theory: alternative theory to, 5–10; conceptual model of, 1–25; essential conditions of, 156; and the family, 15–18; Hegel on, 23–25; and Hobbes, 149–71; Hobbes as natural law theorist and positivist, 114–18, 132–33, 142–48, 155, 165–67, 171, 210; and Locke, 171; medieval and modern, 150–

Natural law theory (*continued*)
54; reactionary thinkers on, 20–22; three kinds of, 157–58; two periods of, 149–50. *See also* Natural law
Natural persons, 187
Natural philosophy, 37
Natural rights, 154–55
Nature: and artifice, 36
Necessity, 9
Nisbet, R. A., 174
Nominalism, 35, 96, 143

Oakeshott, Michael, 70, 211
Obedience: *Leviathan* on, 204; to natural law, 165; to the sovereign, 93–95, 97–99, 126, 140, 158–59, 163–64, 169–70
Objective Spirit, 23, 24
Obligation (duty): internal and external, 125–27; and legal justice, 116; to obey natural law, 165; to obey natural law and civil law, 129–30; to obey the sovereign, 93–95, 97, 98–99, 126, 140, 158–59, 163–64, 169–70; sources of, 15, 134, 210
Oppression, 29
Organic conception of collective bodies, 195

Pacchi, A., 207
Pacta sunt servanda, 146
Pactum societatis, 47, 48
Pactum subiectionis, 48, 50
Palladini, Fiammetta, 180n
Partial societies: corporations and *personae civiles* as, 179; the family as, 178; *Genossenschaften* as, 175, 177; Hobbes on, 172–96; Rousseau on, 174; as systems, 179–93; typology of, 183–86, 193
Parties, 190–91
Passions, 39–40, 67, 97–98
Peace: as dictate of reason, 92; as fundamental problem for Hobbes, 198–99, 203; international, 199–200; mediators of, 125; perpetual,

199; seeking peace as fundamental rule, 45, 120, 144; the state as means of attaining, 122; in state of nature, 43; as supreme end of human beings, 119, 121; virtues indispensable to, 124
Personae civiles, 179, 193
Persons, 187–88, 195
Philosophy: Hobbes on, 31–32, 37; logic, 137; method, 32–35, 86–87; natural and civil, 37; nominalism, 35, 96, 143; traditional idealism of, 99. *See also* Moral philosophy
Physics, 91
Pluralism, 177–78
Polis, 5–6, 177
Political power: abuses of, 59–60; and bourgeois society, 12; conceptions of, 9; and contract founding civil society, 4, 17, 47–49; disintegration of, 29; and domestic power, 15–16; and economic relations, 11; executive, judicial, and legislative, 62; fundamental problem of, 40–41; natural law as foundation of, 158–59, 167; political unity, 85; supremacy of, 75. *See also* Government; Sovereignty; State
Political society. *See* Civil society
Politics: realistic and rationalistic conceptions of, 198. *See also* Political power
Politics (Aristotle), 5, 13
Positive law. *See* Civil law
Positivism, legal. *See* Legal positivism
Power, political. *See* Political power
Primitive societies, 41
Private property: Hobbes on, 71–72, 216; Locke, on, 18–20, 71
Private systems, 184–86, 188–89, 193
Procedural laws, 124–25
Promises, 46, 124, 146
Public officials, 175, 176
Public systems, 184–86, 188–89, 193
Pufendorf, Samuel, 106, 114, 180n
Puritans, 78

Rationalistic conception of politics, 198
Rational society, 14
Realistic conception of politics, 198
Reason. *See* Right reason
Reformed churches, 63–64, 77–78
Regular systems, 186, 188–90, 193
Religion: divine law, 93, 162, 168; Hobbes on, 79, 100–101. *See also* Christianity; Church and state
Representatives, 183, 186–89, 193, 195–96
Revenge, 124
Right of assembly, 191–92
Right of association, 191–92
Right of resistance (civil disobedience), 94–95, 140, 154, 170
Right reason, 44–46; human capacity for, 91; and laws of nature, 118–19; in modern natural law theory, 152–53; peace as dictate of, 92; and sovereignty, 57
Rights, natural, 154, 155
Robertson, George Croom, 205
Roman Catholicism, 63, 77
Rosse, Alexander, 215
Rousseau, Jean-Jacques: on domestic society and the family, 17–18; on partial societies, 174; on political unity, 60, 75; on state of nature, 4–5, 43
Rules, 44–45

Scarcity, 39
Schmitt, Carl, 69, 70, 198, 208, 212–14
Scholasticism, 34, 95
Science: demonstrable and not demonstrable, 35–36, 91; relativistic and absolutist conceptions of, 143
Scientific method, 88, 95
Security, 57, 98, 127, 129
Six Bookes of a Commonweale, The (Bodin), 6, 95
Social contract. *See* Contract
Sovereignty: absoluteness of, 53–56, 75; and civil law, 56, 57, 137; and common law, 56, 112; duties of the sovereign, 190–91; indivisibility of, 60–62, 83; irrevocability of, 49–53, 124; and legitimacy of systems, 185–86; and natural law, 56–57, 58–59, 65, 117–18, 130–31, 136–38, 139, 141–44; obedience to the sovereign, 93–95, 97–99, 126, 140, 158–59, 163–64, 169–70; and right reason, 57; sovereign as representative, 189; source of sovereign's authority, 142; sovereign's relations with subjects and other sovereigns, 138–41. *See also* Government; Political power; State
State: Aristotelian theory of, 6–8; Aristotle on, 5–6, 178; as artificial man, 47; Augustinian-Lutheran conception of, 68; bourgeois state, 10–11, 12; church and state, 29, 63–66, 74, 76–78, 80–81; compliance with laws in, 46; conceptions of, 9; contractual basis of, 91, 94–95; as enforcer of laws of nature, 46; as guarantor of security, 98; and the family, 16; Haller on, 22; Hegel on, 23–25; Hobbes on, 36–38, 74–75, 85–86, 91–92, 94–95, 99–100, 117, 144, 161, 173–78, 194, 195, 213; Hobbes's definitions of, 49, 187–88; as Leviathan, 100, 101, 176; liberal, 194; limitations on power of, 54–55; Locke on, 128; as machine, 36, 37–38, 69, 89, 100, 101, 208, 213; as means of attaining peace, 122; modern, 67, 74–75, 85, 101, 173–74, 213; monistic conception of, 173, 177–78, 183; and natural law, 135, 147, 165; pluralistic conception of, 177–78; public officials, 175, 176; and public worship, 169; and reciprocal consent, 3; and state of nature, 2, 90, 99–100; as a system, 183; unit of, 29–32, 60, 67–69, 74–75, 83, 190. *See also* Government; Political power; Sovereignty

State of nature, 38–41; and anarchy, 29; in Aristotelian model, 8; in conceptual model of natural law theory, 1–2; contradictoriness of, 90; and death penalty, 141; and economic relations, 11, 19; and the family, 13–15; Hegel on, 23, 25; Hobbes on, 10, 38–41, 100, 197; insecurity in, 47; liberty in, 100; Locke on, 4, 10, 43; and market society, 10; natural law in, 133, 159; Rousseau on, 4–5, 43; and the state, 2, 90, 99–100; varying interpretations of, 3–5; war of all against all in, 41–44
Stephen, Sir James Fitzjames, 109
Stillingfleet, Edward, 219
Strauss, L., 209, 212
Subordinate systems, 194
Substantive laws, 124
Synthesis, 88
Systems, 179–83; definition of, 180–81; dependent and independent, 182, 186, 193; legitimate and illegitimate, 185–86, 189–91, 192, 193; public and private, 184–86, 188–89, 193; regular and irregular, 186, 188–92, 193; the state as, 183; subordinate, 194

Tanny, Philip, 219
Taylor, A. E., 209, 211
Tenison, Thomas, 219
Thomas, Keith, 71
Tönnies, Ferdinand, 14, 205–6
Totalitarianism, 69, 211, 218
Traditional society, 14
Trevor Roper, H. R., 211
Trust, theory of, 53
Truth, 96

Unity of the state, 29–32, 60, 67–69, 74–75, 83, 190

Vainglory (vanity), 40, 71, 97–98
Village, 5, 6
Voluntarism, 97

Wallis, John, 201–3
Ward, Seth, 215
War of all against all, 41–44, 198
Warrender, Howard, 159, 160, 207, 210, 211, 220
Watkins, J. W. N., 206, 207, 210–11
Whitehall, John, 215
Witnesses, 126